A WORLD OF HIS OWN

DAVID WILLIAMS

A World of His Own

THE DOUBLE LIFE OF
GEORGE BORROW

Oxford New York
OXFORD UNIVERSITY PRESS
1982

Oxford University Press, Walton Street, Oxford OX2 6DP

London Glasgow New York Toronto
Delhi Bombay Calcutta Madras Karachi
Kuala Lumpur Singapore Hong Kong Tokyo
Nairobi Dar es Salaam Cape Town
Melbourne Auckland
and associates in
Beirut Berlin Ibadan Mexico City Nicosia

British Library Cataloguing in Publication Data
Williams, David
A world of his own: the double life of
George Borrow.
1. Borrow, George   2. Authors, English—19th
century—Biography
I. Title
823'.8   PR4156
ISBN 0-19-211762-9

Set by Oxford Publishing Services
Printed and bound in Great Britain by
Robert Hartnoll Limited
Bodmin Cornwall

CONTENTS

ILLUSTRATIONS

PRELIMINARY

WHEN I was in the sixth form, and getting ready for what was then called the Higher School Certificate, I was required to read, for the English papers, some text-book selections from the works of George Borrow published by the Oxford University Press. Amongst other things on the menu, I remember, was *Silas Marner* by George Eliot. Asked to choose a favourite between the two Georges the form selection fell one hundred per cent on George B. We all enjoyed him.

Not many people studying English literature in the sixth forms of today will so much as have heard of Borrow, never mention read him. George Eliot, blown heavenward by the trumpets of Leavisite praise, is reverentially read by all. Borrow of the mighty stride – he could cover more than thirty miles a day and always counted on doing the last lap to the pub at six miles an hour – Borrow the mysterious, the adventurous, the polyglot, the pugilist, the dodgy lover has been thrown into an unregarded corner.

Up in Valhalla with his favourite old Norsemen, he will not be taking much account of this neglect. It has happened to him before. In 1843 he published *The Bible in Spain*. (His alternative title was *Journeys, Adventures and Imprisonments of an Englishman in an Attempt to Circulate the Scriptures in the Peninsula*.) The book was a huge success. Borrow came up to London from Norwich and attended important balls and soirées. In one year John Murray sold just short of 20,000 copies of it. The original edition of Dickens's *Pickwick Papers*, priced at twenty-one shillings, sold 7,250 copies – but one must remember that there were many other editions, and of course the instalments preceding them. All the same Borrow's sales represent a tremendous success. There was an eight-year gap after that before Murray was able to coax *Lavengro* out of him. But *Lavengro*, surely a better book even than *The Bible in Spain* and his masterpiece, quite failed to win support, and nothing that Borrow could write later was able to arrest the decline. He died lonely, almost unknown and almost unread in 1881 at the age of 78.

Then, slowly, came a revival of interest. People became aware that a uniquely strange creature had been living amongst them and had been writing books that were a wonderful and fascinating mixture of opposites: exotic, flamboyant, dreamlike – and in the same breath dry, argumentative, and harking back to the eighteenth century. Borrow began to be read again and plentiful books and articles were written about him. This revival in turn faltered round about 1939, but now, once again, the swing is the other way, and it is becoming clear at last that Borrow is a genuinely original, strongly creative writer and that limbo has not been and never will be a place capable of holding him.

He is a deliberate mystifier. He dodges about, plays tricks with time and place. How was he on sex? The present generation, hot for certainties on this subject above all others, will press him on this but will never get answers better described than fluid. If he was here to be questioned face to face – you'd need to be a fearless investigator to tackle this – the likeliest answer you would get would be: 'Ask Isopel Berners'. But with her too, being over-inquisitive would be an employed tactic qualifying for danger-money.

His linguistic range is unbelievably wide. Manchu, Moultanee, Romany, Welsh, Spanish, Portuguese, Russian, Armenian – you can go on counting up to forty. Did he really know them? Well, Colonel Napier, a reliable man, heard him talking Moultanee fluently in Spain in 1839, and reasonably asking where he had picked it up got the equally reasonable reply, 'Some years ago in Moultan'. But was he ever there? We can't know, but it is possible, because he had a way of disappearing from human ken for longish periods. Mrs Mary Borrow, the staunch and splendid woman he married, must have had a terrible time with him. Yet she loved him. In spite of his private and particular kind of sexlessness he had a way of making women love him. And as for the languages, well, he had Macaulay's gift of photographic memory. He could read a page, shut the book, and say the page. There are scribbled notes of his in foreign languages – words, phrases, longer passages – these he read and for ever after could see them, as on a screen lighted up in his head. All he lacked was an ear for the tunes of a language. In the pub in Port Dinorwic he aired his *cymraeg*. '". . . your Welsh is very different from ours . . ." "I am the seed not of the sea-snake but of the coiling serpent, for so one of your Welsh poets called the Saxons." "But how did you learn Welsh?" said the old man. "I learned it by the grammar," said I, "a long time ago . . ."' He did no such thing. He learned it by looking at it – the quick method that never teaches you the tune.

And the gipsies. What was the true nature of his intimacy? And why should Mrs Herne seek to poison him? Had he penetrated too far into the secrets of a most secret society? And his matchless dialogue: how did he – so casually – master the difficult art of creating character through dialogue and at the same time of moving the narrative on? Questions, questions. And in the end we have to be satisfied with a single, short, defiant statement.

He was his own man.

CHAPTER 1

THE JOURNEYING BOY

ON 8 September 1853, about the middle of the day, an outstandingly tall, white-haired man was walking along Yarmouth jetty. It was blowing hard and the sea was high. A boat from an anchored ship was making its way ashore for supplies of fresh water. The crew were being thrown about and finally, not far from beaching, a wave thirty feet high washed over them and one man was pitched into the sea.

The tall man – he had had his fiftieth birthday the previous July – jumped from the jetty on to the sand, and then, just as he was, into the frothing water. A life was saved, and beachmen helped with the others. Because the rescuer was George Borrow he wrote about this event – as he did about most of the events of his life at some time or another even if in a disguised, allusive, and manipulative way. He had been, he asserted, the only person who had confronted the billows in deep water. 'I am anxious to give to the beachmen whatever credit is due to them; I am anxious to believe that one of them was once up to his middle in water, but truth compels me to state that I never saw one of them up to his knees.'

This is a typically Borrovian account. The man is fearless. The man is powerful. But the man is also neurotically anxious lest justice should not be done to him. Certainly justice was fully done in this instance. Dr Gordon Hake of Bury St. Edmunds, a friend of Borrow's as well as his medical man and something of a writer, wrote an account of the deed for the *Bury Post* which appeared on 17 September:

The moment was an awful one, when George Borrow, the well-known author of *Lavengro*, and the *Bible in Spain*, dashed into the surf and saved one life, and through his instrumentality the others were saved. We ourselves have known this brave and gifted man for years, and, daring as was this deed, we have known him more than once to risk his life for others. We are happy to add that he has sustained no material injury.

Long afterwards, in 1892, when Borrow was dead and Hake old, the doctor wrote again of Borrow in his *Memoirs of Eighty Years*, but by then his admiration was more qualified.

George Borrow was one of those whose mental powers are strong and whose bodily frame is yet stronger. His temper was good and bad; his pride was humility; his humility was pride; his vanity, in being negative, was of the most positive kind. He was reticent and candid, measured in speech, with an emphasis that made trifles significant.

Borrow was essentially hypochondriacal. Society he loved and hated alike: he loved it that he might be pointed out and talked of; he hated it because he was not the prince that he felt himself in its midst. His figure was tall and his bearing very noble. He had a finely moulded head, and thick white hair – white from his youth; his brown eyes were soft yet piercing; his nose somewhat of the Semitic type, which gave his face the cast of the young Memnon. His mouth had a generous curve; and his features, for beauty and true power, were such as can have no parallel in our portrait gallery.

Borrow, if he had read that, would probably have gone into one of his black moods in which it seemed to him that all those he had dealings with, and large numbers of those whom he did not know at all, were allied in a malignant conspiracy to thwart him and hold him down. But the *Bury Post*, at least, had done right by him. Here was George Borrow, the man of action, fearless and strong to save. It had printed a good, true story and newspapers all over the land thought it worth copying. Even the far-off *Plymouth Mail* copied it, giving the report the title: 'Gallant Conduct of Mr G. Borrow'. This paper circulated across the Tamar, and was read by farming folk in places round about Liskeard – Trethinnick, St. Clear and Menheniot. There were Borrows still in these places, and they asked themselves: could this famous George, author of *The Bible in Spain* which had had such a success back in 1843 be a member of the family? Henry Borrow of Looe Down, an old man of seventy-six, was particularly interested. Henry's father, another Henry, had had a younger brother, Thomas, born in 1758 in the parish of St. Clear. In 1783, aged twenty-five, this Thomas had been obliged to flee the county, and all his family, after some violent behaviour – he had, amongst much else, knocked down the headborough of Liskeard, Edmund Hambley, a maltster in a fair way of business and much respected. This serious crime was made more serious by virtue of the fact that young Thomas was at the time apprenticed to this very Hambley. What he had done therefore was almost as bad as knocking down his own father – just as bad, some might say, because Thomas had no father to knock down: John Borrow of Trethinnick had died in 1758 before his eighth son, Thomas, had been born.

And so young Thomas had swiftly disappeared. He had run for it. Liskeard never saw him again; neither did the county of Cornwall.

But – and this was the question that quite agitated the Borrow descendants still active on Cornish soil – could they claim kinship with this famous son of a prodigal father? Robert Taylor of Penquite Farm, who had married Anne, the daughter of Henry Borrow of Looe Down, was asked to write a letter. He was the best of them all at written self-expression. And so Robert wrote, putting the question that was uppermost in the family mind. He addressed his letter: 'George Borrow Esq., Yarmouth', and this was enough. This was a notable man – not a wholly popular one, but still a notable. Borrow wrote cordially back. Yes, there was this strong Cornish connection. '. . . I am delighted to learn that there are still some living at Trethinnick who remember my honoured father, who had as true a Cornish heart as ever beat' he told them. He said furthermore that he would 'appear amongst them on the first opportunity.' And this was not empty politeness. All his life Borrow was a restless man, watching eagerly for any chance – any excuse – to be on the move. On Christmas Eve of that same year, 1853, he arrived in Liskeard on foot. There was nothing surprising in this: he had in his time arrived on foot in much stranger, much more distant places than Liskeard. But it was, all the same, a special sort of arrival. George Borrow, after a silence of fifty years, had linked up again with his father's people.

'My honoured father, who had as true a Cornish heart as ever beat' – this phrase of Borrow's when writing to his Cornish cousins might have been no more than an epistolary flourish. In 1853 Thomas Borrow had been almost thirty years dead. But in those distant days when George Borrow had been an adolescent – and even sulkier and more incomprehensible than most – relations between father and son had been far from affectionate. These old tensions would hardly have been revived in Borrow's Cornish conversations of 1853 and 1854. His role would have been that of a rather lonely man coming home after more than half a lifetime. He would have listened to memories of his father older than his own.

In 1778, at the age of nineteen, the orphaned Thomas Borrow had been put in the care of his uncle Henry Borrow of Liskeard, who had bound him apprentice to the maltster, Edmund Hambley. The youngster was tough, strong, and aggressive. That same year he had joined the Yeomanry Militia. There were duties attached to this, of course, but not such as to interfere with his obligations towards Hambley. He spent five years in Liskeard, learning his trade, growing stronger, accustoming himself to the military life and developing qualities of leadership; the youth of Liskeard took notice of him.

Then in 1783 the time of the annual Menheniot Fair came round. Between Liskeard and Menheniot there was a fun-feud – an excuse for horseplay and minor violence: and pugilism – the art whereby two men knocked each other about in strictly regulated, scientific fashion – was beginning to be highly popular. Matches were fought in fields, on staked out grass patches outside the big towns. The high nobility came in coaches to watch and wager on them. The ordinary folk streamed out on foot or on horseback.

But at that Menheniot Fair of 1783 the young Thomas Borrow allowed his fighting blood to carry him away. He took charge of the Liskeard forces when they were beginning to flag and enabled them to carry the day. Maltster Hambley with his constables tackled Thomas for causing an affray, and a highly excited Thomas forthwith knocked his master down and so, at one blow struck in an exhilarated thoughtless moment, changed the course of his life. He became a criminal on the run. He disappeared, and nobody, then or now, knows what he did with himself over the next five months. (There is something very Borrovian about this.) Then, on 29 December 1783, he took the King's shilling at Bodmin – Coldstream Guards, Company C. He was twenty-three years old and was packed off to London. The winter of 1783–4 was a hard one, and Thomas Borrow seems to have been sobered by whatever experiences he had been obliged to endure. He did not of course lose the aggressiveness which was part of him but he channelled it. As a soldier he was dutiful, reliable, and attentive. There was no swift climb for him, however, because he lacked both money and influence. All the same, by 1792 he had climbed to be sergeant, and at this point he was transferred to the first Norfolk Regiment of Militia, stationed at East Dereham. He stayed with the regiment, a loyal and devoted servant, for thirty-two years, and when he retired had reached the rank of adjutant-captain.

Thomas Borrow's duties after that transfer were chiefly concerned with the raising and training of recruits. And not long after his arrival those duties became heavy and demanding. The armies of revolutionary France were soon to gain strength and authority and to spread their wings. By the time he was forty in 1799 Bonaparte would have established himself as the foremost military commander of modern times. Thomas Borrow's Regiment of Militia had only just been raised in 1792: he was facing therefore strenuous years. He was thirty-four by then, and doubtless felt the need to be married. His eye fell upon Ann Perfrement.

And here, more than ten years before Borrow was born, comes the first of the many mysteries which surround the man as ink surrounds

an octopus on the defensive. In *Lavengro* Ann Perfrement is presented to us as a gracious old lady of seventy or so. (Borrow wrote the
first part of his autobiography in the winter of 1842–3.) She belonged,
he says, to a Huguenot family which had resisted 'the tyranny of
Rome' as he puts it (something which for Borrow was always prima
facie evidence of virtue), and 'had established themselves in East
Anglia'. When she was young she had been 'strikingly handsome', he
says – but of course this is something he has to take on hearsay. Then
he goes on to pay a stately tribute. 'Hail to thee, dame of the oval face,
olive complexion and Grecian forehead; by thy table seated with the
mighty volume of the good Bishop Hopkins spread out before
thee. . . .' There is genuine affection in his words, and the impression
is conveyed of someone used from youth up to the best of everything
both spiritual and material. Her family 'had established themselves'.

Yet when Thomas first met her he was a sergeant-major and she
was playing a bit part in a theatrical touring company. Even the first
player in such a company must have been a very minor person indeed
– a strolling actor of not much more consequence than a gipsy one
might think – because East Dereham was no more than a large village,
and the best accommodation vagrant actors would be likely to find
there would probably be a rigged-up booth. If the Perfrements had
been the dignified people Borrow conjures up, devoted to agriculture
and to the principles of the reformed church, would Samuel, Ann's
father, have allowed his twenty-year-old daughter to go kicking up
her heels in the company of disreputable barnstormers? Biographers
have on the whole followed the *Lavengro* guidelines, and taken Ann
Perfrement at her (Borrovian) face value. It seems possible, even
likelier however, that she was the daughter of peasants – of gipsy
origin perhaps, since gipsies, or Hungarians as they were known,
sought to give themselves respectability by use of the similar-
sounding epithet 'Huguenot' – and by the age of twenty not unaccustomed to tumbling in the hay.

At all events, if that indeed was her background it was to be a useful
and appropriate one for the sort of life which she was to lead with
Thomas for the next twenty and more years. Apart from shortish lulls
Ann Borrow was always on the move, the camp-follower of her
husband. She had no home other than a tent or barracks. If you drew
a line from Southampton to Edinburgh then it would be true to say
that Ann Perfrement was enabled to familiarize herself, with a painful
thoroughness rare indeed for a woman of her generation, with the
kingdom lying east of that line. Even after the ending of the wars in
1815, when recruiting ceased at last to be an urgent, never-ending

business, the wanderings of Thomas Borrow and his family continued for a while longer. In August 1815 the regiment was sent to
Ireland and the little towns of Clonmel and Templemore knew them
as birds of passage. Borrow, almost thirteen by the time they left in
May 1816, roved and rode round the counties of Waterford and
Tipperary and got to know them well. Ireland and Irishness remained
an abiding influence on him. After all, the Celtic genes seemed from
somewhere to have built themselves into him. Sergeant-major Thomas Borrow was a Cornishman. And was not Thomas his father?
Probably.

Yet here, at the very moment of his conception (October 1802)
Borrow presents us with the first of his innumerable puzzles. Was he,
in fact, the son of Thomas Borrow? Mr Brian Vesey-FitzGerald has
argued persuasively that he was not. Can his view be accepted? The
crucial passage is to be found in chapter 14 of *Lavengro*. Here
Borrow, thirteen years old at the time, reports, or reconstructs, a
conversation between Thomas and Ann which took place in 1816 or
1817, when Thomas was a retired man and beginning to be ailing. '"I
will hear nothing against my first-born [This was John, born in
1800.]" said my father, "even in the way of insinuation: he is my joy
and pride – the very image of myself in my youthful days, long before
I fought Big Ben, though perhaps not quite so tall or strong built. As
for the other, God bless the child! I love him, I'm sure; but I must be
blind not to see the difference between him and his brother. Why, he
has neither my hair nor my eyes; and then his countenance! why, 'tis
absolutely swarthy, God forgive me! I had almost said like that of a
gipsy, but I have nothing to say against that; the boy is not to be
blamed for the colour of his face, nor for his hair and eyes; but then,
his ways and manners! I confess I do not like them, and that they give
me no little uneasiness. I know that he kept very strange company
when he was in Ireland; people of evil report – horse-witches and the
like. . . . That ever son of mine should have been intimate with the
Papist Irish, and have learnt their language!" "But he thinks of other
things now," said my mother. "Other languages you mean," said my
father. "It is strange that he has conceived such a zest for the study of
languages; no sooner did he come home than he persuaded me to send
him to that old priest to learn French and Italian, and, if I remember
right, you abetted him; but, as I said before, it is in the nature of
women invariably to take the part of the second-born. . . ."'

Did Thomas suspect that in October 1802 his wife had had a gipsy
lover? It is true that during their twenty years or so of wandering life
Ann was constantly being left to herself. Thomas's frequently chang-

ing headquarters were still headquarters merely, from which he made
detailed sorties into the surrounding areas in quest of recruits. For
Ann there would have been plentiful opportunities, perhaps also a
need, for extra-marital affairs. But to set against this is the fact that the
only lull, the only stay-at-home time for Thomas Borrow, occurred
between October 1801 and May 1803 – the length of time the pre-
carious Peace of Amiens lasted. And the parish register at East
Dereham says: 'A.D. 1803. Borrow, George Henry, son of Thomas
and Ann his wife (late Perfrement), born July 5th, baptised 17th.' So
Borrow was conceived in October 1802, the most likely time, in all
the wandering years of the marriage of Thomas and Ann, for Thomas
to be quietly at home in East Dereham attending to his husbandly
duties and interests, and the least likely time for Ann to be entertaining a dark-faced stranger, perhaps even a gipsy from one of their
encampments on Mousehold Heath outside Norwich.

The vicar of St. Clear at the time of Borrow's Cornish visit was
J. P. R. Berkeley. He watched Borrow closely: was not this after all
by now a quite famous man? He even gave a dinner for him. Borrow
acted oddly, Berkeley thought.

. . .his feelings were much too excited. He was thinking of the time when his
father's footsteps and his father's voice re-echoed in the room in which we
were sitting. His eyes wandered from point to point, and at times, if I was not
mistaken, a tear could be seen trembling in them. At length he could no
longer control his feelings. He left the hall suddenly, and in a few moments,
but for God's providential care, the career of George Borrow would have
been ended. There was within a few feet of the house a low wall with a drop of
some feet into a paved yard. He walked rapidly out, and, it being nearly dark,
he stepped one side of the gate and fell over the wall. . . .

Does this sound like the behaviour of a man revisiting the childhood
haunts of a father whom he knew to be a fake-father? But Borrow was
an hysterical, mixed-up man. Anyone who, in his case, distinguished
with quick positiveness between appearance and reality, would be
acting rashly. In 1856 Nathaniel Hawthorne wrote: 'Dining at Mr
Rathbone's one evening last week (May 21st), it was mentioned that
Borrow. . . is supposed to be of gipsy descent by his mother's side.
Hereupon Mr Martineau mentioned that . . . though he had never
heard of his gipsy blood, he thought it probable, from Borrow's traits
of character. . . .'

All this has to remain speculative. René Fréchet, who wrote a
thorough and scholarly account of Borrow in 1956, considers that
Vesey-FitzGerald's arguments in favour of a thoroughbred gipsy

Borrow are not at all conclusive. Borrow's behaviour during the Cornish visit of 1853–4 leads us to suppose that he genuinely believed himself to be the son of his father, in spite of the dark rumblings which he puts into Thomas Borrow's mouth in *Lavengro*. It has to be taken, then, that Thomas Borrow did indeed have two sons, first John, then George, both widely different in appearance as well as in temperament, but both his. Whether the second son was a gipsy on his mother's side remains more open to question. If he was, then of course John was too – and the *Lavengro* description of him in early childhood – 'a rosy, angelic face, blue eyes, and light chestnut hair' – does not in any way tally with gipsydom.

Borrow was born three years after his brother, on 5 July 1803, into a land at war. This would not in the ordinary way have made much difference. But as he was the son of a serving soldier, and moreover a soldier concerned primarily with the business of recruiting, it made a very great deal of difference. Until May 1816 – for almost the first thirteen years of his life therefore – Borrow never stayed in one place for long. During the years when he was too young to be aware of anything, Thomas and Ann were marching mainly about Kent and Sussex. Then in 1809–10 they were quartered again in the home town of Norwich, and Borrow went first to school in East Dereham, which was small and quiet and where the patterns of life, war or no war, did not change markedly from generation to generation.

But no sooner settled into a routine than the young beginner had to be up and moving again. The regiment moved to Norman Cross. This was a geographical point rather than a place. It lay a mile or so north of the village of Stilton on the Great North Road where the Peterborough road, bearing north-eastwards, crossed it. The nearest village was either Stilton or Yaxley, and here, in watery flood-prone country, the army had established a camp for prisoners of war. The *casernes* where the prisoners were held impressed the seven-year-old Borrow. He talks about them in *Lavengro*. 'What a strange appearance . . . with their blank, blind walls, without windows or grating, and their slanting roofs, out of which, through orifices where the tiles had been removed, would be protruded dozens of grim heads, feasting their prison-sick eyes on the wide expanse of country. . . .'

Borrow at Norman Cross seems to have gone surprisingly far afield. The living conditions there must have been makeshift, certainly not the kind to supply the sheet-anchor domesticity which the very young need and respond to. Raising healthily enquiring children in a hastily run-up barracks dumped in a watery nowhere must have been a strenuous, even exhausting business. Ann Borrow, who was tough, must occasionally have found her pair too much for her. One or the other, but George the younger more often than John, would have gone missing. Fortunately it was April when they got there: the winter floods were over; the sun was beginning to climb fast. Borrow explored the neighbourhood round Yaxley and Whittlesea Mere: the unimaginable quietness of the older England still just held. Already at East Dereham he had gone a little to school and begun to absorb Lilly's Latin Grammar. A young woman had given him *Robinson Crusoe*, and the wonderful engravings had stirred him to try to master the print. The *grande dame* of the place, the widowed Lady Fenn, was greatly interested in children and had written books for them, concealing her authorship under pleasing pseudonyms like 'Mrs Teachwell' or 'Mrs Lovechild'. Borrow would certainly have come under her eye. He stood out.

By the time they had settled in, summer had come, and Borrow remembered the weather as 'bright and glorious'. He also remembered that he had been 'subjected to but little control', and it was here, about this time, that he had one of those 'encounters' which so strongly characterize all his writing. Near Whittlesea Mere there was an abandoned manor house. The grounds had run wild and here Borrow ran wild too. He plunged about and poked about and when he was tired he sat down with his back against a tree, and tried to see how much further he could get with *Robinson Crusoe*. Sometimes on these jaunts he passed a 'tall, elderly individual'. (All his life Borrow was irritatingly fond of this word 'individual', ugly, unspecific, but helpful to the anonymity he was always dodging behind.) He wore gaiters and a skin cap. He fumbled about in bramble bushes and studied viper trails on the road. Then he would move quickly, there would be some scuffling, and the elderly individual would reappear holding a large viper in his hand. He wanted admiration, but got little from the small boy. '. . . I could do as much myself.' Later on, however, they got to be friendly, and the viper-catcher gave Borrow a tame one for himself.

Carrying the creature about under his shirt, Borrow was ready now for the 'encounter'. In a bit of a clearing he came upon a tent. Two light carts stood outside and horses were grazing nearby. There was a fire, and a man and a woman sat on either side of it. The seven-year-old marched confidently and silently up. He startled them. The man was plaiting straw, the woman, so Borrow thought, was making counterfeit money. The couple rushed threateningly at him. They were both on the young side of middle age and both villainous and savage to look at. Borrow stopped them by producing

the viper from where it lay close to his chest. These two, the Gipsy
Smiths, took Borrow for a magician, a 'sap-engro', one whom the
snakes obeyed. They were eager to show proper deference. Their son,
'a lad of some twelve or thirteen years' Borrow says, came up. The
two fraternized.

This was a relationship that lasted through life. The boy was
Ambrose Smith – or Ambrose Petulengro because the gipsies went
under two names. Borrow called him 'Ambrose' all through *Lavengro* and *The Romany Rye*, but altered it to 'Jasper' just before the
manuscripts were printed. The alterations were in pencil and carried
out in the hand of his wife Mary Borrow. The two were 'brothers' –
blood brothers perhaps, because it is likely that a ceremony of
blood-brotherhood was carried out between them. It might even
have been performed then and there, at that first meeting, because the
two were suitably young. Ambrose was not, as Borrow says, 'a lad of
some twelve or thirteen years' but someone a year or two younger
than Borrow himself. He lived on till October 1878, and Borrow
survived him by a little under three years.

The question that has to be asked of course – and it is a question
that recurs as you come to the numerous dream-sequences in the life
of Borrow – is an urgent and difficult one. How much of all this are
we to believe? Clearly not all of it. Ambrose was six, not twelve.
Borrow was very young indeed to stand his ground when threatened
by wild and ruffianly strangers and to cow them by reaching for a
viper. Did Ann Borrow know where he was? Did the boy tell her
about it when he got back? Did he recount the arrival of the piratical
Nat on a hard-ridden horse, of how he carried some sort of warning
which caused the whole gipsy colony to gather and pack and flee but
not before Nat had been handed two bags of false money? The
improbabilities stand together in a row and shout at you.

But Borrow was not a liar. Rather he was evasive and secretive. He
garbled. His essential truths are of the kind which cannot be conveyed in a down-to-earth realistic way. He needs to hang muffling
curtains round them. He asks us to suspend disbelief willingly and
substitute for it poetic faith. That he gained entry suddenly into a
wild and pagan world, that this world fascinated him and held him
close all his life long – so much is certain. Whether it took place beside
a quiet country track in Huntingdonshire, not far from huge and ugly
prisoner-of-war barracks, when he himself was not much more than a
toddler – that each reader has to decide for himself. Borrow is regally
uninterested in plausibility. His concern is to make a genuine experience memorable.

The family stayed at Norman Cross until July 1811. After that they were back on home ground in East Dereham for a few months, but before the end of the year Captain Borrow was on the move again. Having no settled base he would have worried a great deal over the education of his two sons. He was not a man to duck his responsibilities. Whenever there was a pause on the march (Harwich, Leicester, Melton Mowbray, Tamworth, Macclesfield, Stockport, Ashton-under-Lyne, Huddersfield, Sheffield . . . the list is long), '. . . in every town in which we were stationary,' as Borrow puts it, 'I was invariably (God bless my father!) sent to the classical academy of the place . . . .' But there was no real settling until, in April 1813, the West Norfolks finally arrived in Edinburgh. Here they stayed until the victory of the allies over Bonaparte at Leipzig and the final putting away (as people thought) of the Emperor on Elba in June 1814, and Borrow, enrolled at Edinburgh High School, had at last the opportunity to grow in godliness and good learning.

Here of course there is another question which insistently demands an answer. Why did not the Captain, fully aware quite obviously of his responsibilities over his sons' education, board them out with their maternal grandparents, the Perfrements, at Dumpling Green, and keep them steadily at school either at East Dereham or even at Norwich itself which was only eleven miles and a bit away? But Borrow makes no mention of his maternal grandparents. The Samuel Perfrements, and that farm at Dumpling Green, quite fade away.

At Edinburgh High School, Borrow, ten years old by now, seems to have been something of a wild one, and this, after all his marchings and counter-marchings, is nothing to be surprised at. He was a Sassenach and so, for the Scots boys, a natural enemy to measure their strength against. There was fighting. Borrow was good at fighting always. There was probably plenty of truancy too. He got to know David Haggart, two years older than he was, who had enlisted as a drummer-boy in the regiment. Haggart was very wild indeed, took to banditry, murdered twice whilst attempting to break prison and was hanged in his native Edinburgh in 1821. None of this though really prompts Borrow to reproof. Haggart, Borrow thinks, is a man cast in some respects in the mould of Tamerlane. And all his life Borrow was never in doubt that the world could do with Tamerlanes. Borrow felt a kinship between himself and the rogue-rebel Haggart. He liked the way he stood out in boys' battles, between Old Town and New Town.

A wild-looking figure is descending the hill with terrible bounds; it is a lad of some fifteen years; he is bare-headed, and his red uncombed hair stands on end like hedgehogs' bristles; his frame is lithy, like that of an antelope, but he has prodigious breadth of shoulders; he wears a military undress, that of the regiment, even of a drummer, for it is wild Davy, whom a month before I had seen enlisted. . . .

Borrow casts his story forward eight years in order to take in Haggart's throttled end; and still for him the Tamerlane parallel persists. 'Both these men were robbers and of low birth, yet one perished on an ignoble scaffold, and the other died emperor of the world . . . yet . . . what is the intrinsic difference between them? . . .' Well, yes, there was a difference. Borrow, writing all this in the 1840s by which time he had become a small landed proprietor and respectable, felt that there had, for propriety's sake, to be a difference. But his efforts at separating the two sound rather half-hearted, and he is happier when he reverts to a tone of affectionate apostrophe. 'But peace to thee, poor David! why should a mortal worm be sitting in judgment over thee?' Borrow was still the vagabond, still at heart a reluctant conformist.

In the summer of 1814 the regiment returned to Norwich and was disbanded. Borrow was sent to the Grammar School in Upper Close. John studied painting with Crome. But even now Borrow's wandering years were not over. Bonaparte saw to that. To cope with the threat of the Hundred Days, Captain Borrow, in his mid-fifties by now, was soon busy re-mustering. The regiment reached full strength too late for Waterloo, and instead was sent to Ireland at the end of August 1815 to become established at Clonmel in the south, half way between Waterford and Tipperary. The army's role was 'pacification'. During the long wars Ireland had prospered in a modest way. The British had been eager to import her grain. The victory at Waterloo changed all that. The big landowners went back to dairy-farming ; amongst the tenant-farmers there were evictions; wages fell and prices fell; the Protestant ascendancy grew stronger as did the rebellious mutterings of the Catholic Irish. Why should they pay for the late wars on the same scale as the British? The West Norfolks were required to put a stop to activities much less peaceable than straw-plaiting. The family was nine months altogether in Ireland, mainly at Clonmel but briefly, towards the end, at Templemore. Borrow was enrolled at the only Protestant school Clonmel possessed. There was a rough wildness about the place that appealed to the natural cravings of the youngster Borrow. There was also a strange tongue to listen to because in 1815 the Irish language was still vigorous and widely spoken. '"A queer tongue," said I, "I wonder if I could learn it?" "Learn it!" said my father; "what should you learn it for?"' The son records no reply to this question: nevertheless he was giving expression here for the first time to what was to become one of the driving passions of his life: the acquiring of languages. He was to become 'Lavengro' (with the accent on the first syllable) – the master of words. Irish, Welsh, old Norse, Romany, Russian, Persian, Portuguese, Manchu, and modern Greek – his range was astonishing; the depth of his knowledge, however, perhaps not quite so impressive. To the French word 'jument' for example he gives masculine gender; in Welsh he bothers little about elisions and spells 'eto' (still) 'etto'. None the less his memory for multitudes of words was prodigious, and his ability to get a good, quick grasp of a language utterly remote from English (Manchu for example) quite outstanding.

It was the boy Murtagh, sixteen years old and standing over six foot, who taught him his Irish. He was one of the few papist 'gasoons' whom the Clonmel Protestant school accepted. 'Gasoon' was the name for any poor tenant-farmer's son who came in from the bog in order to acquire enough Greek to qualify him for entrance to a seminary (in Paris perhaps, or Salamanca) and thereafter to the priesthood. Murtagh lived 'at a place called the Wilderness . . . a fearful wild place', and he longed for a pack of cards to alleviate book-learning. Borrow handed over his pack in exchange for Irish lessons – though how reliable a teacher Murtagh was remains a big question. Borrow at any rate contributed enthusiasm and willingness to learn. Irish was not 'a school language . . . but a speech spoken in out-of-the-way desolate places, and in cut-throat kens, where thirty ruffians, at the sight of the King's minions, would spring up with brandished sticks and an 'ubbubboo like the blowing-up of a powder-magazine.' It was a language therefore likely to appeal to Borrow's natural instincts. He was fascinated also by 'the strangeness and singularity of its tones'; and these he was to find in all the Celtic languages – a quality which made them dear to his heart all his life long.

It was in Ireland too that he first came to know and understand horses. He rode magnificently. Whenever he writes about horses he writes at his best. John by now had joined the regiment and was away from the family in barracks. Borrow went to visit him. When he was standing at the door of the barrack stable a groom came up and asked him if he 'would give the cob a breathing this fine morning'. This was to be a bare-back affair, and Borrow, the beginner, confessed to being 'half-afraid'. He nearly slipped off, but he learnt to cling not with hands but with calves and feet. He found too that he had immediately that strange, inexplicable affinity that can exist between horse and

man. He kept going for two hours, and 'Oh, that ride! – most truly it
was an epoch in my existence; and I still look back to it with feelings
of longing and regret. People may talk of first love – it is a very
agreeable event, I dare say – but give me the flush, and triumph, and
glorious sweat of a first ride like mine on the mighty cob!'

The Borrow family returned to England, and Norwich, and stab-
ility in May 1816. The Captain, freed at last from urgent responsibilities – he was to be retired on full pay (eight shillings a day) in 1819 –
took a small house in Willow Lane. His two sons still gave problems.
The standing-down of the regiment lost John his commission. Captain Borrow wrote to the Duke of York to ask whether John, because
of his good service in Ireland, and because he, his father, had a lifetime
of exemplary service to the regiment behind him, might be granted a
commission in the regular army. The reply was bleak. The Duke had
claims which he could not satisfy coming from many who were much
higher in the caste system than the humble Borrows. John was not as
put out by this refusal as his father. His lieutenant's pay continued for
a while, and he was quite content to return to Old Crome's studio and
try to turn himself into a painter. For his younger son the Captain
managed to get a scholarship to the Grammar School, and there, in
the autumn of 1816, in his fourteenth year by now, Borrow returned.

Edward Valpy B.D. reigned there as headmaster between 1810 and
1829. English education was in poor shape all through his time.
Arnold, great initiator, did not begin his work at Rugby until 1828.
Ferocity and flogging were accepted as matters of routine. Rous-
seau's writ did not run in England, and indeed flogging was to remain
as something not in any way unusual for more than a century and a
quarter after Borrow's re-entry into Norwich Grammar School.

But Borrow was not prepared to knuckle under. His pugnacity, his
independence, his tendency always to brood over wrongs real or
imagined – all these were qualities which made him an unsuitable
subject for the Valpy treatment. Added to this his thirteen years of
vagrancy inevitably had its vast and permanent effect on the developing youngster. He had acquired a liking for the company of toughies.
Haggart, Murtagh, the ruffianly gipsies near Norman Cross with
their bags of counterfeit money – there was something in him that
responded to people like these. Edward Valpy aroused in him no
responsiveness at all. He wanted passionately to learn, and to learn
languages especially, but he preferred to follow an out-of-school
programme of his own devising. He bought himself grammars in
second-hand bookshops and defied the languages of France and Italy
to resist his onslaughts. He persuaded his father to agree to private

lessons from Thomas d'Eterville, a priest who had skipped from Caen in 1793, and had since done reasonably well in Norwich, not so much by teaching languages which was his nominal job, as by dealing in contraband. He visited both boys' and girls' schools in Norwich, was rather grubby, and longed still for Caen and his homeland. Borrow made good progress with him and after six months was able to deputize for his master when d'Eterville's other concerns obliged him to miss a teaching appointment.

Yet in school Borrow was indolent, unhappy, and rebellious. The great majority of the pupils were fee-payers, and these looked down on the scholarship boys, but Borrow could never accept a subservient role. He was always ready, even eager, to resist authority – or even a reasonable obedience to rules. When it came to the bullying tyranny of schoolboys he stood up and fought, no matter how hopelessly in the minority. Because he could fight, and fight well, Borrow nevertheless had his followers at school. He told them tales about popery and about the evil doings that popery fostered. Why, at this early age, was his life-long, obsessive hatred of Roman Catholicism apparent? The answer must be that, instinctively and through no conscious process of thought, he saw the Roman Church as the grand symbol of authority, and his immediate reaction, at fourteen as at seventy-four, was to rebel. To his followers he must have seemed wild and strange and exciting. He had been about so much. He had mingled with all sorts and conditions of men. He could talk to them about vipers and the wild Irish. He was tall and swarthy – a foreigner somehow. He rubbed walnut juice into his face to heighten this apartness. 'Borrow, are you suffering from jaundice, or is it only dirt?' Valpy asked him one day. Borrow preserved a sulky silence. He was out of school quite often when he should have been in. He was seen, with his back to the world, hunched in the quiet corners of second-hand bookshops. He walked fast and far across the fens. He went after game in defiance of Captain Borrow's law-abiding dislike of poaching. He wandered in the grounds of Earlham Hall; he even met the wealthy quaker, John Gurney, owner of the estate. Indeed he got to know many people because, in spite of his sulky unresponsiveness at Norwich Grammar School, he had a way with strangers, could talk to them easily and readily. At Harford Bridge, a little way along the road to Ipswich, lived Thomas Thurtell and his son John not long back from the wars. John was a boxer, and taught Borrow the art – one which, as a Norwich scholarship-boy he needed to master, but one which like his father he delighted in for its own sake. On Maundy Thursdays he would go to Tombland Fair, where the sheep-, cattle-, and horse-dealers gathered and where he met again his blood-brother, Ambrose Petulengro, now grown tall.

Not long before the welcome release from school came in 1818 Borrow planned and partly carried through a major truancy. He persuaded three other boys to take part, Dalrymple and the brothers Purland, all of them younger than he was. He told them they would strike eastward, towards the sea and the sand-flats round Caister. And what when they got there? Well, they would find a cave, perhaps, pilfer food as opportunity offered, and make money too. How? By working as porters for smugglers. Purland major and minor, as well as Dalrymple seem to have accepted it all. Borrow could always make an unlikely tale convincing. Very early in the morning they crossed the River Wensum and set briskly off. They had covered only three miles when Dalrymple became scared at the enormity of what they were about. He turned for home. Borrow and the Purlands kept on until they reached Acle, ten miles from Norwich. Here they paused at the roadside to eat the rations they had brought with them. The parent of a grammar-school boy rolled by in a chaise. Not Mr Dalrymple, not Mr Purland, not, certainly Captain Borrow who, all through a hardworking life beset with anxieties could never have afforded a carriage; but none the less someone who recognized them and who could act swiftly and appropriately in surprising situations. He stopped his conveyance, noted that the boys' meal was meagre, and invited them to eat with him at the next inn along. The Purlands who were tired and still hungry, accepted eagerly and even Borrow, still too young to be suspicious of wholesale generosity on the part of comparative strangers, found the prospect of a meal and a rest irresistible. Once arrived at the inn, the parent – he has no name, this putter-down of youthful initiative – immediately sent a man back to Norwich on a fast, fresh horse, carrying the news to Valpy, and Valpy, who had doubtless been through this sort of thing before, immediately dispatched a force sufficient to round the trio up. Replete, comfortable, and still tired enough to want to linger, Borrow and the Purlands were still at the inn when Valpy's lieutenants arrived.

For this Borrow was horsewhipped in the presence of the whole school. James Martineau, brother of Harriet and himself to become a writer on Spinoza and an eminent mid-century theologian, did duty as horse. Borrow never forgave Valpy for this public humiliation; nor did he ever forgive Martineau, when they happened, very much later in life, both to be at the same gathering in London, Borrow refused either to meet or to speak to Martineau; Hawthorne's record of

Martineau's opinion of Borrow on that occasion has already been quoted. Borrow's memory was long, and he was always a man who bore grudges. Norwich Grammar School is wiped clean out of *Lavengro*. His memories of the place, when he came to write were still too painful to be written about: there would have been the risk of a vindictive emotional flare-up which would have destroyed the tone of his book. His resentments were so strong indeed that after he had been withdrawn from school in 1818 he had a strange nervous break-down.

The doctors could not understand it. They thought perhaps he had grown too tall too quickly. He lay on his bed, and 'as for myself, I made up my mind to die, and felt quite resigned. . . . I did not die, for somebody coming, gave me a strange, bitter draught; a decoction, I believe, of a bitter root which grows on commons and desolate places; and the person who gave it me was an ancient female, a kind of doctress who had been my nurse in infancy . . . so I drank the draught, and became a little better. . . .' All this is very Borrovian. The bitter root growing in desolate places, and the ancient crone – are we to take all this as it stands? The core-answer to this must be yes, because Borrow did not fake his facts. The reality, and the import-ance of this illness are further emphasized by the fact that after it came 'the horrors'.

All through his life from that time on Borrow was subject at intervals to fits of intense depression. A powerful, pugnacious man, he could cower before quite insubstantial fears, with a wish only to hide in the dark. He described the first onset of these horrors as he lay convalescent from his mysterious illness. Captain Borrow, ashamed by his son's public disgrace, disappointed that he showed no inclina-tion to make any progress towards manhood in any seemly, conven-tional fashion, seems at this point to lose patience, to want simply to let him lie. But between Borrow and his mother there was always a sympathy strong enough to outlast any lapses or irregularities of behaviour. 'What ails you, my child?' he makes her say . . . 'you seem afraid!' And the conversation goes on: '"And so I am; a dreadful fear is upon me." "But of what; there is no one can harm you; of what are you apprehensive?" "Of nothing that I can express;. . . mine is a dread of I know not what, and there the horror lies. . . ."' '. . . a dread of I know not what. . .' – he never got nearer to it than that.

After Borrow had recovered the Captain determined on a strong line. He would launch this son whether he liked it or not; and he would get rid of him at the same time. He would article him to a firm of solicitors for five years, and Borrow would live on his master's premises, and the little house in Willow Lane would be relieved of a distressful presence. And so, after somewhat under three years, came yet another removal for Borrow. On Monday, 30 March 1819, he was articled to the firm of Simpson and Rackham of Tuck's Court, St Giles in Norwich. He still had not completed his sixteenth year. Borrow's attitude to all this seems to have been listless acceptance. His nerve-storms and his nameless fears had not quite retreated. Indeed they never would again leave him wholly master of himself for any very long stretch.

But it was much, much better than school. '. . . within the womb of a lofty deal desk, behind which I sat for some eight hours every day, transcribing . . . documents of every description . . . Blackstone kept company with ab Gwilym. . . .' Simpson was a good-humoured, indulgent man, as well as being the first in his profession in the city of Norwich and in the whole surrounding area. If his pupil took delight in the disreputable sport of pugilism, if he allowed Blackstone to trail behind a scarcely-known Welsh medieval poet called ab Gwilym (as Borrow insisted on calling him – correctly 'ap'), if he was found at times, black-suited, leaning against the garden railings and chatting to boys from the school he had now mercifully left – well, this was the natural way of youth. He would doubtless settle to the law in due time. Simpson was not to know that his pupil, boy or man, was always to remain the least malleable of mortals, or that, in his middle forties, he would write 'By adopting the law I had not ceased to be Lavengro.'

He had not been long in Tuck's Court before he bought in a Norwich bookshop, Owen Pughe's translation into Welsh of *Paradise Lost*. He compared it with the involved rotundity of Milton's English; and by this means managed to get a smattering of Welsh together. That he was successful shows beyond doubt that here was someone greatly gifted linguistically. To learn Welsh by seeing how Pughe had coped with Milton – Milton of all people – is indeed to learn a hard language the hard way. But Borrow was not satisfied simply with getting the hang of Welsh on the printed page. He had to be able to talk it. Someone in Tuck's Court employed a Welsh ostler. Some of Simpson's clerks made fun of the ostler, called him Taffy, and made him miserable. In this situation Borrow saw an opportunity. He would tell Simpson's young gentlemen that the ostler was to be left alone. If they paid no heed to this instruction then he, Borrow, would knock them down. The ostler was left in peace and in return Borrow was enabled to study oral Welsh. On Sundays he went back to Willow Lane for lunch. The ostler went with him. The visits continued for about a year and Borrow acquired fluent, badly accented Welsh. Captain Borrow did not greatly approve. Even more strongly did he disapprove of his son's talking already of giving up his articles. Giving them up for what? To go about with a Welsh ostler and to watch fist-fights.

Borrow was barely seventeen when, on 17 July 1820, he walked out of Norwich to North Walsham (about fourteen miles) to watch the Painter-Oliver fight, and Borrow, as a pupil of John Thurtell, who almost certainly organized the affair, was able to mingle with Cribb and Belcher and other luminaries who dazzled him as much as ap Gwilym. Thurtell's influence on Borrow is not to be underestimated. He was a tough reprobate. His talent for fixing matches brought the game into the disrepute which caused it to dwindle in popularity from the beginning of the 1820s. He was not a mindless bruiser, but an educated man of considerable intelligence. His father, Thomas, took his turn as Lord Mayor of Norwich. John Thurtell liked to dominate; he dominates many of the best pages in *Lavengro*. Criminals are not notably intelligent; so amongst them Thurtell could act the part of acknowledged leader. He enjoyed the role.

In the autumn of 1823, with robbery as the motive, he committed a brutal and carefully calculated murder. This happened at Elstree where one William Weare died for the sake of £1,000, and Thurtell was hanged for it outside Hertford gaol early in 1824. The North Walsham meeting (there was more than one fight) ended in a violent thunderstorm. Writing with hindsight in middle age, Borrow used this romantically to predict Thurtell's end less than four years ahead, and Ambrose Petulengro is brought in to do the prophesying. (Was Petulengro at North Walsham as well? Perhaps he was; there can be no certainty. It is enough to say that poetic truth requires him to be there, because Petulengro is the symbol for Borrow's gipsydom.)

How exceedingly unlawyerlike it all sounds. Small wonder that Captain Borrow worried lest his second son might possibly be a changeling. And even bruisers, horse-copers, gipsies, and murderers were not the end of it. Even the studious, scholarly side of Borrow plunged down such wild and unconventional by-ways. After Murtagh and the Welsh ostler, it was Mousha Levy, an odd and fraudulent wandering Jew, who offered to teach Borrow German and Hebrew, who cadged a dinner from him, and then asked for the loan of five pounds which Borrow gave. After the fifth dinner Mousha wondered whether a further fifty pounds might not be possible, but here Borrow's indulgence stopped abruptly: Levy's linguistic range was much more limited than he claimed, and at this point he slips out of the Borrovian story, but not before he has introduced his seventeen-year-old to another strong, but –as Captain Borrow would certainly have considered –thoroughly disreputable influence: the drunken, atheistic, revolutionary 'William Taylor of Norwich'.

Taylor was a man of fifty-five when Borrow came to know him in 1820. He was born in 1765, the son of a sober, substantial, Unitarian business man who, in 1780, sent him abroad to acquire culture and languages. He did acquire a considerable range of learning as well as a sympathy for the reformist, subversive notions of the French *philosophes*. (This sympathy, however, did not extend to the violence of 1793. Like so many others who came after him, Taylor much preferred the ideas behind revolution to the realities of it.) He was a man of the left rather in the way that Hazlitt was a man of the left. He travelled a good deal in Germany and met Goethe; German philosophers were probably more to his taste than their more radical French counterparts. After he had returned to Norwich he became a busy journalist and translator; he thought of himself primarily perhaps as an intermediary between insular Britain and western Europe with its freer cultural interchanges.

In Borrow he recognized an eager student. He took him up. He taught him German; he taught him what he knew of Danish, which wasn't much. Together they talked about the art of translation, about myths, about folk ballads, about the death of Balder, about Celtic singers like ap Gwilym, about the interrelationship of popular legend and story between country and country. They enjoyed each other's company. But always, it should be noted, even so early, Borrow is the *linguistic* man. What interests him is word-forms and syntax. To words put together in the interests of imaginative creation there seems never to be more than a small, conventional response. For him a string of words in a language unfamiliar to him constitutes an instant challenge. But there is rarely in his work much evidence of excitement about the literature of his own or any other country considered simply as literature.

Cultured high society in Norwich disapproved of Taylor. He drank too much. He smoked too much. He was a subversive. He corrupted youth. His manners were so coarse and hoggish that Harriet Martineau, being a lady, could scarcely be expected to speak of him from personal knowledge. All the same she did speak of him, and tartly too, making it known that 'his habits of intemperance kept him out of the sight of ladies, and he got round him a set of ignorant and conceited young men, who thought they could set the whole world right by their destructive propensities.' But Taylor the multilingual scholar was exactly the object of veneration this lanky, awkward young man was looking for.

Harriet Martineau's contempt for the impious William Taylor was far from being wholly mistaken. He had travelled certainly; he gave contemporary German writers some currency in England and, between 1828 and 1830, collected his translations and criticisms in a book which he called a *Historic Survey of German Poetry*; he had connections with literary London; he corresponded with Southey, Scott, and Godwin. But he was a fake philosopher. He was pretentious. He wrecked his father's prosperous business. For self-justification he depended upon the plaudits of callow young men. He filled young Borrow up with delusive notions about how easy it would be for him to make a success for himself in London as a writing man. He was right of course to recognize in Borrow a youth of extraordinary quality; but he was far from recognizing – perhaps at that stage he should not be blamed for this – the unique quality of Borrow's genius. He thought of him, as he thought of himself, as a linguist, a translator merely. And when Borrow translates a stanza from Goethe's 'Erlkönig' in the thumping, simple way he does –

> Sweet baby, I doat on that beautiful form,
> And thou shalt ride with me the wings of the storm.
> – O father, my father, he grapples me now,
> And already has done me a mischief, I vow.

– Taylor lacks the wit to see that this won't do at all. He filled the boy up with totally mistaken ideas about himself, pushed him down the wrong road, and in so doing did him incalculable damage. He wrote about him to his friend Southey, once also like Taylor a revolutionary but by 1821 lapsed into the pensionable security of the laureateship:

A Norwich young man is construing with me Schiller's 'William Tell', with a view of translating it for the press. His name is George Henry Borrow, and he has learnt German with extraordinary rapidity; indeed, he has the gift of tongues, and though not yet eighteen, understands twelve languages – English, Welsh, Erse, Latin, Greek, Hebrew, German, Danish, French, Italian, Spanish and Portuguese; he would like to get into the office for foreign affairs, but does not know how.

The Foreign Office, translating Schiller for the press – it was irresponsible, to say the least, for a man in his middle fifties to dazzle an eighteen-year-old articled clerk to a solicitor with such beguiling and inappropriate dreams.

It was at Taylor's house that Borrow met another man, eleven years older than he was, who was to exercise considerable influence upon him. This was John Bowring, a man who in 1821 had done well at precisely the things Borrow wanted to do well at. He had travelled in Russia, Spain, and Scandinavia. He was a linguist. He had recently published *A Specimen of Russian Poets*. He was intent upon a career which was to bring him considerable distinction. He may well have talked to the young Borrow airily and confidently about the golden joys lying just ahead of him in the world of literature; and Borrow would have listened and yearned confusedly, and he would have gone back to Tuck's Court to work at more languages, to toil doggedly at translations from the Danish or from the German – and with all thought of the law fading ever more swiftly from his mind. What Taylor was encouraging him to do, what Bowring only eleven years older than himself had in fact done – he too could do.

When he went home to Willow Lane on Sundays there was now no brother John to talk to about personal matters and about young men's aspirations in general. John had gone to London because Crome died in April 1821 and B. R. Haydon was willing to accept him as a pupil. Captain Borrow had bled his small resources of £150 to enable him to go. John's now being where Borrow wanted to be, strengthened a vague but growing determination never to settle to the law as a profession. Meanwhile however there was nothing to do but to wait until the expiry of his articles in 1824 – with some feeling of guilt about what he must have felt to be a betrayal of his father, a father moreover whose robust strength was now dwindling at an alarming rate – and to walk over to Mousehold Heath to seek the company of the gipsies and of Ambrose Petulengro in particular.

It was a short while before John's departure, if the dating in *Lavengro* is to be relied upon (a very conditional clause indeed), that he came upon Ambrose again after a long gap, and asked him what was his opinion of death. It was a natural question for him at that time. He was himself muddled, frustrated, and despairing – and there was always a suicidal streak in him; watching his father on Sundays too would have put graveyard thoughts into his mind. Petulengro accepts death as the final and inescapable shutter-off, but robustly refuses to have hankerings after it. There follows one of the most famous, and most beautiful of Borrow's many memorable conversation-pieces.

'Life is sweet, brother.' 'Do you think so?' 'Think so! There's night and day, brother, both sweet things; sun, moon, and stars, brother, all sweet things; there's likewise the wind on the heath. Life is very sweet, brother; who would wish to die?' 'I would wish to die.' 'You talk like a gorgio – which is the same as talking like a fool – were you a Romany Chal you would talk wiser. Wish to die, indeed! A Romany Chal would wish to life for ever!' 'In sickness, Jasper?' 'There's the sun and stars, brother.' 'In blindness, Jasper?' 'There's the wind on the heath, brother. . . .'

The passage is too familiar to need quoting in full. It is good to be reminded of it though, good to realize that thanks, perhaps, in part to the lyric certainties of his blood-brother, he was able to shrug off his adolescent death-wish, and come, in due time, to write prose which strongly survives.

John, the favourite son, moved on from Haydon, crossed the channel and started to copy old masters in the Louvre. His letters home began to be widely spaced. His father fretted. He felt that he was moving out of life; and John was not there, was apparently too preoccupied even to write. During these months Borrow came closer to his father than ever before. Growing up a little he recognized that his father had cause for bitterness. 'The military pension which I enjoy will cease with my life. The property which I shall leave behind me will be barely sufficient for the maintenance of your mother respectably. I again ask you what you intend to do. Do you think you can support yourself by your Armenian or your other acquirements?' The long conversation with his father develops into a highly emotional scene: '". . . if I can't succeed, and am driven to the worst, it is but dying . . . .' "What do you mean by dying?" "Leaving the world; my loss would scarcely be felt. . . ."' Captain Borrow turns with forgiveness towards his prodigal. '"I will not reproach you . . . Boy, when I am gone, look up to your brother, and may God bless you both. There, don't weep. . . ."' Borrow had the gift, when he chose to use it, of exact and total recall. There is no reason to suppose that this half-reconciliation between failing father and frustrated son did not take place pretty exactly as, in middle age, Borrow recollected it in *Lavengro*.

Borrow had meanwhile been working hard at what interested him. Godless Billy Taylor and Bowring between them had brought the name of this harum-scarum young man to the notice of Thomas Campbell, at that time editing the *New Monthly*, and Sir Richard Phillips, responsible for the radical *Monthly Magazine*. Phillips printed Borrow's article on 'Danish Poetry and Ballad-writing' which Borrow signed 'George Olaus Borrow' as a tribute to Olaus Wormius who, in 1636, had written an account of ancient Danish literature, a copy of which remains in Norwich Guildhall Library replete with Borrow's copious notes. There were translations also from the German balladist Bürger. Nothing he managed to see in print at this time made anything of a hit. He consoled himself by

producing a bouncy, chest-thumping ballad of his own, about himself – 'Lines to Six-foot Three' – which Edward Thomas thought of as
'already pure Borrow, with a vigour excusing if not quite transmuting
its rant'. The lines had to wait until 1826 before they were printed but
in all probability they had already been written, were part of 'your
other acquirements' which Captain Borrow alluded to during that
famous conversation.

> A lad, who twenty tongues can talk,
> And sixty miles a day can walk;
> Drink at a draught a pint of rum,
> And then be neither sick nor dumb;
> Can tune a song, and make a verse,
> And deeds of northern kings rehearse;
> Who never will forsake his friend,
> While he his bony fist can bend;
> And, though averse to brawl and strife,
> Will fight a Dutchman with a knife.
> O that is just the lad for me,
> And such is honest six-foot-three. . . .

There are four more stanzas of this, but Borrow did not chant them in
vindication to his father. Instead he remembered the injustice of the
world towards him and what he felt to be his hard-won achievements.

To heighten all his personal and domestic stress, there came, in
October 1823, the news of John Thurtell's savage crime. He felt
himself pitched into the middle of the lurid melodrama. He was
confused. He was too young to know with any sort of certainty what
stance he should take up in a situation such as this. That he had
managed a half-reconciliation with his father now that his father was
clearly approaching his end gave him some sort of consolation, but
not enough. He had to leave Norwich. Yet his father was dying and
he could not leave the mother he loved to say the *nunc dimittis* alone;
nor could he leave before the expiry of his articles in February 1824.
But once these two releases were accomplished, he would go. Where
would he go? Where any young man, then as now, would be likeliest
to go: to London, where the action was, where newspapers and
weeklies and monthlies were published, and where his friend Roger
Kerrison, a wealthy youngster whom he had got to know in the
offices of Simpson and Rackham, had already gone.

The waiting and the tensions brought on symptoms of nervous
prostration like the ones he had suffered in 1818. From Norwich he
wrote to Kerrison on 20 January 1824:

Dearest Roger, – I did not imagine when we separated in the street, on the day of your departure from Norwich, that we should not have met again: I had intended to have come and seen you off, but . . . the hour slipped past me unawares. I have been again for the last fortnight laid up with that detestable complaint which destroys my strength, impairs my understanding, and will in all probability send me to the grave, for I am now much worse than when you saw me last. But *nil desperandum est*, if ever my health mends, and possibly it may by the time my clerkship is expired, I intend to live in London, write plays, poetry etc., abuse religion and get myself prosecuted, for I would not for an ocean of gold remain any longer than I am forced in this dull and gloomy town. . . .

There is feverishness in this – in his right mind Borrow was never one to abuse religion unless it was bound up with popery – but there is determination also.

Not long after that letter the outline of things to come became clearer. It began to look as if the expiry of the Captain and the expiry of his son's articles would come pretty close together. In February the condition of the sturdy old soldier began swiftly to deteriorate. John Borrow was sent for urgently from Paris, and arrived in haste. On the last day of February 1824 the Captain died. On the last day of March Borrow was free of the indulgent bondage imposed upon him by lawyer Simpson. He had some thirty or forty pounds' worth of security, his father having made him meagre provision until he reached his majority on 5 July, but enough for Borrow on the evening of the very next day to take an outside seat on the London coach. With him he carried his little green box containing the manuscripts which he hoped would quite soon bring him to public notice. There were his translations from ancient Danish, versions of the songs of ap Gwilym, and some of the German Romantics done into English. He had in addition a letter of introduction written by Taylor to Sir Richard Phillips in whose *Monthly Magazine* he had already appeared. Roger Kerrison was lodging at 16 Millman Street a quarter of a mile to the north of Gray's Inn and had found accommodation for him in the same house – 'a small room, up two pair of stairs, in which I was to sit, and another, still smaller, above it, in which I was to sleep'. Borrow arrived in London in the early morning of 2 April, eager to throw down his challenge to the world.

CHAPTER 2

LONDON

BORROW visited Sir Richard Phillips immediately. He was confident that having read Taylor's letter, Phillips would set about the task of turning him into a successful author with confidence and enthusiasm.

Phillips was a capable man who had had his ups and downs. The son of a Leicestershire farmer, he left agriculture to come to London and prove himself – very much like the enormously tall young man who stood before him that morning in the early spring of 1824. Things had not gone well for him, and he had returned to Leicestershire. Still, however, he could not attune himself to working on the land, and in particular, took a strong dislike to stock-breeding and the consequent butchery. He became a vegetarian, and began to keep a school in Leicester. He prospered moderately and branched out into shopkeeping. Then he became interested in reformist politics, and launched a paper called the *Leicester Herald* in 1792. He was gaoled for selling Tom Paine's *The Rights of Man* but he was able to conduct his radical journalism from prison, and even to start another journal, *The Museum*. Not long after he was released there was a fire in his shop, and, freed from his burdens by the insurance money, he made a second assault on London. He founded the *Monthly Magazine* which had a long and not inglorious career. His premises were in Bridge Street (now New Bridge Street) which runs from Ludgate Circus to Blackfriars Bridge. He engaged very profitably in the publishing of school books, and an industrious Aberdonian, Dr Mavor, produced a *Spelling Book* and a *History of England* which were notable money-spinners. In 1808 Phillips was knighted. When Borrow first faced him Phillips was a man of fifty-seven; he was a faddist, and a tyrant, and he was contemplating retirement to Brighton. Translations by an enthusiastic young man of the works of Dafydd ap Gwilym could not be relied upon to bring colour to his cheeks. Could Borrow produce something saleable on the lines of *The Dairyman's Daughter*, perhaps, a religious tract which was currently enjoying a vast success? 'But, sir,' Borrow asked him, 'surely you would not pander to a scoundrelly taste?' The answer was, yes, Sir Richard would, and perhaps there might be work for Borrow in the six-volume compilation 'Celebrated Trials' which he was thinking of bringing out.

Borrow put Dafydd ap Gwilym back in his green box and, for want of anything else, accepted the role of hack. Perhaps he accepted this because Sir Richard, in addition, offered him some challenging translation work. He had himself composed *Twelve Essays on the Phenomena of Nature*, a work he was proud of and one which, he suspected, might appeal more to the Germans, with their love of abstractions, than to the earthy English. In the letter from his friend Taylor, Borrow's linguistic prowess had been unreservedly praised. To translate the *Twelve Essays* into German would therefore be a congenial challenge in those interstices of time when he was not investigating and putting down on paper the last days of British felons brought to book. All this was a knife thrust into the balloon of Borrow's ambitions. Nevertheless he said yes. Short of taking the next coach back to Norwich, there was nothing much else he could do. Phillips offered terms – £50 on completion for the 'Trials' and payment for the philosophy only after it had gone on sale. These were the terms of a slave-owner. It is probable that he offered them in order simply to get rid of this young man. He could hardly have expected that Borrow would accept them.

Borrow's linguistic abilities, remarkable though they were, were of the swift, rough-and-ready kind. To translate out of a foreign language into his own might have been a possibility for him. To translate out of his own language into the foreign one was, and still is of course, a different matter altogether. Phillips must have realized this. A man of substance and achievement in his time, a man still presumably an upholder of the rights of man even though Tom Paine was fifteen years dead – how could he have brought himself to exploit a youngster so ruthlessly? The young man was clearly in a state of something like exalted despair – Phillips might well have thought he was in the presence of someone close to insanity. To look at, Phillips was ruddy, large, and fat. As he passed, the boys shouted 'Roast beef!' after him. The looks were deceptive. This vegetarian was mean and glum – and perhaps frightened. Borrow was intimidating. Six foot three in 1824 was a very great height indeed. People stared at him. Already his hair was beginning to turn white. He was good-looking, with thick eyebrows, bright eyes different from each other, a nose perhaps a bit too big and aquiline, a well-shaped mouth with a pouting underlip, and long, powerful hands. Added to this he looked, and was, totally fearless – an instant fighter at all times. Phillips's immediate purpose would have been, not so much to drive a ferociously hard bargain as to keep Borrow sweet.

Borrow went back to Millman Street and set to work. He was always willing to work at any task provided it harmonized even remotely with his ambitions. All the same this was not quite the life he had imagined for himself. He was not able to conceal distress and despair. Roger Kerrison found him a difficult man to share lodgings with. Indeed one night, according to Kerrison, he began bellowing and making a disturbance outside number 16. The constables came after him, but, wonderfully quick on his feet, he ran on, dived into the Thames, swam to the south bank and escaped. He threatened suicide. His horrors took hold of him again. One day in May 1824 he stayed home, and, whilst Kerrison was out at his work, wrote him a trembly note: 'Come to me immediately I am I believe dying.' It was at this point that Kerrison began to fear that he might have got himself caught up with a madman. He moved from Millman Street to Litchfield Street near Seven Dials, and wrote a letter to John Borrow, still in Norwich, to say that his brother was behaving oddly, and that he was talking of going to Norwich on the thirty-first. Kerrison's advice to John was that he should hold tight on to his brother until he should have calmed down. This was a friendly act, not a callous one. He did what he thought best for a friend, and then slipped quietly out of his life. Borrow went to Norwich, but neither John nor his mother were able to hold him for long: he returned to fight his battles.

Kerrison's anxieties are important. Borrow's huge drudgeries had not long begun when John received the warning letter. He could scarcely have been reduced to such a state of extravagant despair in under two months. The six-volume compilation of criminal trials which he had undertaken was certainly a colossal task, but it did not chain him to a table and chair in the Millman Street attic. Phillips's hard bargain required that he seek out, and pay for, his own books relevant to his subject. This would mean wandering about the bookstalls and discovering the mazy, narrow streets of a London still clustered closely round the banks of the Thames. He collected his bits of facts here and there, and brought them to Phillips for approval. Phillips was loudly critical: '"How is this?" he exclaims; "I can scarcely believe my eyes – the most important life and trial omitted to be found in the whole criminal record – what gross, what utter negligence! . . ." "What a life! what a dog's life!" I would frequently exclaim, after escaping from the presence of the publisher. . . ."' But still he must have enjoyed the poking about, the conversations with odd characters.

One day he found himself amongst an expectant crowd at the corner of Oxford Street and Tottenham Court Road; there were grouped faces staring out of the upper windows of all the houses. Was all this because someone of the sort he was writing about was on his way to execution ? 'Just then I heard various voices cry "There it comes!" and all heads were turned up Oxford Street, down which a hearse was slowly coming. . . .' In the hearse were the remains of Byron, dead the previous April and now brought back home at last to be buried at Hucknall. Borrow turned away, and

Hurrying down the street to the right, I encountered Francis Ardry. 'What means the multitude yonder?' he demanded. 'They are looking after the hearse which is carrying the remains of Byron up Tottenham Court Road.' . . .'Ah, a great poet.' 'I don't think so,' said I. '. . . Ah!' . . .'Replete with malignity and sensualism.' 'Yes!' 'Not half so great a poet as Milton.' 'No?' . . .'Nor that poor boy Chatterton, who, maddened by rascally patrons and publishers, took poison at last. . . .'

And after some more of this conversation Borrow's friend Ardry (in the manuscript text of *Lavengro* he is given his real name of Francis Arden) takes him along to a fifth-rate inn in St. Martin's Lane, and introduces him to some Irish friends.

Francis Arden was a young man, with a young man's eagerness for sexual exploits and a dashing urban life generally. Did he ever exist, or did Borrow invent him as a symbol of the kind of living-pattern which he both liked and rejected in about equal parts? Someone signing himself 'F. Arden' wrote himself down for five copies of Borrow's *Romantic Ballads* in 1826, and so, unless Borrow bought the copies himself, using for signature a name given to an imaginary companion, he must have existed. Nothing is known of him however except for what Borrow himself tells us about him: he was an Irishman and a Catholic. At that time, Daniel O'Connell was in the middle of his struggle for Catholic emancipation. Borrow needless to say had no sympathy for O'Connell whom he was to describe, much later on, as 'a trumpery fellow'; but Francis Arden's support for O'Connell did not in any way impair the friendship – it meant plotting and secrecy and adventure which Borrow could delight in while disregarding the ultimate ends. Arden was for Borrow simply a young rip who exercised himself in manly sports.

. . .my thoughts are fixed on something better than politics. 'I understand you' said I; 'dog-fighting – well, I can easily conceive that to some minds dog-fighting . . .' 'I was not thinking of dog-fighting,' said Francis Ardry. . . . 'Not thinking of dog-fighting!' I ejaculated. 'No . . . something higher and much more rational than dog-fighting at present occupies my thoughts.' 'Dear me,' said I, 'I thought I heard you say, that there was nothing like it!' 'Like what?' said Francis Ardry. 'Dog-fighting, to be sure.' said I. 'Pooh,' said Francis Ardry . . . 'That which at present engages my waking and sleeping thoughts is love – divine love – there is nothing like *that*. Listen to me, I have a secret to confide to you.'

Arden then tells him about 'the most delightful young Frenchwoman imaginable' whose name is Annette Le Noir.

Annette by herself need not concern us. She simply gives reality to what one might easily guess: that Arden chased women in the normal young man's way. Can it be taken for granted that Borrow, in his company, chased women too? If he chased women he would not with his good looks have had to chase for long. But here the question has to be asked: was there something wrong, something abnormal, something lacking about Borrow's sexuality? The Reverend Augustus Jessopp, who lived to a great age, who was to be headmaster of King Edward VI School, Norwich in the middle decades of the century and afterwards, on retirement, rector of Scarning in Norfolk, who knew of Borrow in his later years, who knew George Meredith too and more or less brought up Arthur, that unfortunate son of Meredith's by Mary Ellen Peacock, wrote about Borrow in the *Daily Chronicle* of 30 April 1900:

Of anything like animal passion there is not a trace in all his many volumes. Not a hint that he ever kissed a woman or ever took a little child upon his knee. He was beardless; his voice was not the voice of a man. His outbursts of wrath never translated themselves into uncontrollable acts of violence; they showed themselves in all the rancorous hatred that could be put into words – the fire smouldered in that sad heart of his. Those big bones and huge muscles and the strong brain were never to be reproduced in an offspring to be proud of. How if he were the Narses of literature – one who could be only what he was, though we are always invited to lament that he was not something more.

This is surprising. Jessopp, from what we know of him, was an intelligent, capable, and kindly man. Earlier, in an article written for the *Athenaeum* of 8 July 1893, he expresses boundless admiration for the author of *Lavengro*, so that there is not, in Jessopp, any discoverable motive for malice. Yet how are we to place reliance on a man who says of Borrow – who was to lay low the Flaming Tinman with the famous 'Long Melford', right-handed blow – that 'His outbursts of wrath never translated themselves into uncontrollable acts of violence'? If Jessopp could be wrong about that – as he surely was – he

could have been wrong about his sexuality. And there are those who
have dismissed such notions as moonshine. Mr Brian Vesey-
FitzGerald took this line – and very persuasively – as late as 1953.
Perhaps Borrow was simply overworked – but he does show signs
too of a young man aware of some deep inadequacy in himself and at a
loss to know what to do about it.

He returned to his labours in early June 1824 after his short visit to
Norwich. His brother John came up to join him briefly soon afterwards, to see Haydon. John had been commissioned to paint the
portrait of Robert Hawkes, Mayor of Norwich in 1824, but, young as
he was, felt daunted by the task (assuredly he was more easily
daunted than his brother), and so came up to London to offer the
commission to his master Benjamin Haydon. He was doubtful
whether a man as eminent as his master would accept such a job; but
one hundred guineas were on offer, and Haydon, hovering always on
the edge of bankruptcy, grabbed at the opportunity. While with
Borrow, John was able to bring Ann Perfrement, always his supporter and consoler in chief, nearer to her second son by telling him
she had been crying a good deal because his letters had been so
infrequent. With Haydon in tow, John went back to Norwich after a
fortnight, leaving his brother more composed, less obsessively concerned about looking in at himself and being terrified at what he saw.
He laboured on at his criminals. Phillips drove him. He increased the
scope of the compilation. No longer was it to be simply insular –
Newgate Calendar stuff. Borrow should scour Europe for his male-
factors as well.

'Where is Brandt and Struensee?' cried the publisher. 'I am sure I don't
know,' I replied; whereupon the publisher falls to squealing like one of
Joey's rats. 'Find me up Brandt and Struensee by next morning, or . . .' 'Have
you found Brandt and Struensee?' cried the publisher, on my appearing
before him next morning. 'No,' I reply, 'I can hear nothing about them';
whereupon the publisher falls to bellowing like Joey's bull. . . .

Did he also, in the middle of all this and whilst wrestling with the
rendering into German of Phillips's opaque philosophizings, translate F. M. von Klinger's novel, *Faustus: His Life, Death and Descent
into Hell*? The *Monthly Magazine* for July 1824 told its readers that
the *Celebrated Trials* would be coming soon, but also added: 'The
editor of the preceding has ready for the press, a Life of Faustus. . .
which will also appear the next winter.' Klinger's *Fausts Leben, Taten
und Hollenfahrt* was a scandalous work which first appeared in St.
Petersburg in 1791, thus being a precursor of the first part of Goethe's

Faust, which did not offer itself to the world till 1808. There is no
mention of Borrow's working at this whilst he was still in Norwich
serving his time with Simpson, and it is easier to believe that he came
across Klinger, probably in a French translation, whilst rummaging
the London bookstalls in search of material sufficient to satisfy
Phillips's exorbitant demands, but when did he find time to work on
it?

Borrow did manage to get his six volumes of trials together, and
they were published in the spring of 1825. Some while before that,
however, there had been brisk skirmishings over Phillips's philosophy. Borrow had shown him his Germanized version of the first
chapter, and had returned a few days later, tired and hard up and
hoping perhaps for something on account.

I found him stamping with fury upon certain fragments of paper. 'Sir,' said
he, 'you know nothing of German; I have shown your translation of the first
chapter of my Philosophy to several Germans: it is utterly unintelligible to
them.' 'Did they see the Philosphy?' I replied. 'They did, sir, but they did not
profess to understand English.' 'No more do I,' I replied, 'if that Philosophy
be English.' The publisher was furious – I was silent. For want of a pinch of
snuff, I had recourse to something which is no bad substitute for a pinch of
snuff to those who can't take it, silent contempt . . . the compilation was
completed, I got paid in the usual manner, and forthwith left him.

Phillips receded to Brighton. His *Universal Review*, with unsigned
notices in it by Borrow, had failed after a few months. The *Monthly
Magazine*, for which half a dozen or so of Borrow's translations,
mostly from Danish balladry, had been accepted, went on, but Sir
Richard, from 1825, had little to do with it. He lived on until 1840,
but already when Borrow knew him this extortionate bully was
clearly showing signs of shakiness so far as his mental faculties were
concerned: how otherwise to explain his belief, passed on to us by
Borrow, that the earth was pear-shaped . . .?

That London year, as Borrow lived it, would have been enough to
prostrate even a young man not naturally given to deep pathological
depressions. The six volumes of the *Celebrated Trials* ran not far
short of four thousand pages. Not even Edgar Wallace, with his
dictaphone, could have achieved such productivity. The work tends
to be dismissed now as simply a compilation, a copying-out job. So,
in some considerable measure it is – indeed it must have been; but all
the same Borrow's hand is apparent, and there is no reason to
disbelieve him when he tells us that it was the compilation of

Celebrated Trials that taught him how to write. In the Thurtell trial, for example, Borrow re-creates his personal experience:

Thurtell was dressed in a plum-coloured frock coat, with a drab waistcoat and gilt buttons, and white corded breeches. His neck had a black stock on, which fitted as usual stiffly up to the bottom of the cheek and end of the chin, and which therefore pushed forward the flesh on this part of the face so as to give an additionally sullen weight to the countenance. The lower part of the face was unusually large, muscular and heavy, and appeared to hang like a load to the head, and to make it drop like the mastiff's jowl. . . .

This is the writing of a man in a hurry but it is urgent, and alive.

By the time he handed his copy in, and received his fifty pounds, the small amount of money he had brought up with him from Norwich must have long been spent and he must have had considerable debts all round. When these had been paid he must have been not far short of penniless again – eighteen pence a page was all he got for his *Review* contributions. And yet he stayed on in London, a London which becomes partly a world of fancy peopled with characters that loom strangely up at us out of fog, partly a world of harsh and sharp reality. The people he meets and talks to as he marches here and there are wraith-like yet grubby. The old apple-woman who sold her bit of fruit sitting daily at one end of London Bridge not doing much business was a fence on the side. She clung to Borrow one day because she thought he was about to throw himself over – though suicide was not in his mind on that particular day. She treasures a book, Defoe's *Moll Flanders*, and Borrow, poor though he is, offers to buy it from her because Defoe is as much his hero as Thurtell for a time had been. But no, not even for his two silver crowns is she prepared to hand it over – '. . . without my book I should mope and pine, and perhaps fling myself into the river. . . .' (One feels that the death-wish, even when suppressed, is alive and often strong in Borrow's mind through this London year: 'Mine was an ill-regulated mind at this period' he tells us.) The Armenian silk-merchant whose pocket Borrow saved from being picked – here is the kind of chance acquaintance Borrow delights in. The Armenian offers him the opportunity for linguistic display. '"In the name of all that is wonderful, how came you to know aught of my language?" "There is nothing wonderful in that," said I; "we are at the commencement of a philological age, everyone studies languages: that is, everyone who is fit for nothing else. . . ."' Borrow parades his specialism and mocks it all at once. The Armenian has bookcases full of Armenian literature. '"I should like to see

Z— in an English dress; you shall translate Z— . . . . He is our
Esop. . . ." "I will have nothing to do with him," said I. "Wherefore?"
"There is an old proverb," said I, "that 'a burnt child avoids the
fire'. I have burnt my hands sufficiently with attempting to translate
philosophy to make me cautious of venturing upon it again. . . .'"
Still Borrow mocks himself. But then the Armenian, already rich,
acquires another £100,000. What to do with it? '"I have heard you
say," says Borrow, "that the grand oppressor of your country is the
Persian; why not attempt to free your country from his oppression –
you have two hundred thousand pound, and money is the sinew of
war?"'

By April 1825 Borrow's money was down to almost nothing. 'One
morning on getting up I discovered that my whole worldly wealth
was reduced to one half-crown. . . . I had determined that I could do
no better than accept the first proposal of the Armenian, and translate. . . .' But when he arrived at the Armenian's premises the Armenian had gone, leaving him a letter but no grateful enclosures. 'I . . .
have come to the conclusion that it is my bounden duty to attack the
Persians. When these lines are delivered to you I shall be on the route
to Ararat. . . . I should scarcely have undertaken the journey but for
your pungent words inciting me to attack. . . .' Unlucky Borrow: not
only a man given to wild adventures himself, but a supplier of motive
for wild adventures in others. . . .

It is at this point that we come to the most mysterious of Borrow's
books, *The Adventures of Joseph Sell*. It is mysterious because all the
records combine to prove that no such book ever existed. Yet Borrow
says he wrote it. He did write something very quickly at a time when
he was very short of cash, but the title was not *The Adventures of
Joseph Sell*. He tells us he went to Greenwich Fair, met Ambrose
Petulengro and had comforting chat. Ambrose offers him £50 but
Borrow refuses it. '"Then the half of it?" "Nor the half of it; but it is
getting towards evening, I must go back to the Great City." "And
what will you do in the Boro Foros?" "I know not. . . ." "Earn
money?" "If I can." "And if you can't?" "Starve." "You look ill,
brother. . . .'" So Borrow, who was always proud, set out for Millman Street, but on the way paused outside a booksellers whom he had
once tried as a possible buyer of ap Gwilym. Stuck to the window was
a notice. 'A novel or Tale is much wanted.' Could he do it? He
thought he could. After all the past year had given fluency and
readiness to his pen. He may not have gained much, but certainly he
had gained that. But how was he to live till the job was finished? He
was down, he tells us, to eighteenpence by now. He thought he might
elaborate upon, and novelize, something from the *Celebrated Trials*.

He stayed awake all night plotting it out. Bread and water and twenty-four hours a day apart from cat-naps could see the thing finished. Tenacity and stamina carried him through. He took the finished product to the bookseller; he haggled; he managed to squeeze £20 on account out of him. He was exhausted. 'I felt that, were I to remain where I was, I should die. . . .' He packed a trunk with clothes and books and sent it off to Norwich. He got ready his bundle and stick, and 'in about three days I was in readiness to start.' As he crossed the Haymarket at the beginning of his journey Francis Arden popped up again. He was in a smart cabriolet with Annette and pulled up on seeing him. '"Holloa, friend . . . whither bound?" "I do not know. . . . all I can say is, that I am about to leave London." "And the means?" "I have them. . . ."' There follows the French conversation in which Borrow gives 'jument' the masculine definite article, and then Arden drives swiftly off.

Now this cannot be right in factual detail. But beyond doubt it is true to the essence of the thing. The dates are muddled. Greenwich Fair took place on 23 May. He left London on the twenty-fourth – he must have done because the events described in the succeeding weeks cannot be made to tally if he left a week earlier or a week later. Therefore he cannot have written 'Joseph Sell' between Greenwich Fair and his departure. 'Joseph Sell' came before the Fair. Because he was flat broke he perhaps scaled down Petulengro's generous offer of a loan, and took instead eighteenpence from him – or he may have won as much by gambling. He collected his £20 advance that same evening, and set off next day. But the dispatching of his trunk to Norwich? He could have left money for that at Millman Street. And the undiscoverable 'Joseph Sell' ('Sell' is a deliberately chosen name; it is his way of telling us that he is practising his favourite ploy of concealment)? Was it perhaps *Tales of the Wild and Wonderful*, published anonymously by Hurst, Robinson, and Co. in 1825? Clement Shorter thought so, and included this in his massive Norwich Edition of Borrow's works where it may be found in volume 15. Certainly there are signs here and there of Borrow's hand in this, but there are other signs, like the dedication, which point the other way. Most likely the book was a compilation in which Borrow had some part – probably small. After all, even that would represent a few days of highly intensive labour.

So there he was, on 24 May 1825, in flight from the city which had refused to accept him. His state of mind must have been desperate and confused. He had taken to the roads – like the gipsies. He was to all intents and purposes – or would be once the remains of his £20 had gone – a tramp. He made for Salisbury Plain.

CHAPTER 3

GONE TO EARTH

'In about two hours I had cleared the Great City. . . .' After nine miles, as evening was coming on, Borrow felt ready for rest. The Amesbury coach came by. He hailed it; and, for sixteen shillings was allowed a place and a chance to sleep. At early light he was in Amesbury and told to get down or pay more. Half awake he got down, 'whereupon off whisked the coach . . . and I was left alone.' He climbed briskly out of the Avon valley, and in the silence of the early morning – a total silence unimaginable to us a century and a half on – he saw Stonehenge. As the stones loomed up in front of Borrow he experienced ecstasy. Here was something out of the ancient world that he could touch and not simply try to translate; 'taking off my hat, I advanced slowly, and cast myself, with my face on the dewy earth, in the middle of the portal of giants, beneath the transverse stone. The spirit of Stonehenge was strong upon me!'

Did it all happen, the three months of wandering that were to follow, exactly as he said? It is, of course, impossible to be categorical about this. Nevertheless certain points need to be made. The single most important point is simply that *Lavengro* was begun, most probably, in 1843. A man of forty was remembering scenes visited, people met, conversations held by an overworked, undernourished, half-hysterical young man who was twenty-one at the beginning of the journey at Stonehenge, and a summer older when he ended it by telling the recruiting-sergeant – a fiery-faced man: was Borrow reminded of his father? – that he thought he'd go to India. A gap therefore of nearly nineteen years stretches between what was done and what was written about. Borrow was not a diarist, not a journaliser, and if he wrote home to Willow Lane, no letters have survived. He had therefore to rely upon memory. Borrow's memory for foreign vocabularies was remarkable. Whether it was good in all other respects may be doubted. How many men of forty could sit down, and set out on paper, exactly what they did, in the fullest detail, during a long walking-tour undertaken almost twenty years earlier? Would they get the events in their right order? Where did

Borrow meet so-and-so? Was it in Warminster or was it in Wil-lenhall? Where was it that the strange, sad man had told him his strange, sad story, all in the dark, and to the accompaniment of rolling thunder and flashes of lightning?

The latter part of *Lavengro* (from chapter 59) and the whole of *The Romany Rye* (except the Appendix) are concerned with that summer of 1825, with a series of intensely lived, spiritual experiences. These mingle and jostle with and against the outside world, and the people walking about in it, and impart to that world, and to those people a strangeness that probably belonged more to the awakening young man than to the people themselves and to the country they lived in and moved through.

Although England was still wonderfully unspoilt and peaceful, the aftermath of the long French wars was having its effect and the industrial revolution was beginning to shoulder-charge a bewildered people into new, and unpleasant, ways of life. One summer later Cobbett rode about the countryside where Borrow began his march and he saw unemployed working folk dizzy from starvation. The most adverse effects and the consequent unrest of the first industrial revolution were found in the south; the Tolpuddle martyrs were Dorset men. The folk-myth hero Captain Swing led his pitchfork army through the southern shires. Borrow saw none of this. That he did not should not be held against him. In the 1930s when Orwell and Priestley made their English journeys it was the rule to be socially committed. In the 1820s it was not so. Then it was Cobbett, and not Borrow, who was the man out of line.

Much time and ingenuity have been expended by able and enthu-siastic scholars in an effort to map out Borrow's itinerary, to bring the time and the place and the loved one all together. George Sampson worked the whole progress out, day by day, from his leaving London on the afternoon of Tuesday, 24 May 1825, to Wednesday, 3 August (the seventy-second day of his travels) when he reached, Sampson thought, the Swan Hotel in Stafford. It is prudent, perhaps, to be less precise than Sampson. From Stonehenge he went to Salisbury, then north-west to (perhaps) Heytesbury. Still in a north-westerly direc-tion he continued for about four days, and then, in a somewhat more northerly direction, for another six. By this time he was in Shrop-shire, and his moves become more limited and less purposeful. He moved westward as far as the Welsh border, and then back into the famous Mumper's Dingle which was probably near Willenhall. There is only quite local movement after that until the visit to Tamworth Fair on 26 July. On 31 July if George Sampson is right, Ambrose

Petulengro lent him £50, enough to buy himself a horse, and two days after that he reached Stafford. The most westerly point of his journey was probably the Welsh border south of Oswestry; after that he made a slow return eastwards through the Midlands.

In the country, [Sampson says at the beginning of the Appendix] it [i.e. the autobiographical work as a whole, both *Lavengro* and *The Romany Rye*] shows him leading a life of roving adventure, becoming tinker, gypsy, postillion, ostler ; associating with various types of people, chiefly of the lower classes, whose ways and habits are described; but, though leading this erratic life, we gather from the book that his habits are neither vulgar nor vicious, that he still follows to a certain extent his favourite pursuits, hunting after strange characters, or analyzing strange words and names. . . .

Borrow's first important encounter was with the well-born, wealthy stranger at the inn. They talk, and the stranger says, 'pray do me the favour to go home with me'. Borrow agrees, and they arrive at 'a large brick house, built something in the French style. . . .' It is grand and well maintained, and they go up 'a spacious flight of steps to the door, which was at once flung open, and two servants with powdered hair, and in livery of blue plush, came out and stood one on either side as we passed. . . .' The two dine well. It is dark and it is hot; there is thunder in the air. The stranger asks Borrow to stay 'for a day or two'. Although he has been oddly silent over the meal he has 'much to talk . . . about .' The scene is set for a spooky, romantic-bizarre story. Wealth and pleasure cannot satisfy this man. 'No sooner has my imagination raised up an image of pleasure than it is sure to conjure up one of distress and gloom; these two antagonistic ideas instantly commence a struggle in my mind, and the gloomy one generally, I may say invariably, prevails.' His mother, whom he deeply loved, had become seriously ill. 'My mother became worse . . . I rested neither day nor night, but roamed about the house like one distracted. Suddenly I found myself doing that which even at the time struck me as being highly singular; I found myself touching particular objects that were near me, and to which my fingers seemed to be attracted by an irresistible impulse. . . .' This compulsion haunts him through life. He strives, in spite of his easy circumstances, to become busy. He tries authorship, but that cannot satisfy or cure him either.

How did I get all the matter which composed it? Out of my own mind, unquestionably; but how did it come there ? – was it the indigenous growth of the mind? And then I would sit down and ponder over the various scenes and adventures in my book, endeavouring to ascertain how I came originally to devise them, and by dint of reflecting I remembered that to a single word in conversation, or some simple accident in a street, or on a road, I was indebted for some of the happiest portions of my work; they were but tiny seeds . . . which in the soil of my imagination had subsequently become stately trees, but . . . I am constantly discovering that, however original I may wish to be, I am continually producing the same things which other people say or write. . . . you saw how I touched, it was to baffle the evil fortune . . . . To baffle it I occasionally perform actions which must appear highly incomprehensible; I have been known, when riding in company with other people, to leave the direct road, and make a long circuit by a miry lane. . . . I have also been seen attempting to ride across a morass. . . . If I touch various objects, and ride into miry places it is to baffle any mischance befalling me as an author. . . .

Theodore Watts-Dunton, who, as a boy of nineteen and admirer of *Lavengro*, had watched Borrow swimming off Yarmouth in the 1850s, before getting to know him some eighteen years later, whose by no means negligible novel *Aylwin* shows him also to be a man greatly interested in gipsydom, wrote about Borrow in an *Athenaeum* article dated 25 March 1899, when Borrow had been nearly twenty years dead:

There was nothing that Borrow strove against with more energy than the curious impulse, which he seems to have shared with Dr Johnson, to touch the objects along his path in order to save himself from the evil chance. He never conquered the superstition. In walking through Richmond Park he would step out of his way constantly to touch a tree, and he was offended if the friend he was with seemed to observe it.

So Borrow had this compulsion like Dr Johnson, and like Beckford of Fonthill also. Could this stranger at the inn have been Beckford? Could Borrow have met him on his journey up from Stonehenge? Beckford had left nearby Fonthill in 1822, but only to go to Bath, still not far off Borrow's route. Would this strange tic that they shared have drawn the, in all senses queer, elderly gentleman – in 1825 Beckford was in his middle sixties – to a white-haired, galloping youngster not quite twenty-two? It has to be said, though, that there is no evidence to suggest that the young Borrow had the touching disease – at least no one who knew him young ever spoke of it. In youth however Borrow would probably have been better able to control or conceal it.

It is tempting to suppose that Borrow put a good deal of self-explanation, self-exploration into the words of this autobiographer. To ride off down a miry lane, leaving a company of horsemen without any word of comment or apology – this is a very Borrovian thing to do: to be worried about his (supposed) powerlessness to be

original in his writing – this too might be strong in the thoughts of an
overdriven hack scarcely out of his adolescence. Did the author of
Vathek and the author of *Lavengro* touch hands in sympathy in
Lansdown Tower on a sultry, thunderous night in June 1825? It is
guesswork of course, but not wild guesswork, to risk saying that they
did. And if Borrow identified himself with Beckford's uncertainties
about himself as a writer – that too is acceptable.

Further on, probably somewhere in Worcestershire, Borrow met a
travelling tinker. The tinker owns a small cart and a pony and the
implements of his trade, and also has a wife. This, though, was no
hardy, prospering ruffian. Things up till quite recently had been
smooth, because like all belonging to his trade, he had his patch, his
querencia; within strict geographical limits he had his clientele. But
now a violent Yorkshireman had challenged his monopoly. He and
his wife Grey Moll were much too aggressive for this timid pair. The
tinker, lamenting, accepts that he has been driven out of business.
Why at least, asked Borrow, does he not sell his stock-in-trade – a
deal that would at least enable him to support himself while he sought
a safer job? The tinker sees no hope in this. What use to anyone can
his pony and cart be now that he can hand over to a buyer no
prospective trading area to work in? 'I'm half inclined to buy your
cart and pony, and your beat too.' This is clearly a sudden impulse,
and the tinker is astounded. 'Why! You would get your head
knocked off. Suppose you were to meet him?' The fighting Borrow
confidently takes command: 'if I were to meet him I could easily
manage him, one way or another.' Like all, or almost all, of Borrow's
travelling acquaintances the tinker so far has remained nameless. But
now Borrow does not ask him his name ; he tells Jack Slingsby what
his name is. 'There, don't stare. . . . I've been in these parts before, at
least not very far from here. Ten years ago, when I was little more
than a child, I was about twenty miles from here in a post-chaise at the
door of an inn. . . . I saw you standing by a gutter. . . . somebody
called you Jack Slingsby. . . . I never forget anything I hear or see; I
can't, I wish I could. . . .'

Borrow's two autobiographical books can be thought of as his
attempt to come to terms with this omnipotent memory unable to
blot out the past. The facts are there; they are in his head; matters
much more terrifying than jittery Jack Slingsby are there. Borrow
puts it all down, but with a slant and that other-worldliness which
will give him the ability to look at it all in a spirit of reluctant
acceptance. It is quite a mistake to take *Lavengro* and *The Romany
Rye* as fantastic rides on a broomstick. Borrow met Beckford and in

meeting him found kinship. He met the tinker and remembered him
from ten years ago when he had seen him some twenty miles from
where they now talked and had heard someone call him by his name –
Jack Slingsby. Twenty miles to the east of wherever precisely they
were, Captain Borrow and Ann and his two sons would about then
have been travelling back to Norwich from Ireland, and ostlers
would have been partnering fresh horses to the post-chaise somewhere along Watling Street; Borrow, coming up to twelve, would
have had eyes for everything and everybody. Once you are prepared
to take account of his idiosyncracies, Borrow tells you no lies.

He drove on with Slingsby's shabby little outfit – to the north-
west, he tells us, and therefore edging towards Wales and the Celts.
With the moonless, starless dark, rain came on, and Borrow is able to
make us see how wild and desolate England could be only a hundred
and fifty years ago. '. . . the country in which I now was seemed
almost uninhabited. . . . I heard occasionally the bark of dogs; but the
sound appeared to come from an immense distance. The rain still
fell. . . . I followed in the rear of the cart . . . till . . . I heard other
hoofs than those of my own nag. . . .' The noise is coming towards
him. Two men on horseback, coming on fast through the dark along a
road far too narrow for any but the slowest, most careful two-way
passage. Borrow yelled for them to stop, but the yell was taken for a
bandit's yell. He tries to calm and reassure the frightened men only to
be kicked on the shoulder by the horse of one of them as he gallops
off, shouting defiance, once he realizes that there is no real danger. A
bit sore, Borrow got into the cart, nodded off, and let the pony take
him. And the pony, in the way of ponies, took him to a place he knew
which was sheltered and suitable for camping. In the morning light,
he checked over the equipment he had bought. Slingsby had not sold
him short. Borrow could now set up either as tinker or as smith. The
weather improved. He stayed where he was for a few days. No one
came near. The desperate, neurotic young Londoner began to flex his
muscles and grow calmer.

A gipsy girl, not more than a child, broke his peace. He gives her a
kettle and, instead of payment, she dances for him and sings him a
Romany song – and he sings for her an answering stanza. Borrow
creates a scene of liveliness, innocence, and charm, but suddenly the
warmth drops out of it and there comes a hint of fear. Has the girl
taken unkindly to the notion of this vastly tall gorgio's talking the
secret language of her clan? A few days later she comes back, still all
innocence but still faintly sinister. She has brought a present for him
tied up in a white napkin: two cakes. They have been baked by her

grandmother, both for him, but 'I know you will give me one, pretty brother, grey-haired brother – which shall I have, brother?' The choice is trivial, but Borrow, in his ballad-strain, conveys to us also the certainty – just as the old balladists could – that the choice is dire. He picks one, but the girl snatches both up and juggles with them: 'here is your cake, this other is mine.' He asked her how she could be sure she was offering him the one he chose. 'Quite sure, brother; but if you like, you can have mine; there's no difference; however – shall I eat?' After much hesitation because he had no appetite, he nibbled at his own cake. The girl watched until he had swallowed a fair portion of his present and then made off. 'Farewell, brother, pretty brother, grey-haired brother.' Borrow sat on under his ash tree, began to feel sleepy, dozed off, awoke and 'something appeared to bear heavy on my breast.' He had been poisoned.

All this is factual. We know who attempted murder and the exact means employed. The details can come in a moment, but the details do not really matter. Borrow is here creating for us a symbol of the tragedy of his life as he saw it; and the symbol is as alive now as on the days when he created it. For anyone who reads Borrow sympathetically he told all in the subtitle of *Lavengro*: he was 'the scholar, the gypsy, the priest'. He intended that subtitle as a summing-up. He saw himself as a scholar whose scholarship was to concern itself primarily with languages and with primitive literature. He saw himself as a 'priest', that is a man living – living uproariously even – in the world of men, but at the same time living apart, forsaking the lusts of the flesh and preaching – or perhaps better 'living out' the brotherhood of man, proclaiming a co-partnership, though not in Wordsworth's sense, with the natural world – and the symbol here is the viper of Norman Cross; finally Borrow was 'the wild one', a wanderer, an opter-out; in other words he admired the way the gipsies lived: what he longed for was to live a wholly private life in some larger, and accepted, society – a mistletoe-parasite living like a clenched fist plunged into the middle of the larger oak.

In London the Borrovian scholar had been slapped in the face; the Borrovian worker-priest, gossiping with the apple-woman-cum-fence plying her trade at one end of London Bridge, had not got very far either. And now, here somewhere in the wildernesses of Shropshire, it suddenly began to look as if Borrow the wild one had been rejected also. The cake was not a cake: it was a murder-weapon. The gipsies whom he looked upon as his allies, one of whom was his blood-brother, wanted him out of the way.

The girl who had danced for him was the niece of Martha Herne, and her name was Joni Boss (Boss, Bosvil, Bosville – they are all forms of the same name, a gipsy name and one she shared with the Flaming Tinman, Jack Slingsby's rival). Martha Herne hated Borrow because he was an outsider trying to associate himself with the secret society of gipsydom. And so, when Joni returned to her after the first meeting with him to tell her she had found him tinkering on the Flaming Tinman's patch, she decided to kill him by administering a dose of the drows (barium carbonate, or witherite – gipsies killed pigs by the same method), which was found round lead mines. An interval of three days was necessary for the journey to the nearest mine, the Snailbeach mine at Minsterley, the return, and the baking of the cake in the efficaceous way known, in her private witchcraft way, to Martha Herne. In the event, however, Borrow never ate more than some half of it, and thus his life was saved – though only because he was a young and very powerful man. The symptoms he describes – the burning of the eyes, the convulsive movements, the suddenly feeling better and then the suddenly feeling worse again – all these are right for poisoning by barium carbonate. Martha Herne came near to finishing him off.

The two women, realizing that Borrow was not going to drop dead before their eyes from what he had eaten – and this was undoubtedly what they expected – attempted to hasten him on his way. They urged the dog that was with them to go into Borrow's tent and maul him; the dog showed reluctance; they tried to poke his eyes out with a stick but were frightened to come too near. Borrow, *in extremis*, was still somehow formidable, still – the symbol holds up – defiant in betrayal. Then the two furies were disturbed by the scrunching of cartwheels on the move, and they ran, leaving Borrow to Peter Williams and his wife Winifred, travelling evangelists of the revivalist Calvinistic movement which began in Wales in the second decade of the nineteenth century. From about 12 to 21 June Borrow travelled with Williams and his wife towards the Welsh border. They nursed him and helped him to regain his strength. During the journey Williams gave Borrow a lengthy account of himself, and a Gothic story it was, one of a man obsessed with the purpose of making atonement for a sin committed by himself in unregenerate days. A haunted man, then: and why should Borrow set it down for us at such length? The explanation must surely be that Borrow was beginning to see himself, like Williams, as a haunted man.

By the time they reached the border he was more his usual hardy physical self. The Williamses pressed him to go on with them, but he refused. The reason? Here Borrow springs his surprise. The Welsh they have been speaking freely is not, as they will have thought, gibberish to him. He is a scholar. He has made translations into English from the ancient Welsh poets. He has no mind to trundle into the country on a tinker's cart. 'When I go into Wales, I should wish to go in a new suit of superfine black, with hat and beaver, mounted on a powerful steed, black and glossy, like that which bore Greduv to the fight of Catraeth. I should wish, moreover, to see the Welshmen assembled on the border ready to welcome me with pipe and fiddle, and much whooping and shouting, and to attend me to Wrexham. . . .'

And so the Williams couple and Borrow parted, Borrow eastwards again, his saviours into Wales, two people mightily impressed and surprised. Borrow was always a man who enjoyed, and strove for, a good exit.

Suddenly, at that parting, Ambrose Petulengro was there – 'in the ford' are the words used. An odd reappearance one might think. Was Ambrose crossing the boundary stream? Or was Peter Williams, knowing Borrow now for the linguist he was, addressing him in Welsh, and did Borrow slyly indicate this to those in the know by putting down a literal 'in the ford' as a translation of Peter's 'yn y ffordd', which would mean, more vaguely, 'in the way' or 'along the road'? Whichever way it was, Borrow was almost certainly bringing this meeting forward in time. Certainly the meeting with Ambrose took place, but further to the east. Ambrose on the Welsh borders was out of his ground by a good way; he would know, just as surely as Jack Slingsby, that this had become the Flaming Tinman's territory. Borrow juggled in this way with the order of events because he wanted to get his ritual fight with Ambrose out of the way in preparation for more important events shortly to follow. And why should there be a ritual fight? Simply because Mrs Herne was of Ambrose's clan, and the word had gone round among the gipsies that she had made away with herself in order to atone for her failure to eliminate the foreign intruder, George Borrow. Ambrose explained the business to his blood-brother: 'There is a point at present between us. . . . I shouldn't like it to be known that I went up and down the country with a pal who was the cause of my mother-in-law's death . . . if I and my pal have a tuzzle, he gives me satisfaction . . . and he who says to the contrary knows nothing of gipsy law. . . .' And so, at a convenient place unspecified, they go at it, bare-fisted, but it is only a formal affair lasting half an hour merely, enough for Borrow to be bloodied and for Ambrose to feel easy in his conscience, having done the proper thing – 'which is all that can be expected reasonably for an old woman who carried so much brimstone about her. . . .'

After a companionable while, the two parted, and Borrow set up his forge ten miles farther on – 'in a dingle'. This was the most famous of all dingles – Mumper's Dingle – and learned men have plotted and charted and timed in order to settle exactly where it was. Majority opinion has decided that it was somewhere close to Willenhall. The difficulty is that, as he counts the days from his parting with Peter Williams at the Welsh border, the journey by pony and trap must have been accomplished at an unbelievable speed for him to have been around Willenhall by 25 June – but George Sampson who made him pass through Much Wenlock and Bridgnorth and who had him in his dingle by the twenty-fifth, is not a man to be lightly contradicted. However, much that was of the greatest importance to Borrow happened in that dingle, and it is quite likely that he played tricks with the unity of time in order to ensure a changeless background to events through which he sought to make sense – for his own purposes more than for us – of his inmost self; a difficult task for any of us, particularly difficult for Borrow. Outside he was a confident, striding giant, the most un-Hamlet-like of men. Yet inside him uncertainty, self-mistrust, melancholia thrashed around.

He stayed in Mumper's Dingle and taught himself the trade of forging horseshoes and fitting them to hoofs. He had the pony to practise on. He got the trick of it in four days, and then came an attack of the horrors. Later on Borrow was to say that he dated his affliction from the time of his poisoning by Martha Herne. Evidence, especially from his time in Millman Street, would suggest that he had suffered before. What distinguished this particular bout so as to make it stand out in his memory as a starting-point was the terrifying, obliterating violence of it. 'I sat down on my stone, and, supporting my arm upon my knee, leaned my head upon my hand. Heaviness had come over me. . . .'

What follows is the finest description of hysteric mania ever set down by a writer of English. He was alone. That is important. And 'the horror was upon me' – that is repeated. 'Every moment I felt it gathering force, and making me more wholly its own. What should I do? – resist, of course: and I did resist. I grasped, I tore, and strove to fling it from me; but of what avail were my efforts? I could only have got rid of it by getting rid of myself---.' This most moving phrase rings on in the reader's ears. He is in the presence of a man possessed. 'I rushed amongst the trees, and struck at them with my bare fists' – one remembers the picture Watts-Dunton gives of the old man walking about Richmond Park and touching the trees – 'and dashed my head against them, but I felt no pain . . . and then I flung myself on the ground, gnawed the earth and swallowed it: and then I looked around; it was almost total darkness in the dingle, and the darkness added to my horror. . . .' He ran up out of the dip in search of reassurance and light, but 'in another minute the sun was gone . . . it was of no use fighting against the horror, that I saw; the more I fought against it the stronger it became. . . .' The fact that Borrow retained his powers of reasoning, that he was not in any sense insane, but, as it were, watching himself intensifies for us the extremity of his situation. 'I again uttered wild cries, so loud that I was apprehensive they would be heard by some chance passenger on the neighbouring road. . . .' Again the reasoning man stands terrifyingly before us. 'I, therefore, went deeper into the dingle; I sat down with my back against a thorn bush; the thorns entered my flesh, and when I felt them I pressed harder against the bush; I thought the pain of the flesh might in some degree counteract the mental agony. . . .' Then at last the grip of the thing weakened slightly. 'I . . . found my little horse . . . I put my hand to his mouth, he licked my hand. I flung myself down by him and put my arms round his neck. . . . I clung to my little horse as if for safety and protection. I laid my head on his neck; and felt almost calm; presently the fear returned, but not so wild as before. . . .' And so, gradually, he returns to mastery of himself.

Two days later Borrow, still weak from the effects of poisoning and hysteria, saddled Ambrol, his little horse, and prepared to set off to the nearest place for provisions. He had decided to stay where he was for a while and recuperate. He might even write a little. Freedom and independence – the comfortable solitariness of beast and man in partnership – more than made up for the loneliness. But just as he was about to set off – probably to Willenhall or to Wolverhampton – there came an interruption: the Tinman appeared. He was accompanied by his woman, his Moll and following behind, a tall girl he called Belle. He stopped at the sight of Borrow ready to go, but the tall girl urged him on. 'Why don't you move forward, Jack?' She seemed to think that here was a place suitable enough for the stags to fight it out. Jack Boswell, the Tinman, was not as tall as Borrow; he was tough, but not nearly as young as Borrow. Borrow tried to avoid hostilities. 'You need not be afraid . . . I bid ye welcome.' But the Tinman was in no mood for a peaceful settlement, and Belle was even more eager for a fight. 'Afraid at what? – at that lad? Why, he looks like a ghost. I would engage to thrash him with one hand.' But Borrow refused to match her hostility. He talked to her as a young man might be expected to talk to a young woman good to look at.

It is the only place in the whole of Borrow's writing where he can be said to make overt, if pedantic, sexual advances to a woman. 'You might beat me with no hands at all, fair damsel, only by looking at me; I never saw such a face and figure, both regal. Why, you look like Ingeborg, Queen of Norway; she had twelve brothers, you know, and could lick them all, though they were heroes. . . .' But Belle rejected all this. Borrow went on to talk to her in Romany and she disliked him all the more for his thinking of her as a gipsy. 'I would have you know that I come of Christian blood and parents, and was born in the great house of Long Melford,' she said, coming forward and striking him a blow on the face which nearly felled him. Borrow – the gentleman – kept a hold on his politeness and kept his hands off her. But by now the Tinman had warmed himself up. '. . . who gave you leave to camp on my ground?' 'Is it your ground?' Borrow retorted. The Tinman got angrier, and Belle suddenly switched sides: 'be civil, or you will rue it' she told her man. Does she sleep with the Tinman when he wants a change from the workworn Moll? Or does she perhaps sleep with him only when she feels like it? Or does she perhaps not sleep with him at all? This is a point which the modern reader might like to have settled. Borrow suggests that she is virtuous, but is clearly not greatly interested in the question. It is typical of him that he should shy away from any discussion, however oblique, of sexual matters.

So follows the best of all literary fights in English. Had Borrow read Hazlitt's essay, 'The Fight', published in the *New Monthly Magazine* in 1822? Probably not. He was never a great reading man. To Defoe he owed much; he had read Bunyan and Smollett and possibly Sterne; obviously he was fond of *Gil Blas*; and like everyone of his generation who could read at all he knew something of *Childe Harold*. But the writers of his time have, on the whole, strangely little to say to him. However it was, Borrow's description of his set-to with the Tinman easily outpoints Hazlitt's account of Bill Neat's victory over the Gasman. Hazlitt's itch to be everlastingly quoting gets in the way of the action. Borrow's treatment is crisp, serviceable, and direct and therefore entirely suitable to the occasion. The dialogue is taut and pared down to what is absolutely necessary. (Borrow's dialogue is always unfailingly good; what a playwright he would have made if only he had had the structural gift.)

Borrow won. It was not an easy victory. He was weak still from his horrors and from his poisoning. Indeed, if it had not been for Belle, by now his Amazon ally, he would not have won at all. He kept jabbing at the Tinman with his left. He went down, spitting blood, and as she was nursing him on her knee Belle told him to use the Long Melford. 'Why,' she explained – because her champion, blurry by now, couldn't grasp the technical term 'Long Melford' – 'this long right of yours. . . .' She felt his right arm. 'If you do, I shouldn't wonder if you yet stand a chance.' The pair of them went at it again, and 'At last he aimed a blow which, had it taken full effect, would doubtless have ended the battle, but owing to his slipping, the fist only grazed my left shoulder, and came with terrific force against a tree, close to which I had been driven; before the Tinman could recover himself, I collected all my strength, and struck him beneath the ear, and then fell to the ground completely exhausted. . . . "Hurrah for Long Melford!"' Borrow muzzily heard Belle exclaim. 'There is nothing like Long Melford for shortness all the world over.' She was a spirited girl. Squabbling, the two women bring their man to. Belle, with debts settled, is for friendship all round, but Moll remains bitterly unforgiving. The Tinman, still too stunned for self-assertiveness, has thought for nothing but to be away from the interloper. Shall Belle go with them? He leaves the decision to his mort. 'Stay where you are, you jade . . . stay with the bit of a mullo ['mullo' means 'ghost': Borrow was clearly still far from himself] whom you helped. . . . Fetch down your mailla [donkey] go-cart and live here with your chabo' (child or nursling – emphasizing again Moll's poor opinion of Borrow's strength and virility – she clearly felt that the Tinman's downfall was attributable to the tree rather than to Borrow, and certainly as he describes the fight and what leads up to it Borrow is at no great pains to make himself out a hero).

He watched the Tinman and Moll off the scene, and then returned to the dingle leading Belle's donkey still drawing the go-cart. Back in the hollow he found Belle, 'her hair . . . all dishevelled,' in tears. 'They were bad people . . . and I did not like them, but they were my only acquaintance in the wide world.' Can this change be in character? Or is this simply Borrow's way of modulating from fisticuffs and flowing blood to the enigmatic, much interrupted passages of sexual encounter between himself and Belle (or Isopel) Berners?

It would be unwise to come up with too positive a reply to this question. Indeed it is clearly Borrow's purpose not so much to lead us astray as to communicate his own uncertainties. There are plenty of inserted stories in *Lavengro* and *The Romany Rye*, but the best and most famous of all – his rueful, vinegary idyll – is not put before us as a rounded whole. He lived with Belle, in Mumper's Dingle, for probably one month, from 28 June to 28 July 1825. The relationship is developed by means of shy hints, snatches of conversation, and hints of a half-embarrassed strength of feeling growing between them. But Borrow keeps running away from it. Old characters – the

Petulengros for example – make reappearances and hold the stage; new ones are introduced such as the Roman Catholic hedge-priest whom Borrow calls 'The Man in Black' who is made to outstay Belle's welcome – and ours – while the tinker Borrow (staunchly Protestant) and the Roman propagandist hold lengthy and tedious debate.

'... but my glass has been empty for a considerable time; perhaps, Bellissima Biondina,' said he, addressing Belle, 'you will deign to replenish it??' 'I shall do no such thing,' said Belle, 'you have drunk quite enough, and talked more than enough, and to tell you the truth I wish you would leave us alone.' 'Shame on you, Belle,' said I, 'consider the obligations of hospitality.' 'I am sick of that word,' said Belle, 'you are so frequently misusing it; were this place not Mumper's Dingle, and consequently as free to the fellow as ourselves, I would lead him out of it.' 'Pray be quiet, Belle,' said I. 'You had better help yourself,' said I, addressing myself to the man in black, 'the lady is angry with you.'

And this is the way it goes. Borrow's marriage, even though only a month long, is nevertheless a broken one.

But was it a marriage at all? His attitude – to her as well as to his readers – is coy. Is Belle simply a creature out of his imagination? Here it needs to be said again, because it is central to Borrow, that he never 'created' characters in the novelist's way. Her name is invented; but there was an Elizabeth Jarvis born in the workhouse at Long Melford in 1803 whose mother died in giving birth to her. Watts-Dunton wrote in the article already quoted that she was 'an East-Anglian road-girl of the finest type, known to the Boswells [the gipsy Boswells, that is], and remembered not many years ago.' Cobbett said that he came upon some gipsies on the move between Cheriton and Alresford, that is eight to ten miles east of Winchester, and with them there was a young woman '*six feet high*' (Cobbett's italics). That was in 1822. Would there be two tramp-women of that size alive and abroad at the same time in England? It is unlikely. Even a man of that stature was a rarity in those days. So that certainly Belle, under whatever name, existed – and Cobbett too says that she had 'most beautiful features'.

On the evening of the day of the fight the two sat together and she told him about her hard young life, the dominant theme of which was 'Fear God, and take your own part.' 'I like truth and constancy, don't you, young man?' He agreed, but 'I feel very strangely.' 'How do you feel, young man?' 'Very much afraid.' ' At the Flaming Tinman? Don't be afraid of him. He won't come back.' 'I'm not afraid of the

Flaming Tinman.' 'What, then, are you afraid of?' 'The evil one.' 'The
evil one,' said the girl, 'where is he?' 'Coming upon me.' 'Never
heed,' said the girl. 'I'll stand by you.'

These exchanges are intentionally enigmatic. Does Borrow, by the
'evil one' mean his horrors? The reader is tempted at first reading to
think so. But Borrow's attacks, we know, were not frequently recur-
rent. Did Borrow, a robust young man if ever there was one, believe
that the demon just conquered was already meditating a second
onslaught? It is unlikely. Since the girl, by chattering with such
frankness to him about herself, has shown a fondness for him, is it not
possible that he is trying to tell her, and us, that Belle the beautiful and
the bold has come upon a man quite different from the ones she has
met in plenty in her unsheltered life – a man who is sexually odd? She
fails to understand him.

And as the four weeks of its lasting go by the relationship develops,
but Borrow's objective becomes steadily clearer: to emphasize an
irremediable inconclusiveness.

'Well, Armenian is the speech of people of that place [Ararat], and I should
like to teach it to you.' 'To prevent ---' 'Ay, ay, to prevent our occasionally
feeling uncomfortable together . . . Belle, I will now give you a lesson in
Armenian.' 'I suppose you mean no harm.' . . . . 'Not in the least; I merely
propose the thing to prevent our occasionally feeling uncomfortable with
each other . . .'

'Feeling uncomfortable' is Borrow's way of saying that Belle, he
recognizes, feels lustfully attracted to him, while he – well, he is
uncomfortable because he is not sure of the nature of his feelings
towards her. All the exchanges between them during the long periods
when they are alone together have these qualities of funniness and
sadness and uniqueness. It is hard to think of any passages in literature where a writer describes the relations between a young man and a
young woman in quite this way.

They both keep to their tents. 'About mid-day Mr and Mrs
Petulengro came to the dingle to pay the promised visit. Belle, at the
time of their arrival, was in her tent, but I was at the fire-place,
engaged in hammering part of the outer-tire . . . which had come off
from one of the wheels of my vehicle. . . .' It is all very domestic.

With the arrival of the Petulengros, bringing Ursula, Ambrose's
unmarried sister with them, Belle left the dingle for a while, probably
having tired of Borrow's refusal to take his fences.

'Then you are going?' said I. . . . 'Yes,' said Belle, 'I am going on a journey;
my affairs compel me.' 'But you will return again?' said I. 'Yes,' said Belle, 'I

shall return once more.' 'Once more,' said I; 'what do you mean by once more?' . . . 'You were alone here,' said Belle, 'before I came, and, I suppose, found it agreeable, or you would not have stayed in it.' 'Yes,' said I, 'that was before I knew you; but having lived with you here, I should be very loth to live here without you.' 'Indeed,' said Belle, 'I did not know that I was of so much consequence to you. . . .'

This is about as near as Borrow ever gets to directness, and even at this point he pushes in an escape word – 'Having lived with you *here*' – as much as to say that once he was out of the dingle, the special, quiet, private place, and out into the world, far off, seeking strangers, listening to fresh tongues, the situation might change again. Yet all the same, once she has gone, Borrow feels that rarest of emotions for him: bereavement. 'I returned to the dingle, where, seating myself on my stone, I remained for upwards of an hour in thought.'

He was nearing the end of his time in the dingle when Belle came back. Belle had made up her mind that there could be no future for her with him. '"I was always kind to you; and if you have made me cry, it's a poor thing to boast of." "I had no idea of making you cry. . . . Come, cheer up Belle. You were talking of parting; don't let us part, but depart, and that together."' Thus, playing with words, Borrow arrived at last at the point. '"Our ways lie different," said Belle. "I don't see why they should," said I. "Come, let us be off to America together?"'

There, he says, they will conjugate the verb *siriel* together. 'Conjugally?' Belle asks, not sure of him. He reassures her, but there is jokiness in it. So that she shall be convinced might they not try wrestling together? And to give some sort of backing to this lunacy he flings off into Norse legend. Did not Brunhild the Valkyrie swear that no one should marry her who could not fling her down? 'You are beginning to look rather wild,' Belle tells him, sadness and despair and fun mixed up all in a flat phrase that Borrow succeeds in making memorable. She will have one more day to consider this joint American idea because on the next day he is to go to the fair with Mr Petulengro – the next day, in fact, he will have important matters to attend to . . . Does he intend Belle to see it like this?

At the fair Ambrose and he find a fine horse. Borrow at first has doubts because of its scrubby tail, but Ambrose dismisses these. '. . . 'tis your scrubby-tailed horses that are your out-and-outers. Did you ever hear of Syntax, brother?' Ambrose offers to lend him seventy pounds in order to buy it. Borrow refuses the offer, and when they return to the dingle, Ambrose with more liquor aboard than he can properly carry, they find not Belle but a gipsy girl 'who told me that Miss Berners when she went away had charged her to keep up the fire, and have the kettle boiling against my arrival.' He is put out by this departure without notice, but not as shattered as one might expect. 'Husbands do not grow upon hedgerows; she is merely gone after a little business and will return tomorrow. Comforted in some degree by these hopeful imaginings, I retired to my tent and went to sleep.' But the parting is final; he has told us so in advance. As Ambrose and he were on their way to the fair in the early morning Borrow had turned and 'at the extremity of the plain, I looked towards the dingle. Isopel Berners stood at the mouth, the beams of the early morning sun shone full on her noble face and figure. I waved my hand towards her. She slowly lifted up her right arm. I turned away, and never saw Isopel Berners again.' For three days after the return from the fair he waited about, unbelieving. Then he hears a cart approaching but it passes above the dingle. The next day after that an old woman arrives with a letter for him. It is a long letter – Belle is literate – and with it, along with her favourite advice: 'Fear God and take your own part,' is a lock of her hair to remember her by. But it is a letter of rejection all the same. Belle is for America, but without him. Her phrase – 'you are beginning to look rather wild' – has remained with her. 'I thought it best to leave you for ever, because, for some time past, I had become almost convinced, that though with an infinite deal of learning, and exceedingly shrewd in some things, you were – pray don't be offended – at the root mad!' He takes this, on the whole, stoically. He has been acting outside the truth of his own nature. The tramp-woman Belle understands him more thoroughly than he understands himself. 'I retired to my dingle and my tent, where I betook myself to my bed, and there, knowing the worst, and *being no longer agitated by apprehension* [my italics], nor agonised by expectation, I was soon buried in a deep slumber, the first which I had fallen into for several nights.' All passion was spent because he never really had any.

The affair was over. It was Saturday 14 July, and Borrow's passage through his dream-world was over too. He had written, three-quarters of a century before Alain-Fournier, his *Grand Meaulnes*. He had, as J. B. Priestley put it, speaking of Fournier, his 'reality beyond reality'. Within about two weeks – in the middle of August 1825, that is – he was back in Norwich and living at the Willow Way house with his mother, having bought a good horse with money lent by Ambrose, leaving with him his donkey, his cart, and his tinker's tools as surety, having ridden to Tamworth for the horse-fair where he sold his animal at a good profit, and then set out for Norwich and home on foot. The last page of *The Romany Rye* finds Borrow marching briskly eastwards – towards his homeland. The recruiting sergeant

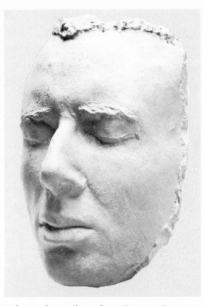

Portrait of George Borrow by his brother John, *c.* 1821.

Life mask attributed to George Borrow, *c.* 1824.

The Borrow house, Willow Lane, Norwich, where Borrow lived at intervals from 1816 to his marriage in 1839 and where his mother lived until 1849.

Gipsies in the mid nineteenth century.

Mumper's Dingle. From a drawing.

tries persuading him to take the King's shilling. India is beckoning.
'The finest country in the world' the sergeant assures him, and drags
in some Indian words to tickle a young man's fancy: 'Kauloes' and
'Lolloes'. Borrow immediately stares at him and becomes excited.
'Why . . . this is the very language of Mr Petulengro . . . and Tawno
Chikno [brother of Mr Petulengro].' This is gipsy-stuff, and the
sergeant immediately backs away. 'I don't like your way of speaking;
no, nor your way of looking. You are mad, sir; you are mad; and
what's this? Why, your hair is grey! You won't do for the Honourable Company – they like red. I'm glad I didn't give you the shilling. . . .' And so Borrow marches on, saying to himself as he goes 'I
shouldn't wonder . . . if Mr Petulengro and Tawno Chikno came
originally from India. I think I'll go there.'

The abruptness of that final sentence is astonishing. Was it
Borrow's way of saying: From this point on you must mind your
own business? Perhaps it was. At any event, he disappeared from
view, popped down a hole like a rabbit, to emerge intermittently. For
example, on a May morning in 1839, in the Posada de la Reyna in
Seville, Lt.-Col. Napier, also staying at the Posada, met someone
who did not give his name. 'He was tall,' says Napier, in his book
Excursions along the shores of the Mediterranean, 'with a commanding appearance; yet, though apparently in the flower of manhood, his
hair was so deeply tinged with the winter of either age or sorrow as to
be nearly snow white.' So this, beyond any doubt, was Borrow. The
time and the place and the elusive one are all together. Napier and
Borrow talked. They rode out together, to the ruins of Italica.
Borrow declaimed some verses and a crowd of *gitanos* gathered. One,
a slight female figure beautiful in the extreme but ragged and grubby,
started to beg: 'Caballeritos, una limosnita!' Borrow told her to stop,
and turning to Napier said (as Napier reports) 'Do you remember
what I told you of the Eastern origin of these people? You shall see
that I am correct.' Then Borrow told the girl to approach, talking in
'Moultanee', and this the girl understood and falteringly replied to.
Later on, Napier, greatly impressed, asked Borrow: 'Where, in the
name of goodness, did you pick up your acquaintance with the
language of these extraordinary people?' And Borrow replied briefly:
'Some years ago, in Moultan.' And Moultan, or Multan, is a town 200
miles or so to the west-south-west of Lahore, now of course just
inside the borders of Pakistan, but to Borrow it would have been,
compendiously, 'India'. There is no reason to suppose that Napier
was anything other than an entirely reliable reporter. And why
should Borrow have said this to him, mentioning quite specifically a
town, unless he had been there?

CHAPTER 4

GONE MISSING

IT will be useful in the first place to set out the hard evidence we have about Borrow's activities and whereabouts between September 1825 and November 1829, the most elusive period of his life.

To begin with he stayed with his mother in Willow Lane and from there resumed his attack on publishers. He had goods to sell and would go on trying to sell them. He wrote to the London publishers of Klinger's *Faust* in his translation to see what, if anything, they owed him, and suggested that, as fire had destroyed two copies in Norwich libraries, he might be prepared to take back remaining copies from Simpkin Marshall, and see what he could do with them himself in Norwich. Then he went again through the material that he had taken with him as ammunition when he first left Norwich for London on 1 April 1824. In Janury 1826 he started to print, in Norwich on his own account, a collection of his translations which he called *Romantic Ballads* and subtitled 'translated from the Danish and Miscellaneous Pieces'. Allan Cunningham, nineteen years older than he, whom he had briefly met in London and who was firmly established as a balladist and as a regular contributor to the *London Magazine*, was asked for a verse preface. Cunningham was kind, and obliged. 'Sing, sing,' he wrote, 'my friend, breathe life again/Through Norway's song and Denmark's strain:/On flowing Thames and Forth, in flood,/Pour Haco's war-song, fierce and rude.' Did Borrow hope that this kettledrum stuff would attract the readers that were so shy of him? If he did, then it is clear that he still had not lost his *naïveté* and trustfulness.

No review of it appeared, although there is evidence that Borrow did not neglect to send it round. Francis Palgrave the historian, father of the *Golden Treasury* anthology Palgrave, and a man to be knighted in 1832, received a copy and responded graciously. The story goes that Borrow also sent a copy to Scott, who made no acknowledgement and earned for himself Borrow's abiding dislike thereafter. His silence (if he ever received the book) strikes one however as both honest and tactful. What comment, other than a wounding one, could the accepted master of balladry both translated and original honestly have made after reading one or two of them here and there?

This is perhaps the most suitable point at which to ask oneself: why did Borrow labour so hard, so long, and with such little reward at translating verse out of a babel of languages? He had little feeling for poetry. 'They are attempting to resuscitate [Keats], I believe,' he said once in the tone of one who found it difficult to believe that 'they' could be so stupid. Wordsworth sent him to sleep. He did enjoy the old rough stuff of balladry and would chant it to himself as he sped along the roads of Britain and Europe. He liked bold simplicity and ruggedness, whether natural or contrived. He liked unsophistication, of poets like ap Gwilym. In Chaucer, who flourished over the same period as ap Gwilym and who was in all essentials highly sophisticated, Borrow never showed any interest at all.

But for all his trying he could never quite catch the darting simplicity, the singing flight of the arrow, which the old poets in their various languages could achieve seemingly effortlessly. Scott could do it – not by any means always but still often enough; and 'Proud Maisie' is a masterpiece without any doubt. Many of the Germans of the *Sturm-und-Drang* had the knack of it, Goethe in particular. Borrow rushed confidently at one of his very best – 'Erlkönig' – and the result is an unqualified disaster. It was not, with Borrow, a case of a writer of genius struggling to find, and failing for a long time to find, the form that suits him. He was writing *Wild Wales* in 1854, when he was fifty-one. By then he had established himself as a writer who could do marvellous things – and things which no other writer before or since has quite managed to do. Yet here he is still at it, preserving ap Gwilym in what Edward Thomas called 'a sort of life in death'.

Why was he afflicted with this blindness about what he could do and could not do? Partly it was the gipsy in him. He liked the rough simplicity of a tramping life; he was at home in the back yards of inns. He saw the old balladists as partakers in a way of life congenial to him. Partly it was his obsession with languages – not so much with their subtleties and complexities as with foreign words simply as foreign words. Syntax and grammar came more slowly than the easily learned vocabulary, but eventually a thorough command of a language could be built up. The oral side was not his strength. He had not much ear for rhythm and cadence. Thus when wandering in Wales at the time of the Crimean War he could understand what the Welshmen said to him. What he said to them was also perfectly comprehensible, but it sounded odd and made them laugh.

He could handle thirty or so languages. Whether he was master in all of them, whether he was quite Lavengro, is more open to question. But it is perfectly natural that anyone with this very special aptitude would want the world, or some part of it, to know about it, hence his huge output of translated material. The job was not done particularly well. It was done at great speed. The following letter to John Bowring, whom Borrow had met and admired in 1821, provides us with a fearful example of Borrow the translator at work. 'To my great pleasure I perceive that the books have all arrived safe. But I find that, instead of an Icelandic Grammar, you have lent me an *Essay on the origin of the Icelandic Language*, which I here return. Thorlakson's Grave-ode is superlatively fine, and I translated it this morning as I breakfasted. I have just finished a translation of Baggesen's beautiful poem, and I send it for your inspection. . . .' Bowring having similar interests to Borrow encouraged Borrow – in all sincerity – to scurry down ways he would have done far better to avoid.

How long exactly he made Norwich his headquarters after September 1825 it is not possible to say, but he was probably there till June 1826, sponging on his mother, and feeling most unhappy about it. He may well have made small, occasional profit out of horse-dealing; but in the main he must have been dependent on her and the small income made available through the late Captain's carefulness and sense of responsibility. This indebtedness to one dead and disapproving of him must have made his situation all the harder to bear. He was in his twenty-third year, and his pride was always easily wounded.

In late June 1826 he was in London, staying briefly at 26 Bryanston Street close to Portman Square, from where he wrote a note to Haydon: 'I should feel extremely obliged if you would allow me to sit to you as soon as possible. I am going to the South of France in a little better than a fortnight, and I would sooner lose a thousand pounds than not have the honour of appearing in the picture.' The connection with Haydon had presumably been loosely maintained since John Borrow's visit to London, when George was staying at Millman Street, to persuade his former master to go to Norwich to paint Robert Hawkes. At that meeting Haydon had been working on a picture to be called *Pharaoh dismissing Moses from Egypt*, and, noticing Borrow's unusual swarthiness, had remarked that here was the man with the face that would do for Pharaoh; but Borrow had replied that he had no wish to appear on canvas. Now, two years later and with money so tight, he was apparently willing to sit to anyone as anybody. Nothing came of this, however; Borrow's likeness does not appear in any picture of Haydon's. But the letter establishes him in

London, and his intention to go to the south of France in July 1826. His brother John sailed for Mexico that summer to take up a job with the Real del Monte Company at £300 a year – a highly paid place indeed, and obtained for him by Allday Kerrison, brother of Roger, with whom Borrow had lodged in Millman Street. John had been granted one year's leave of absence from the West Norfolk Militia on half-pay, with the arrangement renewable. So John appeared settled and prosperous, whilst his brother remained extremely unsettled and with no certainty of income whatsoever.

He went abroad, however, and walked the roads and got casual labour in much the same way as he had the summer before from Salisbury to Staffordshire, tinkering alongside the gipsies, following their 'patterans', or trails, and keeping company with various groups when their directions coincided with his. Few details of his tramping may be pinpointed, but in one of the letters written to his mother from St. Petersburg he speaks of 'London, Paris, Madrid, and other capitals which I have visited.' In *The Zincali* he starts a sentence with 'Once, during my wanderings in Italy . . . it was about four miles from Genoa. . . .'

In Paris he met Vidocq, the scoundrelly thief-turned-thief-taker who put his name to much more in the way of seamy recollection than he actually wrote and whom Borrow found entertaining. It was something partly bred in him, and encouraged and made habitual during his prolonged explorations of the underworld required by his compilation of Phillips's *Celebrated Trials*. From Paris he went on, so he says, to the French Midi, thence across the Pyrenees into Spain and Portugal, and then back through Provence and over the Ligurian Apennines at least as far as Genoa where he took ship for home. It was tough going all the way, and he would have had to work his passage back. (There is no record of a Foreign Office passport having been issued to him at this time – but from beginning to end he would not have been a conventional traveller.) It is unlikely that he got help from his mother: she would not have known where to send it, and besides, out of £100 a year, there could have been little or nothing to send. It is also unlikely that Borrow would have asked for it.

On 12 April 1827 he was back at the Tombland Fair in Norwich, doffing his hat to the trotting stallion Marshland Shales, in acknow-ledgement of the famous animal's age and prowess. He stayed at Willow Lane until the end of November 1827. During September and October there are entries in his mother's cash-book in his handwrit-ing, and entries in her handwriting having to do with Borrow's transactions until the end of the year. After that Borrow plunges off into some dark cloud until July 1829. From Norwich, in that month, he wrote to John in Mexico, and in November 1829 he was back again in London where he took rooms at 17 Great Russell Street and prepared once more for an attack on literary London.

Why did he keep so silent about this year and three quarters? The explanation which tallies best with the kind of man Borrow was goes something like this. Beaten off but not defeated as a writing man, he escapes on to the open road, and experiences the wonderful summer of 1825. Then, after the return to Norwich and the further non-success of the *Romantic Ballads*, comes a second escape, this time to Europe. And still after that there is for him no sure forward move, no way of getting people to see what a champion he was. And so yet another escape? It is probable; but he is not any more a romantic Childe Harold, but a much grubbier sort of chap in danger of becoming inured to humiliation. And so his self-respect would best be defended, if defended at all, by keeping silent. To turn a sizeable passage of time into a mystery might be the least painful method of dealing with it. And in November 1829, back in Bloomsbury again, he is still a man working furiously at self-justification but with abject failure shadowing him more closely than ever. Over the twenty-one months preceding this he was probably back on the English roads, living the life he had lived before, tinkering, horse-dealing, and consorting on and off with the gipsies. The rather over-crowded final pages of *The Romany Rye* may well bring in some of his encounters and experiences at this time.

On 6 December 1829 he sat down in his Bloomsbury room and wrote again to John Bowring, now editor of the Benthamite *Westminster Review*, founded in 1824, and working on a general study of Danish literature.

Lest I should intrude upon you when you are busy, I write to enquire when you will be unoccupied. I wish to shew you my translation of 'The Death of Balder', Ewald's most celebrated production, which, if you approve of, will perhaps render me some assistance in bringing forth, for I don't know many publishers. I think this will be a proper time to introduce it to the British public, as your account of Danish literature will doubtless cause a sensation. . . .

Bowring responded to this more warmly than Borrow had any right to expect. And having received an encouraging reply, Borrow began to push his luck. On 28 December he proposed collaboration. 'Sup-

pose we bring forward the first volume of the Danish Anthology . . .
heroic and supernatural songs of the K.V. [Kampe Viser] . . . they are
quite ready for the press with the necessary notes, and with an
introduction which I am not ashamed of. . . . ' Bowring replied
immediately – and still encouragingly.

On the last day of the year Borrow wrote: 'as it appears that you
will not be disengaged till next Friday evening . . . I will call then. You
think that no more than two volumes can be ventured on. Well! be it
so!' Bowring must have begun to feel that he was astride a hard-
pulling young horse. Borrow worked like mad. Bowring got a prospectus by no later than 7 January – 'for your inspection and for the
correction of your master hand'. Bowring sent it back, having toned
down a certain fulsomeness. Instantly, on 14 January, Borrow replied: 'I approve of the prospectus in every respect; it is business-like,
and there is nothing flashy in it. . . .' He went on to assure Bowring –
although the editor of the *Westminster Review* could scarcely have
been in need of it – of his intense activity. 'Today I translated "The
Duke's Daughter of Skage", a noble ballad of 400 lines. . . .' One
might estimate this output at 4,000 words of verse translation in one
day. How desperate Borrow must have been feeling. And included in
that same letter come still more proposals. Could Bowring get him
some reviewing? and 'enquire whether a *good* article on Welsh poetry
would be received. I have,' he mysteriously added, 'the advantage of
not being a Welshman. . . .' At the same time he had to give notice to
Bowring of a change of address. 'I write this to inform you that I am
at No. 7 Museum St., Bloomsbury. I have been obliged to decamp
from Russell St. for the cogent reason of an execution having been
sent into the house, and I thought myself happy in escaping with my
things.'

According to the prospectus the title of the anthology was to be
The Songs of Scandinavia, and it was to be dedicated, by permission,
to the King of Denmark. At the end of the little booklet two pages
were left blank. These were to enable the subscribers to put their
names down at a guinea a time. Borrow, with that out of the way,
worked on to fill the promised two volumes. There was to be something for everybody, even perhaps something for the King of Denmark. The ancient, the heroic, the supernatural, the domestic, and
thence on down to the moderns with 'the most remarkably lyrical
productions of Ewald, Oelenschlager, Baggersen, Ingemann and
many others'. But all the time the two blank pages at the back
remained blank. The answer from the reading public was: No bid.

By March Borrow accepted defeat, but only on that particular front; he was still ready to jump at other fences. And Bowring was still ready to help in any way he could – the slavery, after all, had not been his. The Danish poet Grundtvig, two months later, bore witness to Borrow's winter labours. Grundtvig, another toiler in unrewarding fields, was over to study and research in Anglo-Saxon literature. He wrote on 26 May: 'On Saturday morning I lunched with Mr Bowring and met there his collaborator in the Danish Anthology, who is the real worker, namely, Mr Borrow, a giant of a fellow, not exactly graceful, but outspoken, and, it seems, straightforward and obliging. He reads Danish much better than Bowring, knows by heart some of my scenes of heroic life.' 'Obliging' – it is not an adjective one would in the ordinary way associate with Borrow, but his yearning to have something put in his way was by now dire and extreme. He presumably recognized the need to be obliging and it is possible here to see the seeds of his later rancour towards Bowring – a capable and well-intentioned man who got himself into the House of Commons, got himself a knighthood, and was British consul in Canton in Palmerston's time where he acted with such Palmerstonian vigour that the Prime Minister himself was put to some embarrassment.

Grundtvig gave him a little treadmill work to do, but before that he had tried for a post in the British Museum. Again Bowring said he would do what he could. 'I should rejoice,' he wrote, 'to see you *niched* in the British Museum,' but again the Bowring influence was not strong enough to get him into harbour. Borrow talked to a Smithfield bookseller and managed to interest him, *en principe*, in a translation of *Y Bardd Cwsg* which he translated as *Visions of the Sleeping Bard*. Elis Wyn, the bard, was a hell-and-damnation priest, born in 1670. His book was full of fiends, and the torments undergone by damned souls once they had crossed the last foul river were described with a vigour which even in translation were too much for the Smithfield bookseller who rejected it. 'The terrible descriptions of vice and torment would frighten the genteel part of the English public out of their wits,' he said, adding: 'I had no idea, till I read him in English, that Elis Wyn had been such a terrible fellow.'

Borrow tried – Bowring again the intermediary – to get himself a commission in the newly formed army of Belgium, but this state-about-to-be-born would not look at him. Grundtvig's little commission petered out – and here, for a change, it was Bowring who blew cold. Bowring was beginning, perhaps, to see Borrow as useful and outstandingly energetic in the role of drudge, and in consequence to warm to the idea of keeping him for himself.

If Belgium would not look at him, what about Greece? On 21 May 1823 he wrote to Bowring:

As at present no doubt seems to be entertained of Prince Leopold's accepting the sovereignty of Greece, would you have any objection to write to him concerning me? I should be very happy to go to Greece in his service. I do not wish to go in a civil or domestic capacity, and I have, moreover, no doubt that all such situations have been long since filled up; I wish to go in a military one, for which I am qualified by birth and early habits. You might inform the Prince that I have been for years on the Commander-in-Chief's list for a commission, but that I have not had sufficient interest to procure an appointment. One of my reasons for wishing to reside in Greece is, that the mines of Eastern Literature would be acceptable to me. I should soon become an adept in Turkish, and weave and transmit to you such an anthology as would gladden your very heart. As for *The Songs of Scandinavia*, all the ballads would be ready before departure, and, as I should take books, I would in a few months, send you translations of the modern lyric poetry. I hope this letter will not displease you. I do not write it from *flightiness*, but from thoughtfulness. I am uneasy to find myself at four and twenty drifting on the sea of the world, and likely to continue so. . . .

It is difficult to see Borrow the tough, Borrow the nearly always combative, in a pathetic light. But there is pathos in this letter, particularly the last lines – and a touch of hysteria too. He is beginning to dart a bit wildly from project to project; he is beginning to delude himself about successes which never come. The Danish translations he knew, must have known, by now were dead ducks, yet he persists in talking of them as if they were still alive and as if just a few more months would see them whirring up in splendid flight. If he cannot be a translator of poetry, then he will be a soldier – somewhere far away if necessary – but he will still remain Lavengro and be prepared to take a dive into the complexities of Turkish. He makes himself out to be two years younger than he is, thus allowing himself an illusory two years for recovery and rehabilitation. 'Poor George' – this came in a letter from his brother John to his mother written in the autumn of 1830 from Mexico – 'I wish he was making money. . . . He works hard and remains poor.' Borrow, in fact, was coming very close to the state of mind which brought him to flight and the abandonment of everything at the end of the summer of 1825. And indeed in September 1830 he did leave Museum Street and return to Willow Lane. 'I am going to Norwich for some short time as I am very unwell . . . cold bathing in October and November may prove of service to me. . . .' Before that, in July, it seems, he had spent some time in Paris.

On 25 July, Charles X had issued three repressive ordinances: he had declared the recent French elections to be invalid, he had set more stringent limits to the franchise, and he had curbed the press. On 26 July Paris, urged on chiefly by the journalists, took to the barricades. Lafayette the arch-survivor headed a provisional government and Louis Philippe, most flexible of the Bourbons, was offered the Crown. It is probable that Borrow, realizing as everybody did that a crisis in French affairs was approaching, went to Paris in the hope of selling on-the-spot articles in some newspaper provincial or metropolitan. There is no evidence that he did so, but he was desperate for a job and prepared to try anything. In *The Bible in Spain* there is a passage where he, in company with an English journalist, watches sword-play and cavalry-charging in the Calle Mayor in Madrid; he breaks off to talk generally of English reporters and their fearlessness in the pursuit of riot and mayhem:

I saw them, during the three days at Paris, mingled with the *canaille* and *gamins* behind the barriers, whilst the *mitraille* was flying in all directions, and the desperate cuirassiers were dashing their fierce horses against these seemingly feeble bulwarks. There stood they, dotting down their observations in their pocket-books as if reporting the proceedings of a reform meeting in Covent Garden or Finsbury Square. . . .

There is no reason whatsoever why Borrow should have indulged in this aside unless he had indeed been in Paris in July 1830.

Between September 1830 and October 1832 it is not possible to keep Borrow closely in view from month to month. He had no settled job that can be discovered. He worried much about the spread of riot and disaffection in England. In January 1831 he wrote to Bowring: 'I have been very busy, endeavouring to the utmost of my ability to check radicalism and disaffection, to seize upon machine-breakers and to bring them to condign punishment . . . but notwithstanding we contrived to stow 260 of them into our old Saxon castle, the greatest part of them have been acquitted, to my profound sorrow. . . .' How did Bowring, who was a strong radical, react to that? He did not, at any rate, turn against Borrow, because in the September of that year Borrow was writing to him again and still full of the dark days threatening.

His brother John in Mexico was having something of a struggle; he moved three times from job to job in almost as many years, but at least he was never like Borrow rejected and idle. He wrote home regularly. When Borrow was asking for Bowring's support in his attempts at an army career – in any army, anywhere – John wrote advising him against this in strong terms. 'Do not enter the army; it is a bad spec,' he told him. And again, more strongly still: 'If you can, raise the pewter, come out here rather than that, and *rob*.' In 1830 in a letter to his mother he said: 'Neither he nor I have any luck.' As the months went by and Borrow seemed still no nearer to settling, John came to have second thoughts about the army. In February 1831 he was thinking that a commission in the Regiment would be better than living hand to mouth. In the summer of 1831 he was recommending a return to the law which Borrow had abandoned with such alacrity for the sour rewards of literary London; and in the same letter he showed that he understood his brother very well indeed: 'I am convinced that your want of success in life is more owing to your being unlike other people than to any other cause.'

During the autumn of 1831 Borrow wrote four letters to the War Office claiming arrears of half-pay on John's behalf. The Pay Office said there could be nothing now due to John Borrow until he attended for training. Borrow replied with passionate pleading. John was (17 September) 'lying sick in the Mountains above Vera Cruz, the pest-house of the New World . . . it would be certain death for him to descend into the level country. . . .' In the end the Pay Office did make some concession. Half-pay arrears were paid from 25 June 1829 to 24 December 1830. 'I am glad you got the half-pay,' John wrote. 'You never tell me what you are doing; you can't be living on nothing.' The elder brother sounds a bit resentful here. Perhaps he was feeling ill, and consequently ill-tempered, in his pest-house. (He died of a fever, still in Mexico, in November 1833, and never saw either his brother or his mother again after his departure from England in 1826.) The likelihood is that Borrow and his mother shared the money between them – with the firm intention of making repayment to John once he returned. Borrow's letters to the War Office are all dated from Norwich. But that should not be taken as proof that he was consistently there between October 1831 and October 1832.

Borrow may at this time have tried to dabble in political journalism – on the Tory side.

. . .at that critical period of my life [he tells us in the Appendix to *The Romany Rye*] that entering into the world, he finds himself without any earthly friend to help him [Bowring having long ceased to count] yet he manages to make his way . . . he is hack author, gypsy, tinker, and postillion . . . and when the reader loses sight of him, he has money in his pocket honestly acquired, to enable him to commence a journey quite as laudable as those which the younger sons of earls generally undertake. Surely all this is a manifestation of the kindness and providence of God: and yet he is not a religious person; up to the time when the reader loses sight of him he is decidedly not a religious person. . . .

This of course is vague in the characteristically Borrovian way. 'The reader loses sight of him' is twice repeated. For how long? we ask. Is he referring to the summer of 1825 or to the much longer stretch from 1825 to 1832? He has a firm intention not to make this clear, but it is much more likely that he is talking about seven years rather than three months; there is the firm indication that he went abroad with money in his pocket like any younger son of a grandee – and the money, not the lordly sum he hints at, came from horse-coping. Willow Lane was his base after September 1830, but there were certainly long absences. During the later years of this period, he took to the English roads again, especially in summer, and lived the vagrant, ruffianly – and probably not unprofitable – life that fascinated him all his days. And did Belle leave for America with the immediate sad finality which Borrow describes in *Lavengro* as published? Well, just possibly she did not. Perhaps she took to the roads in company with him for the occasional business round. They would have made a formidable pair. Perhaps America did not see her until 1832. But then, at the very latest, the break came and lasted, because, suddenly, in that year, at the age of thirty, Borrow became respectable: he got a job, and a job which, in most respects at any rate, suited him admirably, a job which was to enable him to write one of the great literary successes of the nineteenth century.

CHAPTER 5

A MAN WITH SUITABLE EMPLOYMENT

How did Borrow get to know the Skeppers of Oulton Hall? They were pious evangelicals and comfortably off. They had no knowledge of, no understanding of, raffish Borrovian types like the Petulengros; they did not drink ale in public houses. They shrank from the Godless Billy Taylor – drunken, dissolute, snuff-taking, disreputable. Harriet Martineau was astonished when she got to know of this new association entered into by her fellow-citizen, and more astonished still when the news of what this association had led to became general. 'When this polyglott gentleman appeared before the public as a devout agent of the Bible Society in foreign parts' she wrote, 'there was *one burst of laughter* from all who remembered the old Norwich days.'

John Gurney of Earlham Hall, a Quaker, a banker of Norwich, a wealthy man and one markedly devoted to the public good and wedded to reformist principles, was the one who probably forged the initial link. As a youngster, it may be recalled, Borrow had frequented the grounds of Earlham Hall and had fished its streams. The benevolent Gurney had talked with this most striking of youths and had doubtless found him interesting. Gurney would know – he was a man who made it his business to know such things – that here was Borrow, greatly talented and rising thirty, still drifting about and so far as anyone could tell coming to no good at all. It would be entirely in his character to want to introduce such an apparent – and unnecessary – failure to influential people eager to do good.

Edmund Skepper had married Anne Breame, an heiress worth £9,000, and they had bought the Oulton Hall estate. Anne bore two children, a boy born in 1794 and a girl, Mary, born in 1796. Mary married a lieutenant in the navy, Henry Clarke, in 1817, but he died before his first child, Henrietta Mary, was born. Mary Clarke and the baby Henrietta went back to live with her parents. She had £450 a year at that time of her own. They were a pious family to whom Gurney would naturally feel sympathetic. A young widow? Seven

years older than Borrow admittedly, but still. . . . A wild idea might
have crossed Gurney's mind.

However it was, on 22 October 1832, Borrow was writing a
characteristic letter to Mary Clarke.

Dear Madam, According to promise I transmit to you a piece of Oriental
writing, namely the tale of Blue Beard, translated into Turkish by myself. I
wish it were in my power to send you something more worthy of your
acceptance, but I hope you will not disdain the gift, insignificant though it be.
Desiring to be kindly remembered to Mr and Mrs Skepper and the remainder
of the family, – I remain, dear Madam, your most obedient humble servant.

Well, at least it was a present. It demonstrated, in his own peculiar
way, a wish on Borrow's part to show interest. Whether a widow
woman in her middle thirties, with a child of fifteen, would jump
around with delight at receiving a Turkish version of Blue Beard is
open to doubt. Perhaps she would. She would be thinking, doubtless,
not of Blue Beard but of Borrow who was an unusually fine sight to
see. At all events in the month following he was introduced by the
Skeppers to Francis Cunningham, Vicar of St. Margaret's, Lowestoft,
and a strong supporter of the Bible Society. This body, founded
twenty-eight years earlier in 1804, was an influential force in the
evangelical movement. Important Clapham Sect people like Zachary
Macaulay and Wilberforce had fostered its early growth. The Skeppers' idea – Mary's anyway – was that the Bible Society, having
dealings all over the world, concerned as it was with the translation of
the Scriptures into innumerable and exotic heathen languages, might
be the sort of organization which could have an appropriate job for
Borrow. Cunningham was impressed by the young man also. He
wrote to Gurney, who was his brother-in-law and who, on admittedly small acquaintanceship, might be willing to speak for Borrow, and,
having satisfied himself, Cunningham then wrote to Andrew Brandram. This was the letter which was to change Borrow's life, make a
great writer of him and – indirectly at any rate – give him immortality.

Andrew Brandram, of Winchester and Oriel and Rector of Beck-
enham, was Secretary of the Society from 1823 until his death in 1850.
Joseph Jowett, Rector of Dick Willoughby in Lincolnshire and of the
family of the Master of Balliol, was shortly (1833) to become the
Editorial Superintendent of the Society and to hold that post until
1848. These were the two men with whom Borrow was to have most
to do during his association of over seven years with the Society.
Brandram, stiff, cautious, competent, did the appointing and was

probably the stronger character of the two. At the end of December 1832 he received a letter from his friend Cunningham:

My dear Friend, A young farmer in this neighbourhood [Breame Skepper might have preferred a loftier description of himself] has introduced me today to a person of whom I have long heard, who appears to me to promise so much that I am induced to offer him to you as a successor of Platt and Greenfield. He is a person without University education, but who has read the Bible in thirteen languages. He is independent in circumstances, of no very exactly defined denomination of Christians, but I think of certain Christian principle. I shall make more enquiry about him and see him again. Next week I propose to meet him in London, and I could wish that you should see him, and, if you please, take him under your charge for a few days. He is of the middle order in society, and a very produceable person. . . . He may be in town on Monday evening, and will attend to any appointment. . . .

Thirteen languages! This was the sort of phenomenon the Bible Society was seeking. They needed someone who knew, or failing that who was willing to learn at speed, the official diplomatic language of China – Manchu. A Russian scholar, Lipovtzov, had in fact achieved this miracle between 1821 and 1826, and a small part, the Gospel according to St. Matthew, had been printed in St. Petersburg – the characters had been specially cast for the purpose – in 1821. No distribution of the 550 copies of St. Matthew had however taken place because the Neva had flooded, the characters had been damaged while in store in the vaults of the Bible Society's bankers at Sarepta House, and no further progress after the first Gospel had been possible, although in 1826 Lipovtzov had deposited two copies of a completed New Testament translation with the Bible Society in London. The same year Nicholas I had put a stop to any Bible Society activity in Imperial Russia. But the urge to evangelize, checked for five years by natural disasters, had nevertheless, Nicholas or no Nicholas, been revived in 1826 because the Reverend William Swan, of the London Missionary Society, returning from conversion labours amongst the Buryat Mongols living to the south of Lake Baikal, discovered in St. Petersburg a transcript version into Manchu of most of the Old Testament and two books of the New. This had been made at the end of the eighteenth century by a French Jesuit father called Puerot, and Swan had immediately written to the Bible Society, rightly thinking that this find would interest them. Of course Brandram was interested. What Brandram had to do was find a man linguistically capable of coping with Lipovtzov and Swan, practical enough to rehabilitate muddied and muddled type, young and vigorous enough to make at least some headway against Russian obstructiveness ordered by the most despotic of tsars. Cunningham's letter, coming when it did, must have sounded like divine intervention.

Borrow was still a godless Billy Taylor Man rather than a Zachary Macaulay–William Wilberforce Man, yet after long years he recognized Opportunity: a responsible and respectable job with doubtless an appropriate salary, a job involving journeys, inviting risks and, perhaps, an aggressive response, demanding the ability to absorb a remote and difficult language at speed. He walked from Norwich to London. He was outside the Bible Society's offices in Earl Street early on 4 January 1833 and had to wait for the first clerk to arrive and open the place up.

The Secretary and the Librarian did not rush at their decision – they had a young man called Hattersley, also eager and willing, in reserve. They probed. Thirteen languages really was a considerable number. Borrow was confident and fluent. He talked of Arabic; he may even have talked of Armenian. And what of the Reverend Francis Cunningham's remarks about the solidity of his Christian beliefs, 'No very exactly defined denomination of Christians'? – would Borrow perhaps care to amplify? Certainly. He talked about gipsies, of their regrettable paganism, of his knowledge of Romany which was enabling him to shed a light, if only a feeble one, on the black darkness brooding over such as Ambrose Petulengro. Here we see Borrow exercising his gift – a considerable one – for self-persuasion. He desperately wanted a job. If the Bible Society had made it clear to him that the man they appointed would need to be a fire-worshipper, Borrow would have been instantly ready with proofs of how he felt drawn to Zoroastrianism. The truth of it was that Borrow had no religion. He felt an affinity to the earth, to earthiness, to wildness, to people who lived untamed and in some sort of communion with the natural world. But doctrinal questions, the Christian mysteries – these were matters which did not interest him in any committed sense. He passionately disliked the Pope and the Roman Catholic Church, but this dislike was based on political, not on religious grounds. He saw Rome as a danger to the integrity and independence of the British nation, and after the election of Pius IX – most unecumenical of popes – in 1846 that opposition became obsessive, but it was totally different in kind from the opposition which Gurney or Wilberforce, or Brandram himself might have felt.

At all events Borrow managed to make a good impression. On 14 January he was, on certain conditions, offered an appointment. The

job would be in Petersburg, the appointee would have to know
Manchu, but would be given six months in which to learn it. A tall
order, but Borrow had been convincing about his thirteen languages
and had doubtless conveyed confidence at being able to master the
obscurest language in the tower of Babel in six months. He was sent
back to Norwich and told to get on with his studies and given
travelling expenses of £10. Jowett, who perhaps suspected those
'independent circumstances', gave him some proof-correcting to do
as well, and for this some small fee was forthcoming, probably out of
the petty cash because there is no record of any disbursement.

The Society had lent him books to prop him up on his laborious
journey: Amyot's *Dictionnaire Tartare-Mantchou François* (Paris,
1789–90), the *Alphabet Mantchou* by Langlès (Paris, 1807), and a
copy of the Society's already published Gospel according to St.
Matthew in Manchu. In February they sent him von Klaproth's
Chrestomathie Mandchou, ou recueil de textes Mandchous (Paris,
1828). On 10 February, Borrow wrote buoyantly:

I have just received your communication, and notwithstanding it is Sunday
morning, and the bells with their loud and clear voices are calling me to
church [church bells had rung their changes in his unresponsive ears on
hundreds of Sundays before this one, but now he was writing to two
gentlemen of the cloth, Brandram and Jowett, it was important that he
reassure them on his churchmanship as well as on his quick-fire proficiency
in foreign languages] I have sat down to answer it by return of post. It is
scarcely necessary for me to say that I was rejoiced to see the Chrestomathie
Mandchou, which will be of no slight assistance in learning the Tartar dialect,
on which ever since I left London I have been almost incessantly occupied. It
is, then, your opinion, that from the lack of anything in the form of grammar
I have scarcely made any progress towards the attainment of Mandchou;
perhaps you will not be perfectly miserable at being informed that you were
never more mistaken in your life. I can already, with the assistance of Amyot,
translate Mandchou with no great difficulty, and am perfectly qualified to
write a critique on the version of St Matthew's Gospel, which I brought with
me into the country. . . .

Borrow goes on to show them how critical he could be. '. . . the
author has been frequently too paraphrastical, and . . . in various
places he must be utterly unintelligible to the Mandchous from
having unnecessarily made use of words which are not Mandchou,
and with which the Tartars cannot be acquainted. . . .' More sharp
details follow. And then he turns to other aspects of his usefulness.
He has told them that his brother John will be just the man to vet the
Society's recently published translation of the Gospel according to

St. Luke into Mexican, and so here is John's address, with a reminder that outward-going parcels must be paid for by the senders in London: Don Juan Borrow, Compagnia Anglo Mexicana, Guanajuato, Mexico. And then, because he has talked to them of his knowledge of Romany, 'my best thanks for his [Brandram's] present of *The Gypsies' Advocate* . . . next to the acquirement of Mandchou, the conversion and enlightening of those interesting people occupy the principal place in my mind. . . .' To round off his letter, he returns to the Mandchou affair with greater confidence, if that was possible, than before: '. . . had I a Grammar, I should in a month's time be able to send a Mandchou translation of Jonah. . . .' How Brandram and Jowett reacted to this jaunty display of self-confidence we have no means of knowing, but anyone aware of Borrow's hard past years, of his horrors, of his frustrations, of his efforts to combine dignity with job-chasing and woo the suport of busy, successful people like Bowring, will immediately recognize a revitalized young man. Borrow will fulfil his promises and – much more importantly – is about to fulfil his promise.

He boned up feverishly on Manchu. There was to be no salary till he had, within six months, been subjected to further linguistic trials and satisfied the Society as to his competence. This was mean. Borrow was gambling six months of his life away on what to most people would seem an outside chance. But he was a specialist. 'I am advancing at full gallop' he told Jowett on 18 March: 'the want of a Grammar has been, particularly in the beginning of my course, a great clog to my speed. . . .' He told them he agreed with Hattersley, his rival for the job, that Amyot's dictionary was something not very first-rate. He also told them that he had sent his brother John 'one copy of St Luke's Gospel with a letter'. The postage had cost him 15*s*. 5*d*. He did not ask for reimbursement and it is most unlikely that he got it. Finally he added a specimen translation from Manchu – quite a substantial piece from the Mongol History 'which, not being translated by Klaproth, I have selected as most adapted to the present occasion. . . .' On 9 June he addressed Jowett again, and began with Borrovian flourish. 'Revd and Dear Sir, I have mastered Mandchou. . . .' He went on to say that the task had been hard, and, writing to a clergyman and to the Editorial Superintendent of the Bible Society, felt it appropriate to bring in the deity. '. . . the helps afforded me in this undertaking have been sadly inadequate. However, with the assistance of God, I have performed my engagement. . . .' He knew nothing of course of Cunningham's remark about his being 'independent in circumstances', and went on to speak

up for himself frankly in a way that may well have surprised both
Brandram and Jowett. 'I shall now be happy to be regularly employed, for though I am not in want, my affairs are not in a very
flourishing condition. . . .'

On 5 July a sub-committee met at Bible House, and decided to
recommend his appointment to the General Committee. On 22 July
the General Committee met and confirmed the recommendation.
Borrow had his job. From 31 July 1833 he had a salary of £200 a year,
and his travelling expenses to and from St. Petersburg would of
course be paid. He sailed from London on 31 July. Jowett, a less
brusque, more understanding man than Brandram, wrote him a letter
on 5 July which shows that he was perceptive and shrewd about his
recruit.

Now ruminate well on this proposition, and hold yourself in readiness, in
case it be palatable to you, to start on your journey without delay, as soon as
the above recommendation shall be approved by the General Committee . . .
there is occasionally a tone of confidence in speaking of yourself, which has
alarmed some of the excellent members of our Committee. It may have been
this feeling, more than once displayed before, which prepared one or two of
them to stumble at an expression in your letter of yesterday, in which, till
pointed out, I confess I was not struck with anything objectionable, but at
which, nevertheless, a humble Christian might not unreasonably take
umbrage. It is where you speak of the prospect of becoming 'useful to the
Deity, to man, and to yourself'. Doubtless you meant, 'the prospect of
glorifying God' . . . .

Borrow doubtless meant nothing of the sort, and Jowett, aware of
this, wanted to signal to him tactfully that now he was working for
evangelicals. It would not have been in Borrow's nature to attend
very closely to this friendly warning on Jowett's part.

He crossed the North Sea on one of the first steamboats ever to ply,
The Tourist, and the wind blew, and Borrow was sick. He never
managed to accustom himself to rough seas. He wrote to Jowett from
Hamburg on 4 August, and he did manage to remember to bring in
the Lord.

I suffered much from sea-sickness. . . . I landed about seven o'clock in the
morning, and the sun, notwithstanding the earliness of the hour, shone so
fiercely that it brought upon me a transient fit of delirium, which is scarcely
to be wondered at, if my previous state of exhaustion is considered. . . . I did
not come, however, to the slightest harm, for the Lord took care of me
through two of his instruments, Messrs Weil and Valentin, highly respectable Jews. . . .

The Lord, for Borrow, was always very much the Lord of the Old Testament.

His letter was long and informative. About Hamburg he told the Bible Society more perhaps than it wanted to know. '. . . the dancing saloons, which I am informed are most infamous places, are open to the public this evening. . . .' As for his 'transient fit of delirium', beyond doubt that was the horrors once again – the lifetime travelling companion which he would not have wanted the Bible Society to know about in detail. He told them simply that a doctor had dosed him with forty drops of laudanum – a considerable dose – and had ordered his head to be swathed in hot towels. It sounds a strange and drastic cure for a man in great perturbation on a hot summer's day in Hamburg, but after a laudanum-sleep he 'awoke in the evening perfectly recovered and in the best spirits possible'. That was a Sunday. Describing the dancing-saloons, he had been careful to add 'England with all her faults has still some regard to decency and will not tolerate such a shameless display of vice on so sacred a season. . . .' On the 6th (Tuesday) he sailed from Lübeck for Petersburg.

What precisely had he been charged to do? He was instructed by the Bible Society to

assist Mr Lipovtzov in the editing of such portions of the Manchu Testament as we may choose to print (Luke and Acts have been resolved upon already), if the Government shall consent to the work being executed there; if not, to assist Rev Wm Swan in transcribing and collating the MS version of a large part of the Old Testament in this language, and to avail yourself meanwhile of all the facilities which may offer for correcting and perfecting your acquaintance with the Manchu.

The assistance to Swan referred of course to Puerot's Bible translations into Manchu which Swan had come upon in the library of Baron Schilling de Canstadt in St. Petersburg. Borrow felt confident. Out of a first salary-advance of £37 he had placed to his mother's account in her bank the sum of £17 – something towards what he owed her for her support through his failures of a decade.

The paddle-steamer *Nikolai* docked in Petersburg on the 31st. Borrow sought out Swan – 'one of the most amiable and interesting characters I have ever met with' – who, over-tired and ailing after his labours, was relieved to see him. He presented Borrow to Baron Schilling de Canstadt, and he was made free of his library – more especially of the wonderful works of the Jesuit Puerot. He was impressed. 'Staunch Protestant though I be,' he told Jowett, 'I am not ashamed to say that all the skill and talent of our own missionaries, in acquiring languages and making versions of the Scriptures, are, when compared with the capabilities displayed by the seminary priests, faint and seemingly insignificant. . . .' He also of course met Lipovtzov, who knew nothing whatever about Puerot, Schilling, or Swan, and was not much concerned about the rescue and rehabilitation of his drowned and dislocated type. To Borrow's young eyes he appeared immensely old and perhaps – although he does not exactly say so – a bit fussy. 'Mr L speaks no European language but Russ,' Borrow said, 'which I am not sorry for, because frequent conversation and intercourse with him will improve my knowledge of that language.'

The town itself delighted him:

neither London nor Paris nor any other European capital which I have visited [how many exactly *had* he visited by then?] has sufficient pretensions to enter into comparison with it in respect to beauty and grandeur. Many of the streets are miles in length, as straight as an arrow and adorned with the most superb edifices. The so-called Nevsky Prospect . . . is nearly three miles in length and for the greatest part of the way floored with small blocks of wood shaped octagonally.

And he was careful to reassure his employers back home that their wares, in spite of the hostility of the autocratic Tsar Nicholas I, were not likely to be faced with an unresponsive market.

A young man of the name of Nobbs, in the employ of an English farmer residing a few versts from Petersburg, is in the habit on his return from the latter place, whither he is frequently sent by his master, to carry with him a satchel filled with Russian New Testaments and religious tracts, with which he is supplied by an excellent English lady who dwells there. He says that before he has reached home, he has invariably disposed of his whole cargo to the surrounding peasantry.

The implication is that what young Nobbs could do, young Borrow could do better.

He stayed first at 221 Galernoy Ulitza, a house belonging to Egerton Hubbard to whom he had been given a letter of introduction by John Venning, a retired Russian merchant living in Norwich. Venning's son lived there too, as well as other student-boarders – so many, in fact, that after three months Borrow found his quarters altogether too noisy for the pursuit of intensive linguistics, and took a small place where he could be quiet and where he paid only nine shillings a week, including fires. He ate at a Russian restaurant where dinner could be had for five shillings. He told his mother: 'I am not at much expense, being able to live for about sixty pounds a year, and

pay a Russian teacher, who has five shillings for one lesson a week.'
He was dutiful and kept his tendency to impulsive bizarreries under
careful control. After all, he at last had a safe and interesting job, one
that suited at any rate some of his remarkable talents. But his employers were prim, prudent, devout men and he must try his best not
to scare them. The primary requirement, as the Bible Society saw it,
was that Borrow should get in immediate touch with Lipovtzov so
that his translations should be rescued from the flood, put in proper
order and made marketable; and Dr Schmidt, the Society's cor-
respondent in Petersburg and also a member of the Russian Board of
Censors, would be on hand, so they thought in London, to help in
setting this business afoot. Always careful in money matters, the
Bible Society was in no mood to write off an advance to Lipovtzov of
£560, a considerable outlay, on which it seemed likely it would see no
return whatsoever. In Borrow the Society saw a man young, strong,
with fire in his belly, who might find his way – in of course an entirely
meek and Christian manner – out of this impasse. He must not on any
account get into any political trouble, but he must save invested
capital – and, it went without saying, souls.

But Borrow found no eagerness. The Tsar had spoken, and it was
healthy for his subjects not to step out of line. Lipovtzov was affable,
but did not see, in the circumstances, that there was much positive
that he could do. Schmidt too was affable, promised to look into
things, but prudently did nothing. There was a Mongolian Grammar
and Dictionary he was working on, and this, Borrow would readily
understand, took up a large amount of his time. . . . Surprisingly,
Borrow did seem to understand; he did not rage. Faced with polite
obstructionism he simply, for the time being, moved away and set to
work on the other tack. With Swan he worked on Puerot's manuscripts. Schilling was friendly and co-operative and wealthy; here in
his library a man could use his talents and not have his equanimity put
at risk through frustrations.

Moreover in Petersburg Borrow made friends. He was never good
at making friends. With Belle Berners and Ambrose Petulengro he
lived in a kind of exalted other-world; 'friendly' was hardly the word
to describe his relations with them. But in Petersburg, even though
the conditions of his job obliged him to operate largely in a studious
and elderly world, he did find companionship with people of his own
generation. It must have been a relief, for one who had until so
recently been playing the role of athletic young vagabond, to meet
Hasfeld.

Hasfeld came from Denmark, and like Borrow he picked up

foreign languages very easily. Three years older than Borrow, he was already installed in Petersburg when Borrow arrived. His Russian was good, and his chief job was to act as interpreter for the Danish legation. This was an official, not an *ad hoc* appointment, and Hasfeld's salary must have been reasonably comfortable. He supplemented it none the less by teaching languages in specialist schools in the city. Here he taught mainly English, the language Europeans chiefly wanted to learn. Hasfeld's English was astonishingly good – as were his knowledge and appreciation of English literature. He was a mocker and a doubter – a most unevangelical sort of man; and in the early stages of the Borrow-Hasfeld friendship it would have been this side of him that Borrow, a bit stifled by Brandram, Jowett, Swan, and Lipovtzov, would have felt most attracted to. They seem to have gone the rounds of the town in the way young men commonly do. They kept in touch long after Borrow had left Petersburg. Hasfeld visited him in Oulton in 1852 and 1857 by which time Borrow had become a combative country gentleman. After 1857 Hasfeld drops out – perhaps he died.

Borrow kept some of his letters, and these shed light on the recipient as well as on the writer. In November 1836 for example, when Borrow was in Spain, Hasfeld writes him a long letter from Petersburg in reply to one now lost, dated Madrid, 23 May. He had been in Stockholm.

I received the Spanish letter a day or two before I left for Stockholm, and it made the journey with me, for it was in my mind to send you an epistle from Svea's capital, but there were so many petty hindrances that I was nearly forgetting myself, let alone correspondence. I lived in Stockholm as if each day were to be my last, swam in champagne, or rested in girls' embraces. You doubtless blush for me; you may do so, but I don't think that that conviction will murder my almost shameless candour, the only virtue which I possess, in a superfluous degree. In Sweden I tried to be lovable, and succeeded, to the astonishment of myself and everybody else. I reaped the reward on the most beautiful lips, which only too often had to complain that the fascinating Dane was faithless like the foam of the sea and the ice of spring. . . .

But Hasfeld was more than a companion on jaunts. He was a genuine admirer of Borrow as a writer, and Borrow, finding it so difficult to make headway in this line, would have been glad to take comfort from someone intelligent who was eager to praise. Hasfeld understood him. Very few people over the course of his long life found it possible to do that. He dabbled in literature himself so that the two could share their experiences of the averted faces of publishers. In the letter of November 1836 already quoted Hasfeld writes later: 'my

manuscript has been promenading about, calling on publishers without having been well received, because it smelt of Russian leather;
others kept it for three or six weeks and sent it back with "Thanks for
the loan". They probably used it to get rid of the moth out of their old
clothes. . . .'

By the end of October or the beginning of November Borrow's
work in collaboration with Swan on the Puerot manuscripts was
over. Swan departed to his Siberian missionary outpost, and
Borrow's difficulties began to thicken. It was time he turned to the
main business he had been hired for; but Lipovtzov and Schmidt
were still unwilling to help him. Borrow wrote to the Bible Society
telling them how busy he had been in Schilling's library. Jowett
replied politely but not without reminding him that the Manchu New
Testament had been and still was his primary, indeed sole, objective,
and how was that coming along? '. . . more especially, we wish to
know how far your introduction to the literary circle of St Petersburg
has opened the way towards printing in that city any further portions
of the New Testament in the Mandchou, of which you took a MS
copy out with you. . . .' Borrow wrote back on the 20th. 'I determined to take a bold step, and directly and without further feeling my
way to petition the Government in my own name for permission to
print the Mandchou scriptures. . . .' Bludov, Minister of the Interior,
was coy. Did he have jurisdiction in this? He would have to consider.
Borrow went to Bligh, the British Minister, to ask for support. Bligh
was not at home. Borrow wrote to Bligh. But Bligh handed the whole
business straight back to him. Would it not be best if Borrow tried for
a personal interview with Bludov and played upon any human sym-
pathies this administrative man might have? Borrow would not give
up. He knocked on doors. He applied and he reapplied. He was
passed from official to official. At last officialdom generally began to
realize that here was a man against whom the usual cooling-off tactics
would not work. At the end of January Borrow wrote to Jowett: 'On
calling there [by this time he had been shunted off to the Asiatic
Department] I found that permission had been granted to print the
Mandchou scripture.'

He had won the first round, and went on in the same letter to show
that he was keeping his Manchu in good repair. On 4 February he
wrote again to tell them that he had found the chest of Manchu
characters in Sarepta House and was checking them for rust. He also
was bold enough to look some way ahead. The testaments, once
printed, would have to be smuggled into the Chinese Empire. Would

it not be prudent for the Bible Society to post a man in, say, Kiachta, a frontier town inhabited by a medley 'of Tartars, Chinese and Russ', and would not he, George Borrow, be a suitably enterprising holder of such a commission? Jowett, writing on 21 March, tried to rein him in – but politely. This noble offer, to 'wander, Testament in hand to the town of Kiachta, if not to Pekin, with side-glances at Tartar hordes' – well, the Society had thought about something like this before, and had been warned that such an attempt 'would be, in more senses than the literal one, tramontane; . . . such a speculator might probably find not Kiachta, but Siberia, as the end of his journey. . . .' But 'convince us, if you can, that you have the practical wisdom of experienced men on your side, as well as the sanguine temperament of your own enterprising disposition. . . .'

By the end of April he was wrestling hard with the business end of publishing – matters of which he had not the slightest experience. Printing costs – how they could vary from firm to firm; how many Russian *stopes* went to a ream. He travelled about, and it cost him money, and he was careful to point out to the Bible Society that this was so. He found a couple of young German printers, Schultz and Beneze, who tendered very modestly for the job as they were not burdened by an overcrowded order-book. He found paper-makers at Peterhof thirty versts away who could supply paper of the right quality and at what he thought a reasonable price. But he would need credit to pay for it, and he would need somewhere to store it, and when it came to quantity and price, to reams and roubles, he found his arithmetic wilting under unaccustomed strain. He sent a frenziedly busy letter to Earl Street which was full of his practical problems and ended with a postscript: 'I have been laid up for some time with a nervous fever, but thank God I am quite recovered. . . .' The Petersburg winter cold was something he had never before experienced. 'The cold when you go out into it cuts your face like a razor, and were you not to cover it with furs the flesh would be bitten off. . . .' This was to his mother to whom he could be more open about his physical sufferings. 'I went mad, and when the fever subsided, I was seized with the "Horrors", which never left me day or night for a week. . . .' The doctor prescribed a bottle of port a day. Borrow took willingly to this treatment, and it seems to have worked. But it was expensive. He had to reduce by a little in consequence the money he was regularly sending home.

The letter Ann Perfrement sent her son on receiving this dealt a hard blow to an already grievously beset young man.

I am sorry to hear you have been so unwell, and particularly 'the horrors'. I am afraid you do not live regular. When you find yourself low, take a little wine, but not too much at one time; it will do you the more good; I find that by myself. My dear George, take care of your *health*, for you are now my *only hope*. It grieves me to tell you, but I must. Our dear John is no more! He died the 22nd November rather suddenly. . . . Do not grieve, my dear George. I trust we shall all meet in heaven. Put a crape on your hat for some time. . . .

Borrow was distressed. Strong affection (now and then tempered by good-humoured impatience on John's part) and mutual support had always marked the way they stood with each other.

Hasfeld was a comforter through all these emotional and practical upsets, and on the doctor's port wine recommendations he came down strongly on Borrow's side and against Mrs Borrow's more timid advice. In reply to her Borrow showed himself both obedient and disobedient. He told her he was learning to cure his disorders by experience (where we would write 'experiment'), and 'The "horrors" for example. Whenever they come I must drink strong Port Wine, and then they are instantly stopped. . . . How came you, my dear mother, to think I live irregularly? . . . I have got the crape. . . .' And his mother got her due share of his earnings, no matter what expense he might be put to in his travels in search of the cheapest possible means of producing decent copies of the New Testament which would neither shake the Society's finances nor lower its standards.

The extravagant cold gave way to un-English heat. He struggled on, experiencing the frustrations of any man charged with the supervision of contractors engaged on commissioned work. Deadlines receded in the way they have the habit of doing in all ages. Hasfeld remembered that summer and revived it in a letter to Borrow long afterwards: 'how you toiled over your Manchu Testament; how thin you grew, and how you almost killed Beneze and his lads!' Small wonder that his letters to Jowett and Brandram – at the beginning so full and frequent – began to drop off. On 7 October Jowett cracked his whip:

I mention that the date of your last communication *to me* is April 28, o.s. . . . the publication of the Mandchou Scriptures is a work in which our Committee have taken a very lively interest. You may, therefore, readily conceive of their disappointment at receiving so very few notices of your progress in accelerating that work. . . .you ought to reflect that the Committee, who stand between you and the public, should be enabled to give an answer to the question, What is Mr Borrow doing?. . .

This letter, coming from a pious do-gooder comfortably housed and fed in London, coming moreover from one upon whom Borrow had showered busy, vivid, enthusiastic words ever since his arrival in Russia, strikes one as starchy, spiky, ungenerous, and uncomprehending in about equal proportions. As soon as Borrow received it he sat down, spat on his hands, and wrote a letter of some 2,500 words to his employers. It caused no small sensation in Earl Street and it remains one of the greatest letters in our language. It is spirited, manly, direct. It breathes fire. Here speaks a man maligned, yet a man keeping his dignity, abjuring tantrums.

He tells them everything: how nothing gets done unless you, the employer, are tirelessly on watch, how nothing gets done at a price which is reasonable unless you are prepared to be ruthlessly firm. He tells them how he himself has laboured in the heat. They hear how he found Lipovtzov's types 'in a kind of warehouse, or rather cellar. They had originally been confined in two cases; but these having burst, the type lay on the floor trampled amidst mud and filth. They were, moreover, not improved by having been immersed within the waters of the inundation. . . .' They are informed of how he, George Borrow, by his own efforts, hired 'two rude Esthonian peasants, who previously could barely compose with decency in a plain language which they spoke and were accustomed to, [who] have received such instruction that with ease they can each compose at the rate of a sheet a day in the Mandchou. . . .' Nor were the rude Esthonians unaccompanied. 'I have been working in the printing-office, as a common compositor, between ten and thirteen hours every day. . . .' They are made to realize the extent of his vigilance. Mr Beneze, the paper man, slipped in fifteen and a half reams which were below specification. 'I accordingly instantly stopped the press. . . . I sent all the strange paper back, and caused Mr Beneze to recompose three sheets, which had been broken up, at his own expense. . . .' Despite all the difficulties, all the frustrations, he can now say that, with the help of true friends like Schilling and Hasfeld, 'there is not the slightest risk of the progress of our work being retarded . . . but the trouble, anxiety, and misery which have till lately harassed me, *alone* in a situation of great responsibility, have almost reduced me to a skeleton. . . .' At this point Borrow gathers up all his dignity, all his sense of injustice done, into one ball, and sails down upon Earl Street like a man o'war, bringing every possible gun it can to bear.

My dearest Sir, do me the favour to ask our excellent Committee, Would it have answered any useful purpose if, instead of continuing to struggle with difficulties . . . I had written in the following strain. . . 'I was sent out to St Petersburg to assist Mr Lipoftsoff in the editing of the Mandchou Testament. That gentleman, *who holds three important situations under the Russian Government, and who is far advanced in years*, has neither the time, inclination, or eyesight for the task, and I am apprehensive that my strength and powers are incompetent to it . . . therefore I should be glad to return home. Moreover the compositors say that they are unaccustomed to compose in an unknown tongue from such scribbled and illegible copy, and they will scarcely assist me to compose. Moreover the working printers say (several went away in disgust) that the paper on which they have to print is too thin to be wetted, and that to print on dry requires a twofold exertion of strength, and that they will not do such work for double wages, for it ruptures them.' Would that have been a welcome communication to the Committee? Would that have been a communication suited to the public? I was resolved 'to do or die'. . . . I have toiled in a close printing-office the whole day, during 90 degrees of heat for the purpose of setting an example, and I have bribed people to work whom nothing but bribes would induce so to do.

I am obliged to say all this in self-justification. No member of the Bible Society would ever have heard a syllable respecting what I have undergone but for the question, 'What has Mr Borrow been about?'. I hope and trust that question is now answered to the satisfaction of those who do Mr Borrow the honour to employ him. . . . Commend me to our most respected Committee. Assure them that in whatever I have done or left undone, I have been influenced by a desire to promote the glory of the Trinity and to give my employers ultimate and permanent satisfaction. If I have erred, it has been from a defect of judgment, and I ask pardon of God and of them. . . .

But Borrow of course did not believe one word of this last conditional sentence. In his own eyes, and in the eyes of the world and of the Deity, he stood not simply guiltless but heroic. The struggle had availed much more than nothing. The commission given him would, quite soon now, be seen to have been accomplished. And what was more, as if this mammoth blockbuster of a letter was not enough, 'In the course of a week I shall write again. . . .' And this he did, not in seven days but in five. The tone now was more triumphant and forward-looking. He took it for granted that the enemies back home, the whisperers and the doubters, had been flattened – as indeed they had. This letter again was lengthy. He enclosed a signed certificate from Lipovtzov the indolent and useless: 'Testifio:- Dominum Burro ab initio usque ad hoc tempus summa cum deligentia et studio in re Mantshurica laborasse. LIPOVZOFF.' The man had been of some use in the end after all, even if 'Burro' – the Spanish word for donkey – was surely never the word for Borrow.

Clearly in a few months Borrow's work in Petersburg would be over. He therefore took the opportunity of raising again the matter of further Far Eastern duties for himself. Kiachta was a mere 800 miles from Pekin, only 400 from Manchuria. An agent dispatched there

might therefore, trusting in the Lord, not unreasonably hope to be able to penetrate to the Tartar of the capital and the desert. . . . I am a person of few words [the high-handed disregard of obvious falsity here shows just how manic Borrow could become when the mood was on him], and will therefore state without circumlocution that I am willing to become that agent. I speak Russ, Mandchou, and the Tartar or broken Turkish of the Russian steppes, and have also some knowledge of Chinese, which I might easily improve at Kiachta, half of the inhabitants of which town are Chinamen. I am therefore not altogether unqualified for such an adventure. . . .

Jowett wrote back on 18 November. He was apologetic. He was fulsome. He gave in on everything except for the further adventures which Borrow had proposed. 'Thus far, and not one word of Kiachta! Well, be not disheartened, even though the Committee postpone for the present the consideration of your enterprising – not to say in-trepid – proposal. . . .' The Bible Society was reluctant to be positive, then and there, about the prospect of missionary adventures in Tartary, but 'the offer is more likely to be accepted now, than when you first made it. . . .' At almost any cost Jowett was anxious to soothe.

Borrow stayed on in Petersburg for the first nine months of 1835. They were less stressful months. Lipovtzov was a stubborn old nuisance, when it came to translation, a stickler for minute detail, which was never Borrow's style, but all the same the old man became more amenable towards the end. The spring came gradually on and the end of his New Testament labours took clear shape. Borrow had bullied his way through to success. Beneze had been disciplined. Pluchard, the paper-supplier, had been sacked in favour of a Mon-sieur Alquin. Borrow, Tall George, as he was known, strode about Petersburg and knew that Petersburg by now also knew that he was a man who would be heeded. He kept working away at his goal of Kiachta, but China continued to look remote. On 3 May (o.s.) he told Jowett: 'I shall not be able to obtain a passport for Siberia, except on the condition that I carry not one single Mandchou Bible thither.' At least he felt assured now that it was not his employers who were dragging their feet. After all, what was the use of printing such quantities of translated New Testaments, at such cost in human labour and Russian roubles, if they were not to be carried to the point of sale? Perhaps Schilling, with his ample resources and good will, might be of help? In any event – and Borrow underlined this because the last thing he wanted was to be denied the opportunity to continue in service – '*I again repeat that I am at command*'.

Jowett was empowered to reply to this reassuringly. Borrow had impressed, perhaps even cowed, those devout men. 'We are far from being surprised by the impossibility which exists for your desired pilgrimage to Kiachta. But you are not hence to infer that we shall have no further employment for you, when the last copy of the Mandchou New Testament shall have received its full dress.' Those two mighty letters of his had shored him up. A copy of them had been sent to Cunningham in Norwich, and Mrs Clarke of Oulton Hall wrote to him. '. . .dear Mr Cunningham spoke so nicely of you at our Oulton gathering held in a malt office near Mutford Lock. . . . He mentioned you as one of the most extraordinary and interesting individuals of the present day. . . . How much you have been able to save the Society by good management and perseverance. . . .' Later, when she heard that he was planning to go to Tartary she wrote again a letter full of concern. Perhaps the heart of Mrs Borrow-to-be was already won. 'Your letter chilled me when I read your intention of going . . . to the Tartars, that land of incalculable dangers. . . .' Well, it was good to know that someone other than his mother was mindful of him and anxious about him. He gained some weight. Strain dropped from him.

Indeed he found time for more personal interests. Now that Schulz and Beneze were in some sort at his command, he could at last arrange for some of his own rejected translations to be printed. He produced two thin volumes. One he called *Targum*, the other *Talisman*, and of each one hundred copies were printed. As usual with Borrow, what is remarkable about these little books (*Talisman* had only fourteen pages) is not the literary quality so much as the astonishing range of languages from which he translated. Counting languages and dialects separately the reader finds a total of thirty-five – from Ancient British through Latin to Russian, Turkish, and Welsh. The Russian pieces appeared mainly in the *Talisman*, and included two by Pushkin. When Pushkin came to Petersburg Hasfeld personally gave him a copy, and Pushkin wrote in thanks, saying how sorry he was that Borrow had left for home before he could have the chance of getting to know him. 'A pearl in literature' Hasfeld said. In foul or fair weather Hasfeld was Borrow's friend.

As Kiachta seemed to recede – though never altogether out of Borrow's mind – he turned to thoughts of smaller explorations on Russian soil. He had, after all, been a long time in Petersburg, and the final sheets of the Testament were at the printer's. He went by coach

to Moscow in the late summer weather. A priest showed him round
the Kremlin – 'a most intelligent and seemingly truly pious person,
and well acquainted with English spiritual literature, especially with
the writings of Bishops Taylor and Tillotson'. But his own countryman, Archbishop Teekon, the priest said, was more replete with
'spiritual manna', and Borrow, having read, so he said, his Teekon
and derived much comfort and satisfaction from him, was quite
willing to accept the truth of this. Borrow through those last Russian
months seems to have been all amiability. For him, however, the
important event of his Moscow visit was not the Kremlin but his visit
to Marina Rotche, about two versts from the city. He talked a great
deal about the Russian gipsies in the grand summing-up report which
he submitted to the Bible Society on 23 September after he had
returned to England. Would the Bible Society's committee be likely
to have enough interest in gipsies to read through all of his Romany
details? The question does not seem to have occurred to him. He,
naturally, was abundantly interested, and that was enough.

It is worth noticing though how Borrow tailors his account to suit
the taste of Brandram, Jowett, Lord Bexley, and the rest. Borrow the
blood-brother of Ambrose Petulengro, the author-to-be of *Lavengro* is pushed firmly into the background. Some of the gipsy women,
he informed Earl Street, were fine singers, lived in style in Moscow,
made much money 'enabling them to live in luxury of every description and to maintain their husbands in a princely way'. Life in Marina
Rotche was not like this at all. Here 'are a great number of low,
vulgar, and profligate females . . . whose husbands and male connections subsist by horse-jobbing and such kinds of low traffic.
. . . Their countenances exactly resembled those of their race in
England . . . beautiful, their eyes fiery and wildly intelligent. . . .'
Feeling himself being carried away, he slows the tempo down. 'I . . .
spoke to them upon their sinful manner of living, upon the advent
and suffering of Christ Jesus, and expressed, upon my taking a final
leave of them, a hope that they would be in a short period furnished
with the word of eternal life in their own language. . . .'

There is much that is characteristic of the essential Borrow in this
part of his report to the Bible Society. He was aware that he himself
was living at a time when the old world of small groups and small
individual liberties was beginning to disappear and to give way
slowly to massive urbanization and the submergence of quirky,
separate folk into industrial areas that spoke not so much with one
voice as with no voice at all. He did not consciously formulate this in
speech or writing, but he was alive to it. At the same time he accepted

that there must be order in human society, and that order, or orderliness, meant conformity. In no hypocritical, Tartuffian sense, he was a self-persuader. The little parting sermon to the wild ones at Marina Rotche would have been quite sincerely spoken and Slingsby and Thurtell, Belle Berners and the old apple-woman carrying on her crooked dealings at the end of London Bridge, and Ambrose Petulengro and Tawno Chikno – all these would be alive and lovingly remembered in his mind as he spoke and in no sense would he have thought of himself as being fraudulent.

He went back to Petersburg, tidied up his affairs. For rather more than two years he had toiled to turn the scrawls of Puerot and Lipovtzov into something printed, something bound, something saleable. Because there was a ban on any movement of his Testaments to the eastward, he had to make arrangements for casing them so that they could be shipped with him home. About this the Russians were dour and difficult; they were reluctant even to give him a passport which would enable him to leave the country. Borrow overcame these difficulties as he had already overcome so many during his tour of duty. He still felt certain that one day George Borrow would be enabled to set forth for Tartary where there would be adventures as well as languages and dialects, rank on rank, waiting to be conquered by Lavengro. He had himself seen Nicholas, cloaked and plumed, striding the Nevsky Prospect, an immensely tall man, taller even than he was himself, a true descendant of Peter the Great who was seven feet high; and surely such a forceful autocrat would have enough largeness of spirit to change his mind? The thousand New Testaments, together with Borrow's work on Puerot, had cost the Bible Society £2,600, and because of the Tsar their destination could only be for the present the cellars in Earl Street. Borrow rightly felt no sense of personal defeat about this. If it had not been for his devotion and vigilance the outlay would have been significantly more. He had, he felt sure, the confidence of his employers.

On the night before he sailed he and Hasfeld celebrated. Hasfeld gave him an ancient Jewish shekel to remember him by. They drank a great deal, sang songs in Danish, and swore an oath – which was kept – that this was an alliance that time could do nothing to alter. The next day he sailed down the canal to the watching guardship at Kronstadt, thence by the regular boat to Lübeck, and so home. He reached London on 19 September 1835, wrote his report, and then, on one of the last days of the month, returned to Norwich. Would the Bible Society put some fresh proposal to him? He felt certain that they would, especially when he discovered that in Norwich he had

The Nevsky Prospect, St. Petersburg, in the early nineteenth century.

Portrait of John Hasfeld by an unknown artist, 1835. Formerly belonging to Borrow.

Portrait of John Bowring by John King, 1826.

John Murray III. Photo (calotype) by Hill and Adamson, 1843–8.

The Revd Andrew Brandram.

Thomas Gordon Hake. From a photograph of a silhouette, c. 1837

acquired some fame. Perhaps his mother was not so confident about future employment: she had carefully put aside all the remittances he had sent her from Petersburg. She wanted some insurance against the hard years he and she had lived through before 1833.

He did not stay in Willow Lane for long. He kept up his spirits, but waiting was hard. He must go to Oulton to visit the people responsible for giving him his start. He must give Cunningham fuller details. Above all, he must personally give his regards and express his gratitude to Mary Clarke.

CHAPTER 6

THE SPANISH GIPSY

THERE can be no doubt that, even during the last relatively happy and leisured weeks in Petersburg, worry kept biting at him. Had he done enough to ensure some follow-up job with the Bible Society? At the end of June he had written home to his mother: 'I dread the thought of having nothing to do except studying as formerly. . . . I can do anything if it is to turn to any account; but it is very hard to dig holes in the sand and fill them up again, as I used to do. . . . I should like very much to get into the Church, though I suppose that that, like all other professions, is overstocked.' This is indeed what now might be called a mayday signal. He must have known that no man was less suited than he to ministry in any Christian Church.

Mary Clarke was glad to see him back, and her daughter Henrietta, by now in her eighteenth year, must also have felt attracted to this rangy, high-voiced, strange, and glamorous man. Through Cunningham, who got his news from Earl Street, mother and daughter had been able to follow his struggles with fraudulent paper-makers, slow-witted compositors, and prudent, elderly scholars like Lipovtzov. Mary Clarke's inviting of him to Oulton, so quickly after his return, was proof of the genuineness of her relief that he was not going on to the East, proof too, perhaps, of feelings stronger than those of simple relief: because Oulton Hall had been a house of mourning since May when Mrs Skepper, Mary's mother, had died. It had also been a house filled with strong dissensions, because Breame, her brother, had persuaded his father into making a will whereby the whole of his estate, with that of his late wife, should descend to Breame. And Mary Clarke, knowing that her mother's property had been considerable, felt, and pointed out, the injustice of this so far as she was concerned. Mary Clarke had strong understanding and will-power, and a head for business.

Borrow, keeping firmly to his role of Christian missioner, spoke at a Bible Society meeting in Oulton on 9 October. This made an impression, and Borrow was careful to tell Brandram about it. In a letter dated 27 October, and written after his return from Oulton to

Norwich, he added a postscript: 'There has been a Bible meeting at Oulton in Suffolk, to which I was invited. The speaking produced such an effect that some of the most vicious characters in the neighbourhood have become weekly subscribers to the Branch Society. So says the *Norfolk Chronicle* in its report.' And indeed the *Norfolk Chronicle* had given him plenty of space.

Mr. Geo. Borrow from Russia, then rose and communicated much information respecting the Greek Church, the bigotted [*sic*] intolerance of its priesthood and the blind and fanatical devotion of the lower classes in Russia to its superstitious ceremonies. . . . the minds of the higher classes . . . are seldom illumined by the beautiful rays of Christ's Gospel, but too often by the will-o'-the-wisp meteors of human philosophy . . . most arrogant, pretending, and shallow of all human delusions. [They] account for all the wonders which our eyes are every day beholding on natural principles . . . are more absurdly inconsistent than the followers of Buddh, the Indian idol. . . .

'Notwithstanding the unfavourable state of the weather' the *Norfolk Chronicle* reported, 'the number of individuals who attended was by no means scanty. . . .' But it was not the faithful of Oulton that Borrow was primarily addressing, but Cunningham, who was in the chair, and through him the policy-makers in London who would, he hoped, accord a strong *nihil obstat* to the views which he expressed with such picturesque trenchancy.

There had been vague talk, before he left London, of a possible journey to Portugal and Spain, and, thinking of those lessons he had persisted in giving Belle Berners two years earlier, he had stressed to the committee his suitability as a translator or editor of a New Testament in Armenian. Why were they so slow in making a positive decision? He gave them a reminder that here he was, still ready and waiting, on 26 October. 'I am weary of doing nothing, and am sighing for employment.' This letter crossed with one from Brandram which dithered.

Shortly after your departure [from London] we passed a resolution that you should go to Portugal; but when it came to confirmation my heart misgave me. . . . I suggested the *suspension* of the Resolution. What do you think yourself? What do your imaginings lead you to think of China? Supposing yourself arrived on its shores, from all the information you have picked up, do you imagine that you could make any progress in distribution? Favour us with your thoughts. Experimental agency in a Society like ours is a formidable undertaking. May God direct us!

Borrow sat down and wrote again on the instant. He was grateful to Brandram for his hesitancy because he realized that that good man

wished only to spare him, Borrow, peril and difficulty. But he wanted
to emphasize that in him the Bible Society had found a man, young,
robust, and powerful, who was capable of confronting peril and
difficulty and keep his head.

Therefore I wish it to be clearly understood that I am perfectly willing to
undertake the expedition, nay, to extend it into Spain, to visit the town and
country, to discourse with the people, especially those connected with
institutions for infantine education, and to learn what ways and opportunities present themselves for conveying the Gospel into those benighted
countries. I will moreover undertake [and here comes the first open hint that
Borrow the writing man still lived, still nursed projects] with the blessing of
God, to draw up a small volume of what I shall have seen and heard there
which cannot fail to be interesting. . . .

This letter steadied Brandram's nerve. In less than a week Borrow
was back in London, and on 2 November the resolution he longed for
was adopted. 'Resolved that Mr Borrow be requested to proceed
forthwith to Lisbon and Oporto for the purpose of visiting the
Society's correspondents there, and of making further enquiries
respecting the means and channels which may offer for promoting
the circulation of the Holy Scriptures in Portugal.' Borrow hurled
himself into action. On 6 November he boarded ship in London. On
12 November he landed at Lisbon. The correspondents to whom
Brandram referred were John Wilby, an English merchant working
in Lisbon, and the Revd E. Whiteley, chaplain at Oporto. Borrow
carried a letter from Brandram to Whiteley. It outlined plans. It
spoke confidently of the young man bearing the letter.

We have some prospect of his eventually going to China; but . . . in the
interval we have thought that he might advantageously visit Portugal. . . . Mr
Borrow possesses no little tact in addressing himself to anything. With
Portugal he is already acquainted, and speaks the language. Our correspondence about Spain is at this moment singularly interesting, and if it continues
so, and the way seems to open, Mr Borrow will cross the frontier and go and
enquire what can be done there.

Here Brandram's talent for clerical meiosis is well displayed. 'Singularly interesting' was certainly one way of describing the state of
affairs in the Peninsula in 1835. 'Shifting, chaotic, riotous' were other
adjectives equally applicable. In Portugal six years of no-quarter civil
war had ended the year before with the defeat of Dom Miguel, the
pro-Roman Catholic pretender. Dom Pedro, the Regent, had also
died in 1834, and Maria II had become queen at the age of fifteen – a
child-queen, then, with neither the experience nor ability to control

and tame plots, counter-plots, and rebellions. However, she had around her a government that wanted to promote a less strictly Church-orientated educational system. The Bible Society were eager to strike while this opportunity served.

In Spain Ferdinand VII, still childless, married in 1829, as consort number four, Maria Cristina of the Two Sicilies. She gave birth to a daughter, Isabella, in 1830, and proclaimed her heir apparent, thus challenging the succession hopes of Don Carlos, the rightist, absolutist, 'illiberal' younger brother of Ferdinand. Spain as a whole divided sharply on whether to recognize Isabella, and out of this division sprang the beginnings of 'Carlism'. The conflict became stringent and immediate on the death of Ferdinand in September 1833. Isabella was without delay proclaimed queen, with Maria Cristina as Regent. The result was the first Carlist war of 1833–9 with the clergy, all those having views tending to the right, the Basques, and the Catalans supporting Don Carlos. Maria Cristina, not without authoritarian ambition herself, seeing that opposition to Don Carlos was what mattered above all else, was obliged to accept the idea of parliamentary institutions. With the new constitution of 1837, Spain saw the establishment of a two-chamber Cortes, and the country, on paper at least, was keeping step with the English Reform Bill of 1832; but on Maria Cristina's part there was no genuine attempt to make the new arrangements work, and the Carlist war went on until the Convention of Vergara in August 1839 registered an at any rate temporary acceptance of defeat for the Carlists.

Did Borrow know in advance what sort of shambles he was committing himself to? He had assured Brandram that with Portugal he was already acquainted. This exemplifies a strong and constant trait in Borrow's character: his fondness for giving people the clearest possible opportunity to misunderstand him. His linguistic many-sidedness had certainly given him a knowledge of the language of Portugal, and, in his eagerness to reassure his employers on all points, could he not therefore say that he 'knew Portugal'? It is unlikely – though not impossible – that he knew Portugal in the sense of ever having been there. Of course the newspapers would have told him that the Peninsula was troubled, and the Bible Society, whose business it partly was to keep the wider world under close scrutiny, would have had a much fuller picture of the realities of the situation. Brandram's dithering letter of 27 October had included this: 'I had in imagination set you down at Oporto, had inquired what you would do, and the more I turned it in my mind the less did it appear that the door was sufficiently open. . . .' Borrow's remark that he wishes 'to

discourse with the people, especially those connected with institutions for infantine education' argues strongly for the view that he
had, in fact, not the slightest idea of what he was letting himself in for.

In his preface to *The Bible in Spain* Borrow has this to say:

Many things, it is true, will be found in the following volume which have
little connexion with religion or religious enterprise; I offer, however, no
apology for introducing them. I was, as I may say, from first to last adrift in
Spain, the land of old renown, the land of wonder and mystery, with better
opportunities of becoming acquainted with its strange secrets and peculiarities than, perhaps, ever yet were afforded to any individual, certainly to a
foreigner; and if, in many instances, I have introduced scenes and characters
perhaps unprecedented in a work of this description, I have only to observe,
that, during my sojourn in Spain, I was so unavoidably mixed up with such,
that I could scarcely have given a faithful narrative of what befell me had I not
brought them forward in the manner in which I have done.

This is Borrow's way of saying that *The Bible in Spain*, like
Lavengro and *The Romany Rye* which were written later but go back
earlier, is dreamlike. 'I was . . . from first to last adrift in Spain' – this
points a finger at the very heart of a wonderful book. At one level it is
a picturesque adventure story about rough encounters with zanies
and bandits, about stop-overs in dubious inns; at another it is about a
unique man (himself) moving around in a state of interrupted trance
through a wild country torn by violence. He starts, for example, in
the hour before dawn, for Monte Moro. There are two mules, one for
himself, one for his guide, an idiot youth:

Such was my intended companion in a journey of nearly a hundred miles,
which . . . lay over the most savage and ill-noted track in the whole kingdom.
I took leave of my servant almost with tears, for he had always served me
with the greatest fidelity, and had exhibited an assiduity . . . which afforded
me the utmost satisfaction. We started, my uncouth guide sitting tailor-
fashion on the sumpter mule, upon the baggage. The moon had just gone
down, and the morning was pitchy dark, and, as usual, piercingly cold. We
soon entered the dismal wood . . . through which we wended our way . . .
slowly and mournfully. Not a sound was to be heard save the trampling of
the animals, not a breath of air moved the leafless branches, no animal stirred
in the thickets, no bird, not even the owl, flew over our heads, all seemed
desolate and dead; and during my many and far wanderings, I never experienced a greater sensation of loneliness. . . . At twelve next day we arrived at
Monte Moro. . . . I determined upon viewing the ruins which cover the top
and middle part of the stately hill which towers above the town. . . . I
ascended till I arrived at a large wall or rampart. . . . I crossed a rude bridge of
stones . . . and passing by a large tower, entered through a portal into the
enclosed part of the hill. . . . I stumbled on amongst ruined walls . . . treading

over vaults, as I suddenly started back from a yawning orifice. . . . I heard a
tremendous bark, and presently an immense dog, such as those which guard
the flocks in the neighbourhood against the wolves, came bounding to attack
me 'with eyes that glowed, and fangs that grinned'. . . . The barking of the
dog brought out from a kind of alley an elderly man [who] was civil, and
informed me that he served as a soldier in the British army, under the 'great
Lord', during the Peninsula (*sic*) war. He said there was a convent of nuns a
little farther on. . . . We entered a dark stone apartment, at one corner of
which was a kind of window occupied by a turning table, at which articles
were received into the convent or delivered out. He rang the bell, and,
without saying a word, retired, leaving me rather perplexed; but presently I
heard, though the speaker was invisible, a soft feminine voice demanding
who I was. . . .

This is not Borrow trying to sell New Testaments in foreign parts
from panniers strapped to the flanks of a mule. This is Childe Roland
to the Dark Tower Came. And all through the book Borrow switches
from one role to the other. The book is confused and confusing, and
Borrow was entirely right to make it so. He was travelling through a
country living through confused and confusing times.

His mission divides into three tours. His first sortie took in princi-
pally Lisbon-Evora-Badajoz-Madrid, and it lasted eleven months,
from November 1835 to October 1836. He stayed only briefly in
London, and, in the same month, he was on his way back, landing at
Cádiz. This time he was away longer, for twenty-three months until
September 1838, and his main staging-posts were Lisbon-Seville-
Madrid-Salamanca-Corunna-Oviedo-Toledo. After that he stayed
in England until December when he embarked on his third and final
foray which came to an end in April 1840. His 'undertaking to draw
up a small volume' was never lost sight of throughout the four years
and five months of his Spanish adventure. He kept his employers
regularly informed. Jowett's question on 7 October 1834 – 'What is
Mr Borrow doing?' – still rankled. His long letters arrived at Earl
Street with almost the regularity of the serial stories which were just
beginning to be popular: *Pickwick* inaugurated its fortnightly leaps
upward to national fame in April 1836, when Borrow, five months
abroad, was in Madrid trying to cope with the fresh confusions
arising from the resignation of the Prime Minister Mendizabal the
month before. And at Bible Society headquarters his instalments
were being looked forward to with almost the same eager anticipation
as the nation's for Dickens's. 'Your letters are very welcome,' Brandram had told him on 6 April; 'let them be more frequent. . . .' Did
Borrow take this as a rebuke or a compliment?

Letters of George Borrow to the British and Foreign Bible Society, edited by T. H. Darlow, were published by Hodder and Stoughton in 1911. Following Dr Knapp's first biography of Borrow (1899) in which he wrote 'important letters . . . almost all that Borrow wrote to the Bible Society during the eight years of his association with them, do not appear to have been preserved . . .', Watt and Darlow, at that time the successors of Brandram and Jowett, made, as Darlow says, 'further search among the archives stored in the crypt of the Bible House. . . . Mr Watt was fortunate enough to discover nearly the whole of the missing letters, to the number of over a hundred, as well as several reports. . . .' Publication was delayed through the premature death of Watt to whom the editorship of the letters had been entrusted, but in the end, after more than a decade, Darlow managed to bring them out.

The interesting question arises: are the *Letters* and *The Bible in Spain* to be treated as two entirely separate works? There is no doubt that in writing *The Bible in Spain* Borrow referred closely to the Bible Society in London. It would take a whole book to trace out in detail where the two books resemble each other and where they diverge. We might listen, for example, to Borrow on his arrival in Corunna, after the perilous excursion which enabled him to tell Brandram on 15 September 1837: 'I have carried the Gospel to the extreme point of the Old World.' Here is part of the account as he sent it to Brandram, and as it first appeared to the world in 1911.

I have a depot of five hundred Testaments at Corunna, from which it is my intention to supply the principal towns of Galicia. I have as usual published my advertisements, and the work enjoys a tolerable sale – seven or eight copies per day on the average. Perhaps some will say that these are small matters and not worthy of being mentioned; but let these bethink them that till within a few months the very existence of the Gospel was almost unknown in Spain, and that it must necessarily be a difficult task to induce a people like the Spaniards, who read very little and who in general consider money expended in books of any kind as cast away, to purchase a work like the New Testament, offering them little prospect of amusement, and which, though the basis of all true religion, they never have been told is useful as a guide to salvation. Let us hope that the present is the dawning of better and more enlightened times. . . .

In *The Bible in Spain* this became:

I had a depot of five hundred Testaments in Corunna, from which it was my intention to supply the principal towns of Galicia. Immediately on my arrival I published advertisements, according to my usual practice, and the book achieved a tolerable sale – seven or eight copies per day on the average. Some people, perhaps, on perusing these details, will be tempted to exclaim, 'These are small matters, and scarcely worthy of being mentioned.' But let such bethink them that till within a few months previous to the time of which I am speaking, the very existence of the Gospel was almost unknown in Spain, that it must be a necessarily difficult task to induce a people like the Spaniards, who read very little, to purchase a work like the New Testament, which, though of paramount importance to the soul, affords but slight prospect of amusement to the frivolous and carnally minded. I hoped that the present was the dawning of better and more enlightened times. . . .

Here we see Borrow with the Earl Street files close about him. But it is not exactly a transcript; clearly he has it in mind that in the letter he is addressing clerical gentlemen of strong and strict evangelical principles and there is no mention of the Spaniard's being frivolous and carnally minded – a remark perhaps wounding to refined and delicate sensibilities. He tells the general reader that the New Testament is of paramount importance to the soul; in talking to Jowett and Brandram he brings somewhat more amplitude to his fervour. The letters are unique. They prove beyond doubt that Borrow was energetic, honest, fearless, direct in his dealings, and possessed of a freshness of vision which sets him apart from his fellows; they dispose, once and for all, of the notion, put busily about by many, that he was a half-crazed charlatan. The officers of the Bible Society no doubt found him trying and difficult at times; they knew that he was rash, wayward, and unpredictable; they knew that he could make enemies and that he had a long memory for slights and injuries, sometimes real, sometimes imagined. But they knew also that he was a man of honour, faithful and thorough in the carrying out of a commission however hazardous, though his methods were all his own and 'normal channels' not a phrase he recognized. They kept their good opinion of him all his life long. His letters to them show how wise they were to take this line. There are not many collections of letters in English that can match them for interest, variety, and vital energy. *The Bible in Spain* on the other hand shows Borrow the intuitive creative artist at the height of his powers.

When Borrow first arrived in Lisbon, Wilby was away. He had some days to look round before plunging into Bible Society business. He hired a servant to help him polish up his Portuguese, and a horse. Lisbon was dirty and run down. The nine years of civil war the country had just been through had left multiple unhealed scars; even marks of the great devastation caused by the earthquake of 1755 still lingered. He kissed Henry Fielding's tomb – one of the rare occasions when Borrow paid tribute to a relatively modern author – and then

Wilby was back, to tell him that he had just taken delivery of four hundred New Testaments sent out from London. Borrow was eager to be off at once. Wilby, knowing far more than Brandram and Jowett about the situation on the spot, counselled caution. Borrow agreed to make an exploratory tour, taking no Testaments with him. He crossed the Tagus on 6 December and explored the Alentejo – wild scrub land with a scattering of flea-bitten villages. He made for Evora, the only place of importance. He distributed tracts. He stood toweringly beside village-pumps and made no-popery speeches to the inhabitants. The reception he got was affable but amused. It seems probable that his audience understood very little of what he said. He was a most remarkable linguist, but pronunciation, the tune of a language, he always found elusive. He deciphered a magic charm carried by a smuggler; he persuaded 'the fine girl' Geronima to burn Volney's *Ruins of Empires* because it was a book written 'with the sole view of bringing all religion into contempt'; he met a minister, Dom José Agostinho Freire, due for assassination before the year was out. On the whole he enjoyed himself. Living rough and meeting odd characters always suited him. But the people were not as wholeheartedly pro-British as they might have been. After all, was it not Britain that had saved the Portuguese from Napoleonic tyranny? Was he not bringing to the people the word of God, a treasure beyond price? Borrow always had difficulty in understanding the subtly diverse forms which ingratitude could take. Still, he felt that there was no decisive reason for discouragement. He returned to Lisbon full of hope after his reconnaissance.

He could, however, now see for himself that the Peninsula was not under any harsh firm thumb like the Tsar Nicholas's in Russia. Turmoil was everywhere. Carlists and Cristinos fought fiercely against each other but in no very co-ordinated way. The 'Eliot Convention' negotiated between the two sides in the spring of 1835 had been a dead letter from the beginning. Palmerston sent a small army and a naval squadron to San Sebastian in August 1835 to assist the Cristinos in their endeavours to suppress the Carlist forces in the Basque provinces, but the fighting was still going on, as ferocious as it was indecisive. Borrow felt that to have simply Jowett, Brandram, and Lord Bexley behind him in the hazardous venture lying ahead might not be enough. He needed letters of credence from very important people. Although he could be independent to the point of freakishness, he was never shy of asking for help if he saw the strong necessity for it. He wrote to Bowring, by now Member of Parliament for Kilmarnock.

I returned from dear, glorious Russia about three months since. . . . I am now in Portugal, for the Society still do me the honour of employing me . . . as it is much more easy to introduce oneself to the cottage than the hall (though I am not entirely unknown in the latter), I want you to give or procure me letters to the most liberal and influential minds of Portugal. I likewise want a letter from the Foreign Office to Lord De Walden [he was the current British Minister in Portugal], in a word, I want to make what interest I can towards obtaining the admission of the Gospel of Jesus into the public schools of Portugal which are about to be established. I beg leave to state that this is *my plan*, and not other persons', as I was merely sent over to Portugal to observe the disposition of the people . . .should I receive *these letters* within the space of six weeks it will be time enough, for before setting up my machine in Portugal I wish to lay the foundation of something similar in Spain. . . . I start for Spain tomorrow, and I want letters something similar [there is impudence for you] for Madrid, *which I should like to have as soon as possible*. . . . PS. – I am told that Mendizabal is liberal, and has been in England; perhaps he would assist me. . . .

Brisk, businesslike, a bit airy, a bit cheeky even: these were probably some of the adjectives which occurred to Bowring – quite an important man by now – as he digested Borrow's confident demands for immediate action. He did write letters for him, however, but his tone lacked warmth.

On New Year's Day, 1836, Borrow crossed the Tagus again, bound now for Madrid. Antonio, his servant, went with him as far as Aldea Gallega, but after that he had as attendant only the idiot boy who was with him during the Monte Moro experience. At Elvas, near the Spanish border, he too was sent back and Borrow went on alone, crossing the Guadiana and reaching Badajoz on 6 January. He tells us he 'cried in ecstasy': 'Santiago y cierra España' – 'Saint James, and may Spain be kept tight shut,' the war-cry of Spanish knighthood for over a thousand years. Then he went to the Inn of the Three Nations, the place that had been recommended to him in Elvas. He stayed in Badajoz for at least ten days, much longer than he had intended. There were two reasons for his lingering.

First, he had to adapt himself to the realities of the Spanish situation. He had been thinking of a comfortable coach trip up to Madrid all done in a day or two, but would that be wise, the way things were? Second, there was the matter of the gipsies. Standing outside his inn on the day after his arrival in Badajoz he saw two men passing with gipsy faces. He said 'a certain word' to them, and in next to no time the two were about the place passing on the news that a stranger was amongst them who spoke Romany.

They were a filthy, depraved lot, Borrow admitted this; but for all

that he could not resist this strange feeling of kinship. They had fallen
far below the rough standards of the English Smith clan: the women
were whores and pickpockets; the men were violent. All of them
treated Borrow as if he were a *guru*. Borrow enjoyed it. He felt
somehow at home. His notebook began to fill with linguistic variations. Antonio Lopez, the principal one, had business to the north
about, as he said, 'the affairs of Egypt'. He would accompany Borrow
because 'there are . . . wars in the land'; he had, furthermore, as was
always the way with gipsies, a spare horse. The horse was 'spectral
white, short in the body, but with remarkably long legs'. Antonio
spoke of it to Borrow with the warmth of a practised salesman. They
set off for Mérida. Antonio's affairs of Egypt proved to be smuggling,
and, after a juicily adventurous three days in Mérida, Antonio's
daughter, riding up on a donkey, brought news requiring Antonio's
quick return to Badajoz. Borrow bought the donkey and rode on
alone. The Bible Society heard little of all this. He had passed into his
periodic dream-vagabond state. But on 25 January he set himself up
in a large room looking out on to the Puerta del Sol in Madrid. It was
cold. How was he to make a start?

Nothing so far had come from Bowring. But Mendizabal was
undoubtedly the man to seek out, the man to beguile. He was, for the
moment at any rate, Prime Minister. The British ambassador was
George Villiers, an intelligent man, no time-server, not lacking in
courage and sympathetic, if in no totally committed way, to the
evangelical movement. Borrow asked him for help, and got it. Early
on 7 February he went to the prime-ministerial palace, hung about
for three hours, and at last was shown in to Mendizabal – 'a huge
athletic man, somewhat taller than myself. . . . His complexion was
florid, his features fine and regular . . . though scarcely fifty years of
age, his hair was remarkably grey. . . .' (It is odd to find the white-
haired Borrow, not yet thirty-three, noting with surprise the grey-
ness of a man nearing fifty.) Borrow had been told by Villiers that
relations between the Spanish government and the Vatican were far
from cordial. From Mendizabal therefore he looked forward to
affability and co-operativeness. He got neither. Mendizabal was a
supple Spanish jew, most skilful in financial affairs. He wanted no
Bible-talk; he was not interested in promises of the imminent return
of the Saviour; he wanted guns. He had lived for thirteen years in
England. He knew the evangelicals and their ways and he had more
important matters to attend to. But Borrow was not a man to be easily
intimidated. He stood his ground. He argued. Was not Mendizabal
mixing the Bible Society up with cranks and enthusiasts who were

not wholly right in the head? Borrow's organization was in no way turbulent or outrageous, 'they were for the most part staid, quiet gentlemen, who attended to their own affairs. . . .' All Borrow was asking for was permission to print the New Testament in Spanish at Madrid. And he implied the question: was that anything to get excited about? Mendizabal switched to other tactics. He talked of postponement, promises for the future. 'I will not give you per-mission now: but let the war be concluded, let the factious be beaten, and the case will be altered; come to me six months hence. . . .' Borrow decided that the prudent course, so far as the Bible Society was concerned, was to accept this as victory. 'The game is now in our hands,' he told them.

He went back to his lodgings prepared to cultivate patience – and support in any quarter where he might be lucky enough to find it. In March the liberal paper *El Español* printed articles very favourable to the aims of the English evangelicals. In March also Mendizabal fell from power. Two of his party, Francisco de Isturitz and Alcala Galiano, withdrew their support of him and were enabled by this to form their own 'moderate' government which was backed by Maria Cristina and her general, Córdova. Isturitz took over as Prime Minis-ter and the Duke of Rivas became Minister of the Interior. But where Borrow was concerned this new cabinet seemed in no way disposed to change direction over Mendizabal's policy of postponement. Richard Ford, England's greatest authority on Spain and Spanish affairs in the nineteenth century, had journeyed extensively there not long before Borrow's arrival. About the Spaniards generally Ford noted that 'There is no via media, no Protestantism, no Bible in Spain . . . only two classes: infidels and bigots. . . .'

Borrow wrote to Brandram complaining that Wilby was either dilatory in sending him cash for daily needs, or Wilby's cash was being intercepted on the hard way by bandits. Could not the Bible Society let him have a letter of credit on some Madrid banking house? He had not a suit of clothes fit to put on. He showed signs in the same letter of wanting to plunge into the Spanish in-fighting. Brandram took fright at this. He sent him some money, but, as for political matters, he sternly warned: 'You must not as an Agent of our Society pursue the course you have described. . . .'

During the heat of the early summer ('the very Spaniards are afraid to stay out, and lie gasping and naked on their brick floors') he spent on average ten hours of every day dancing attendance on ministers waiting for permission to go ahead. And he was all the more eager to be able to announce progress to his employers because he was becoming increasingly aware that he had a competitor in the field. In the Bible Society's 32nd annual report issued in the summer of 1836 one finds: 'Spain and Portugal have occupied . . . much of the anxious attention of your Committee. They have met with two excellent and devoted friends, who . . . have been exerting themselves . . . in Spain. . . .' *Two*? Indeed yes. And at this point Lieutenant J. N. Graydon makes his entrance on the troubled scene. Graydon was a half-pay officer of the Royal Navy, wild, unpredictable, and ferociously Protestant. Without bothering about any formal commission from the Society he began promoting Bible sales along Spain's east coast in 1835. He printed Catalan translations in Barcelona. He was a firebrand with little specifically naval to do. Working from Gibraltar, a far better base than either Lisbon or Madrid, Graydon had been showing results much more positively than Borrow.

The strong impression left by his letter of 30 June is of a depressed and dehydrated Borrow. When would one of these governments, constantly shifting, living perilously from day to day, at last give him leave to make a start? Graydon came up to Madrid. 'I saw him twice or thrice. He left Madrid for Barcelona about a month since, because the heat of the former place in the summer months is more than he can bear. . . .' The mention is cool but the coolness between them was to change into hot enmity before the end. In June Borrow moved his living quarters, and this was to prove a continuing source of comfort to him throughout his Spanish time. Maria Diaz belonged to Villa Seca, a village in New Castille. She had married below herself for her father was an architect while her husband Lopez simply tilled the land. She had come to Madrid in order to secure a suitable education for her children, and in her Borrow found the perfect landlady. She was intelligent, composed, sympathetic. When he chanted round the house, filling the place with his squeaky voice and his vast range of incomprehensible languages, she showed no impatience, did not even ask him please to stop. She saw that here was a man, however tiresome, with qualities far beyond the common. Borrow came to rely on her greatly.

By now Borrow had also become friendly with Don Luis de Usoz y Rio, one of the editors of *El Español*. Usoz was and remained throughout his Spanish time friendly – and useful. He was wealthy and a scholar. He had friends in the right places. He had a strong sympathy – rare in Spaniards of whatever party at that time – for the aims and objects of the Bible Society, and, late in July, he became a subscribing member. He was the only Spaniard singled out by Borrow for thankful recognition when he came to write his preface to

The Bible in Spain. 'I am most happy to take this opportunity of speaking of Luis de Usoz y Rio, the scion of an ancient and honourable family of Old Castile, my coadjutor. . . .'

In July came the breakthrough. Isturitz was willing to let him print. Villiers had worked hard in support of Borrow. But Borrow himself had also shown a surprising aptitude for manoeuvring and diplomacy. The picture of him as an impatient blunderer needs to be toned down. 'The affair is settled – thank God!' he told Brandram, 'and we may begin to print whenever we think proper . . . for a thousand pounds I would not undergo again all the mortifications and disappointments of the last two months. . . . I am not aware that there is any great necessity for my continuance in Spain . . .when the heats are over Mr Graydon might return. . . .' For the time being Borrow had had enough.

The following month, the temporary quietness in the capital gave way again to violence. To escape the sweltering city Maria Cristina had gone off with her lover Muñoz to La Granja forty miles from the capital. She supposed the army to be solidly behind her, but this was a miscalculation, and her *villégiature* in La Granja equally misjudged. The Regent, with her Bourbon taste for asbolutism, was more unpopular than she thought. Her refusal to recognize the Cádiz Constitution of 1812, with its provisions for popular liberties, rankled. On 12 August her personal guards at La Granja marched into her apartments demanding that she should sign a document promising a return to the Cádiz Constitution. This was refused, and so she was taken down to the courtyard. There they held Muñoz, his eyes bandaged: if she remained obdurate they would blow his head off. Only then did Maria Cristina come round to the views of Sergeant Garcia and his rebel guards. ('Garcia' is Borrow's name for him; historians call him Gomez. The mistake might be due to the fact that Borrow was forty miles away in Madrid while the affair was going on. It is more likely though that here is one more example of the odd, neurotic compulsion he always had either to suppress or to falsify proper names.) Borrow, in the company of English journalists, watched the repercussions of the La Granja coup in Madrid. He watched Quesada, with a handful of loyalist soldiers, quell a teeming riot. He owed no special allegiance to Maria Cristina, but he loved guts. 'His [Quesada's] burst into the Puerta del Sol was the most tremendous and successful piece of daring ever witnessed. I admired so much the spirit of the "brute bull" that I frequently, during his wild onset, shouted "Viva Quesada!" for I wished him well. . . .'

But Captain-General Quesada's courage of the bull was not

enough. Isturitz and his cabinet fled forthwith without waiting to see whether Quesada's *démarche* would work. Borrow himself thought that if Isturitz, Rivas, and the rest had been less lily-livered things might have turned out well for them because mob violence for the moment at least had been put down, and there were loyalist troops already on the march for Madrid. As it was, Quesada himself doubted the wisdom of pursuing tough tactics in isolation. He put on civilian clothes, and like the rest stole away – only later. He was recognized when only just clear of the city and gaoled. Then he was brought back to Madrid and torn to pieces.

That night Borrow sat in a famous coffee-house in the Calle de Alcal. Outside he heard the sound of rekindled violence, and a crowd burst in, singing and stamping. They asked for a huge bowl of coffee, and it was brought. Then someone shouted 'El pañuelo!' ('The swaddling-cloth!'), and 'a blue kerchief was forthwith produced, which appeared to contain a substance of some kind; it was untied, and a gory hand and three or four dissevered fingers made their appearance, and with these the contents of the bowl were stirred up. . . .' Baltasar, one of Borrow's many Madrileño familiars, his 'little soldier-tailor', was amongst the mob. '"Ho, hom Don Jorge," cried Baltasarito, coming up to me with a cup of coffee, "pray do me the favour to drink upon this glorious occasion. . . . Yesterday the brute had it all his own way, but today the *toreros* have prevailed, as you see. Pray drink. . . . You shake your head, Don Jorge. Ha ha; I am young, and youth is the time for pleasure. . . ."' Borrow's shake of the head should be noted. He enjoyed living rough, and he enjoyed a fight; but butchery on this scale was far more than he could stomach – even though it was true that in a way he would be benefiting. Calatrava, the so-called liberal, would become Prime Minister. All Spaniards, all Englishmen too, would be free to print what they chose. His patient struggle with Mendizabal became meaningless on the instant. It was time he returned to England. Earl Street wanted personal discussions with him. He wrote to John Jackson, the assistant foreign secretary: 'I shall make the provisional engagement (to print) as soon as possible; but I must here inform you that I shall find much difficulty in returning to England, as all the provinces are disturbed in consequence of the Constitution of 1812 having been proclaimed, and the roads are swarming with robbers and banditti . . . . Do not be surprised therefore, if I am tardy in making my appearance.'

Borrow left Madrid on 20 August. The short way, across the Pyrenees, was impossible because the Carlists held the passes. So he headed south, pausing in Granada on the 30th to sign himself in the visitors' book: George Borrow Norvicensis. And there the signature and provenance still stand, in the Alhambra. Ten days from Madrid to Granada was quick, but this time, unusually for him, he was in a coach. There can be no doubt that he was tired of Spain. He enjoyed wildness, but only when it was played out against a background of solid, establishmentarian order. Here was total lawlessness. He hurried from Granada to Málaga, from Málaga to Gibraltar, and thence home. He was in London on 3 October, and went on immediately to Norwich to prepare his report.

CHAPTER 7

SPAIN AGAIN

DURING his first days at home he talked again of entering the ministry. The taste of Spain must still have been bitter in his mouth. But the Society was eager to see him go back, and the report he wrote strengthened its desire. With Calatrava in power any agent of the Society was bound to find himself freer to carry out policies previously barred. Borrow wrote: 'The present appears to be a moment peculiarly well adapted for commencing operations in Spain, the aim and view of which should be the introducing into that singularly unhappy portion of the world the knowledge of the Saviour. . . .' It is usually the case that when Borrow drops his natural tone in an endeavour to soothe and sway the evangelical enthusiasts who paid his salary he can sound dangerously like the Reverend Mr Chadband.

In a week or two the lust for wandering took control of him again. He had a conference in London where plans of action were decided upon and on 7 November he sailed on the *Manchester* from Falmouth to Lisbon. This voyage was the most terrifying he ever experienced. Hurricane and thunder, broken engines and idle paddles, the *Manchester* drifting broadside on towards the sharp crags of Finisterre, the steersman's gloomy certainty that 'None of us will see the morning' – and then a miraculous change of wind-direction which saved everybody from immediate disaster and allowed a switch to the relatively routine exercise of coping with a ship that had taken fire. After repairs at Lisbon they sailed on in calmer waters and reached Cádiz two days later.

The Reverend Wentworth Webster of St. Jean de Luz heard something of what happened when Borrow stepped ashore, from his friend, the Carlist agent the Marquez de Santa Coloma, who had been aboard the ramshackle *Manchester* along with Borrow. 'Borrow looked around,' wrote Webster, 'saw some Gypsies lounging there, said something that the Marquis could not understand, and immediately [and here he quotes Santa Coloma directly] "that man became *une grappe de gitanos*. They hung round his neck, clung to his knees, seized his hands, kissed his feet. . . ."' Borrow had come home.

But it was a very troubled home indeed. Gomez, the Carlist general, had been on the rampage in Extremadura to the north. It looked as though quite soon he would be master of Seville, and Carlist groups were close to Cádiz. To add to his problems, Borrow fell ill on the very first night in the city. People thought it was cholera but two days later he was sailing up the Guadalquivir to Seville.

He travelled on the paddle-steamer *Betis*. It was 24 November and misty in the mornings. Borrow lay on the deck feeling seedy. What chances were there of his making missionary progress in this anarchic country? It was even possible that Seville itself would have fallen into the hands of Gomez and his guerrillas before ever the slow-moving *Betis* got there. 'There is not much in the appearance of the Guadalquivir to interest the traveller,' he told Brandram: 'the banks are low and destitute of trees, the adjacent country is flat, and only in the distance is seen a range of tall blue sierras. The water is turbid and muddy, and in colour closely resembling a duck-pool. . . . I repeated Latin verses and fragments of old Spanish ballads, till we reached Seville at about nine o'clock of a lovely moonlight night.'

The place was pretty well cut off. No *diligences* ran between the city and Madrid. Not even muleteers were willing to hire themselves for long journeys, so great were the risks. Gomez was said to be at Ecija, half-way between Córdoba and Seville. Borrow put up at the Posada del Turco and hired a courier, an elderly Genoese who assured him 'I have been accustomed to bookselling.' He explored the city, crossed by boat-bridge to the suburb of Triana, and, as he returned to the *posada* after a country walk in the winter Andalusian sunshine, met Baron Taylor, a naturalized Frenchman though of Irish, Flemish, and English blood. He had collaborated with Charles Nodier on the play *Bertram*, and was now a kind of roving fine arts commissioner sifting through the bric-à-brac of Western Europe for chance treasures that might embellish French collections. He was accompanied by a Mr Wetherell, an English businessman. The encounter is a typically Borrovian affair – sudden, mysterious, with hints of a remembrance of things past, exotic, and far-called. They talk fluently of old times, and Borrow concludes the scene with

He [Taylor] has visited most portions of the earth; and it is remarkable enough that we are continually encountering each other in strange places and under singular circumstances. Whenever he descries me, whether in the street

or the desert, the brilliant hall or amongst Bedouin *haimas*, at Novgorod or
Stamboul, he flings up his arms and exclaims. '*O ciel*! I have again the felicity
of seeing my cherished and most respectable B---'

Respectable? Truthful? Well, as almost always with Borrow it would
be unwise to dismiss this meeting simply as a rococo flourish. There is
mention of this coming-together of supposedly old friends in the
unpublished travel-diaries of a painter called Dauzats who was one of
Taylor's assistants in this singularly ill-timed treasure-hunt. As for
Mr Wetherell, he seems to have taken to Borrow who was invited to
his quarters, shown an Arabic inscription which Wetherell couldn't
make any sense of but of which Borrow naturally and immediately
could. The delighted Wetherell gave him a copy of the *Zohar*, a
collection of Jewish writings; but this, like Mr Wetherell, has slipped
away into limbo.

These ties of suddenly resumed friendship were not strong enough
to hold him in Seville. He was determined to make for Madrid in spite
of the perils of partial encirclement by Gomez's Aragonese-Basque
forces. The elderly Genoese bookseller, hypnotized into foolhardi-
ness, went with him. They reached Córdoba three days later. Borrow
was careful to notify Brandram that 'it has pleased the Lord to protect
me through the perils of a most dismal journey'. There were the usual
fascinating conversations on the way, with innkeepers in the main
who, as is common with people living through dangerous times,
expressed the party opinions they thought likeliest to suit those they
were talking to. Borrow took the same line. The aged Genoese, more
of a stickler for principles, got himself involved in angry exchanges,
decided the whole expedition was too wearing, and told Borrow he
was returning forthwith to Seville. 'My good man,' Borrow surprisingly told him at parting, 'I am invariably of the politics of the
people at whose table I sit, or beneath whose roof I sleep; at least I
never say anything which can lead them to suspect the contrary. . . .'
This is a lickspittle Borrow we rarely catch a glimpse of, but all
through his Spanish time it is clear that neither party, Cristino nor
Carlista, ever succeeded in arousing in him any strong partisanship.

He went sight-seeing in Córdoba – 'a mean, dark, gloomy place',
he thought – and then, partnered by a smuggler, he set off on the
dangerous road to Madrid. The bitter winter which had set in kept the
bandits off the roads, so that by Christmas Day he was in Aranjuez
and warming his frozen innards with brandy. Next day he was in
Madrid and settling down on Piso 3, Calle de Santiago 16, and
looking out for a horse. It was a comfort to be back with Maria Diaz.

Villiers was still *en poste*, and it was to Villiers, an unfailing supporter, that Borrow first turned. He wanted to know whether the permission to print, granted to him by Isturitz, would still stand now that Calatrava was in power. Villiers was entirely reassuring. If Borrow had gained Isturitz's consent how possibly could that now be withdrawn by Calatrava, a more liberal man? If he encountered the slightest trouble, Villiers stoutly said, Borrow should refer immediately to him. So Borrow immediately set about the by now familiar business of finding the right paper and the right printer.

I found that during my absence from Madrid Mr Wood had quitted Mr Borrego, and had accepted a situation in another printing establishment; but as Mr Borrego is in possession of the only English press at Madrid . . . and . . . enjoys the good opinions of Mr Villiers . . . I am determined to entrust the printing to him. . . . And in order that the edition should be as scholarly as he could make it . . . I have engaged the literary assistance of Dr Usoz . . . one of the best Castilian scholars in Madrid [who] will, I have no doubt, prove eminently useful. . . .

Between January and April 1837 Borrow was correcting proofs, and relieving the monotony of office work by being sociable with the Madrid gipsies. The Revd W. H. Rule, a Wesleyan proselytizer in Spain at that time, wrote later about Borrow whom he met while Borrow was busy preparing his stock of merchandise. 'It was rather amusing to find him receiving a morning visit and taking wine with two gypsy ladies, whom he did me the honour to introduce, one as "an accomplished highwaywoman", and the other as "an expert pickpocket".' He also took up another linguistic challenge, this time Basque, most mysterious and most intractable of languages.

He was preparing for a sortie into very dangerous country. He would go westwards, edging all the time towards the north – Salamanca, Leon, then up into Galicia and to Vigo and thence a return eastwards into the Basque country. He wanted permission to appoint Usoz as secretary of a Madrid branch of the Bible Society; he wanted a translation of the New Testament into Romany, a pilot translation of Saint Luke into Basque; he wanted money for a second horse. 'I will ride forth . . . into the wildest parts of Spain, where the Word is most wanted. . . .' he told Brandram. He was full of demands, full of self-confidence; and Brandram, who never managed thoroughly to reconcile himself to Borrovian high-handedness, wrote him a slightly testy letter on 22 March:

You will perceive . . . that nearly all your requests are complied with. You have authority to go forth with your horses, and may you have a prosperous

journey. . . . Respecting Dr Usoz, you can hardly have forgotten that you
were to say to him personally all that could be written. With regard to
forming a Bible Society in Madrid, and appointing Dr U. secretary, it is so
out of our usual course that the Committee for various reasons cannot
comply with your wishes.

He got rid of the knife-happy smuggling henchman who had come
up with him from Córdoba, and, through O'Shea, a Madrid banker,
discovered Antonio Buchini, a Greek from Constantinople. Buchini
was picturesque and violent, and Borrow, when he wrote to Hasfeld
about him on 29 April, tried but failed to conceal his delight in him.

I have a servant, a person who has been a soldier for fifteen years, who will go
with me for the purpose of attending to the horses and otherwise assisting me
in my labours. His conduct on the journey is the only thing to which I look
forward with uneasiness; for though he has some good points, yet in many
respects a more atrocious fellow never existed. He is inordinately given to
drink, and of so quarrelsome a disposition that he is almost constantly
involved in some broil . . . he carries an exceedingly long knife, which he
frequently unsheathes and brandishes in the faces of those who are unfortunate enough to awaken his choler. It is only a few days since I rescued from
his grasp the maidservant of the house, whom otherwise he would undoubtedly have killed, and all because she too much burnt a red herring
which he had given her to cook . . . but, bad as he is, he is the best servant I can
obtain; he is very honest, a virtue which is rarely to be found in a Spanish
servant, and I have no fear of his running away with the horses during the
journey after having perhaps knocked me on the head in some lone
posada. . . .

Buchini indeed proved staunch. 'Many was the wild spot to which he
. . . accompanied me; many the wild adventure of which he was the
sharer. His behaviour was frequently in the highest degree extraordinary, but he served me courageously and faithfully. . . . *Kosko
bakh, Anton* [Good luck to thee, Antonio].' He also bought another
horse, a ferocious black Andalusian.

Towards the end of April Borrow went down with feverish in-
fluenza, and this was followed by a heavy cold and a barking cough.
Villiers, seeming to grow fonder of Borrow as the British Embassy as
a whole became more bored with his too regular calls, sent a messenger to his lodgings to say that he was himself proposing to buy a
useful quantity of the Testaments and to send them out to the various
British consulates in the country. Eager to be off, Borrow called in an
expensive surgeon-barber to see if he could cure him. The man was
confident, bled him of sixteen ounces, pocketed his fee and assured
him he would be ready to start next day. And so next day, 15 May

1837, preferring his drastic doctor's assurances to what his own enfeebled body told him, Borrow came carefully downstairs, climbed slowly on to the back of his black stallion, and set off towards the north-west. He was bound for the Guadarrama and thence, provided he could keep a grip on himself and his charger, to Salamanca.

This was the beginning of Borrow's greatest Spanish journey. It was to last for five and a half months, and he was not to see Madrid again until 31 October. Sixteen chapters – 20 to 35 inclusive – of *The Bible in Spain* are devoted to it, and the whole 236 pages of it are brilliant, absorbing, and diversified. Strange people, bizarre adventures, lilting conversations, fun, and above all the neurotic, daredevil, unpredictable, indomitable character of Borrow himself. At the remotest point of his travels, the *alcalde* of Finisterre – a buffoon perhaps but none the less dangerous – decides that he (Borrow) is the Pretender, Don Carlos in person. 'I was aware,' says Borrow, keeping a straight face with obvious difficulty, 'that I had, indeed, committed a great imprudence in coming to this wild place, and among these barbarous people without being able to assign any motive which could appear at all valid in their eyes. . . . "What did you ascend the mountain for?"' the *alcalde* reasonably enough inquires. '"To see prospects." "*Disparate*! I have lived at Finisterra forty years and never ascended that mountain. I would not do it in a day like this for two ounces of gold. You went to take altitudes, and to mark out a camp."' But the guard on the door, one Antonio de la Trava, speaks up now for this strange, gigantic, wandering man. 'This man is not Carlos; he is what he declares himself to be, an Englishman, and whosoever seeks to injure him shall have to do with Antonio de la Trava, el valiente de Finisterra.' The *alcalde* allows himself to be persuaded by this, and decides that Borrow shall be sent on to Corcuvion, there to be examined by the *alcalde* of the district. 'But,' said the *alcalde* of Finisterre, 'what is to be done with the other fellow? He at least is no Englishman. . . . Now, fellow, who are you, and what is your master?' 'You' is Sebastianillo, 'a poor broken mariner of Padron' whom Borrow has picked up to serve him as guide through these north-western wilds of Spain, and Sebastianillo is in deep trouble with the *alcalde*. '. . . since you have no passport, and have confessed that your name is Sebastian, you shall be shot. Antonio de la Trava, do you and the musketeers lead this Sebastianillo forth, and shoot him before the door. . . .'

The lunatic *alcalde* is persuaded to back down. Borrow and Sebastianillo are sent on to Corcuvion to be interrogated by another, weightier *alcalde* – Don Laureano Maria Muñoz – and Sebastianillo arrives drunk. Never mind. This *alcalde*, though short, is fashionably dressed and altogether more in touch with the amenities of civilized life. Borrow tells him of the troubles heaped on him in Finisterre. Ridiculous, says this *alcalde*, that Borrow should have been arrested as a Carlist.

'Not only as a Carlist, but as Don Carlos himself.' 'Oh! most ridiculous; mistake a countryman of the grand Baintham for such a Goth!' 'Excuse me, sir, you speak of the grand somebody.' 'The grand Baintham. He who invented laws for all the world. I hope shortly to see them adopted in this unhappy country of ours.' 'Oh! you mean Jeremy Bentham. Yes! a very remarkable man in his way.' 'In his way! In all ways. The most universal genius which the world ever produced:- a Solon, a Plato, and a Lope de Vega.' 'I have never read his writings. I have no doubt that he was a Solon; and as you say a Plato. I should scarcely have thought, however, that he could be ranked as a poet with Lope de Vega.' 'How surprising! I see indeed, that you know nothing of his writings, though an Englishman. Now, here am I, a simple alcalde of Galicia, yet I possess all the writings of Baintham on that shelf, and I study them day and night.' 'You doubtless, sir, possess the English language.' 'I do. I mean that part of it which is contained in the writings of Baintham. I am most truly glad to see a countryman of his in these Gothic wildernesses. . . . Stay, I think I see a book in your hand.' 'The New Testament . . . how very singular. Yes, I remember. I have heard that the English highly prize this eccentric book. How very singular that the countrymen of the grand Baintham should set any value upon that old monkish book!'

And there are the wonderful coincidences. Benedict Mol, for example, he meets in Madrid during his first tour. Strolling in the pleasant and fertile meadows between the canal and the Manzanares, Borrow chats to the hawkers and is introduced by one selling oranges by a deserted water-tower to another, the unlikeliest huckster of them all. 'Senõr Don Benito Mol, how do you do?' There follows a vivid description of this bulky old man whose stock-in-trade appears to be 'two scented wash-balls' – which would make him a soap-boiler by trade. He speaks not Spanish, but 'a rough dissonant jargon' 'You speak the language of Spain very imperfectly' Borrow tells him. 'How long have you been in the country?' Then there follows – told not in narrative but in conversation – the life-story of Benedict Mol, a man beset by much misfortune and want, all of it somehow picturesque, but a man still nourishing a hope. And, being a German-Swiss, he speaks to Borrow in that testing variation of High German because he recognizes in Borrow a man capable of switching linguistic trails with the deft swiftness of a train picking its pauseless way through Clapham Junction. Benedict, once a soldier in the Walloon

Guard and son of the Lucerne hangman, has lived in Minorca but behold him now, after the death of his wife, perilously short of funds and living in Madrid; however, 'I intend shortly to return to Lucerne, and live there like a duke.' How is this to be managed, Borrow wonders, after he has coaxed out of him the candid tale of his poverty. 'When I go,' Benedict insists, 'it shall be in a coach drawn by six mules, with a treasure, a mighty *Schatz* which lies in the church of Saint James of Compostella, in Galicia. . . .' The man's mind must be wilder even than his looks: is he meditating after so long a bandit raid upon a holy place? No, not quite that. Long ago, fellow-soldiers of the Walloon Guard placed a great booty in a large copper kettle and buried this in Santiago de Compostella, and the last of the Walloons, before expiring gave Benedict the exact details of where in the great cathedral to look – Benedict hurries on before Borrow has the chance to put the obvious question: 'several times I have been on the point of setting out on the journey, but something has always happened to stop me. [There is a lot of life in that remark.] I fell into the hands of a Basque woman who persuaded me to live with her, which I have done for several years. She is a great *Hax* . . .' and Borrow would have been ready to accept this, because Borrow knows by now that all women are *Hexen* (witches).

Here, employing the instant-blackout technique he always enjoys, Borrow breaks off the tale. But it is not the end of it. Walking in the alameda of Santiago, probably in the second week in August, with much on his mind and many adventures behind him, he rested on a quiet bench. Then 'I perceived what at first appeared a shapeless bulk slowly advancing: nearer and nearer it drew, and I could now distinguish the outline of a man dressed in coarse brown garments, a kind of Andalusian hat, and using as a staff the long peeled branch of a tree. . . . The moon shone on grey locks and on a ruddy weather-beaten countenance which I at once recognized. "Benedict Mol," said I, "is it possible that I see you at Compostella?"'

Benedict Mol the seeker after treasure did indeed visit Santiago in the summer of 1837 – and in 1838 as well – on the pursuit of his particular kettleful of gold. There was a bookseller in Santiago called Rey Romero; Borrow made a friend of him as an itinerant salesman of New Testaments should. Two years later Romero wrote Borrow a letter which is circumstantial and clinches the whole thing as being more than a figment of Borrow's imagination.

The German of the *Treasure* came here last year bearing letters from the Government for the purpose of discovering it. But, a few days after his arrival, they threw him into prison; from thence he wrote me, making himself known as the one you introduced to me; wherefore my son went to see him in prison. He told my son that you also had been arrested, but I could not credit it. A short time after, they took him off to Corunna; then they brought him back here again, and I do not know what has become of him since.

Rey Romero was right about Benedict – and right about Borrow too.

So Borrow's missionary journey in the north-west continued. He kept Brandram faithfully informed. Writing from Corunna on 15 September he told him:

Having now arranged matters in Galicia, as well as circumstances will permit, I am about to quit this province, directing my course to Oviedo in the Asturias. The way is long, and is infested by robbers and factions; yet I go forth without much fear, hoping that the Lord will prove my shield and guard as on other occasions. From Oviedo I proceed to Santander, and from thence to the Basque provinces. . . .

And then comes another instalment. He had arrived at Oviedo. He makes no attempt to enlist sympathy by telling them of his bodily health – of his terrible dysentery, of his ophthalmia – but sticks to the outward perils.

This journey was a terrible one; during the greatest part of it we had to toil up and down mountain gorges and ravines, to force our way through bushes and thickets, and to wade rivers and torrents swollen by the rain, which descended continually . . . we had to bribe various peasants to accompany us, though we incurred great risk by so doing of being conducted to some den of thieves and stripped and murdered. At Ribadeo we procured a fresh horse and guide, and continued our way to Oviedo, encountering still greater difficulties, the ground being still more rugged and broken than that which we had previously passed over. My own horse rolled down a precipice, and was much maimed, whilst that of the guide was so worn out by the time he reached Gijon, that he foundered. As for Antonio and myself, we arrived barefooted and bleeding, for I need scarcely say that during all this journey, which amounted at least to 130 miles, we went on foot, the poor horses being scarcely able to carry our books and baggage. . . .

Let nobody say that George Borrow was not earning his stipend.

Besides, he had small triumphs to record for them as well as a recital of disasters, escapes, and suffering, and one that happened in Oviedo itself where he occupied a scantily furnished room in an ancient *posada*. Sitting there, past ten in the evening, with the rain drumming outside, and working on his report, he heard footsteps climbing the stairs: 'in walked nine men of tall stature, marshalled by a little hunch-backed personage. They were all muffled in the long cloaks of Spain, but I instantly knew by their demeanour that they were *caballeros*. . . .' Lining up before him, 'suddenly and simultaneously they all flung back their cloaks, and I perceived that every one bore a book in his hand. . .!' They had all bought New Testaments in the Oviedo bookshop which Borrow had just supplied. Recalling uncomfortable past experiences, Borrow thought that they must be a deputation of civil notables come to take him into custody. But no. The little hunchback was the spokesman. 'Be under no misapprehension, Sir Cavalier; these gentlemen are my friends. We have just purchased these books in the shop where you have placed them for sale, and have taken the liberty of calling upon you in order to return you our thanks for the treasure you have brought us. I hope you can furnish us with the Old Testament also. . . .' Borrow contrives, as so often, to build an eerie, hallucinatory quality into this scene. 'After about half an hour's conversation, he [the hunchback] suddenly said in the English language, "Good-night, sir," wrapped his cloak about him, and walked out as he had come. His companions, who had hitherto not uttered a word, all repeated, "Good-night, sir," and adjusting their cloaks followed him.' Borrow felt gratified.

And the morning after, 30 September, he put in a postscript: 'Morning 30th, twenty Testaments have been sold.' Having received these accounts, Brandram wrote back in characteristic style. He was pleased of course – who could not be when asked to contemplate devotion, tenacity, and pluck on the scale offered by Borrow – but Brandram was at all times a great taskmaster, ready and eager to knock uppitiness on the head. 'I know you are no accountant,' he wrote in reply, 'but do not forget that there are some who are. My memory was jogged on this subject the other day, and I was expected to say to you that a letter of figures would be acceptable.' And then came another calculated prod, on the subject of the enthusiastic Lieutenant Graydon, whom Borrow so much disliked: 'Mr Graydon's letters, as well as yours, are deeply interesting, yet two more different men were never cast in Nature's mould. Of each I hope they have their own peculiar post [Brandram's prose is not often obscure in this kind of way] and are occupying it well, and to each I trust it will be given to see that their labour is not in vain in the Lord.' This was not the talk calculated to sound soothingly in Borrow's ear. He was soon to see how infuriatingly zealous Graydon could be at others' expense. Meanwhile he felt that he merited praise. He had spent dangerous months in what was largely enemy country, planting stocks of the Word here and there, and making personal contacts. For him there had been no skulking à la Graydon in the warmth and security of Gibraltar.

From Oviedo he followed the coast road to Santander, expecting a stock of Testaments to be awaiting him there, but 'I found to my great sorrow that the two hundred Testaments which I had ordered to be sent from Madrid were not come'. He supposed they must have been seized by Carlists, and so, still 'afflicted with a terrible dysentery', he decided to risk an encounter with Carlist guerrillas and return directly to Madrid. He got there on 31 October, and felt he deserved well of the Bible Society; indeed on the very next day he wrote to tell them so.

I am a frail foolish vessel. . . .Yet something, though but little, has been effected by this journey. . . .The New Testament of Christ is enjoying a quiet sale in the principal towns of the north of Spain, and I have secured the *friendly interest* and co-operation of the booksellers of those parts, particularly him, the most considerable of them all, Rey Romero of Compostella. I have, moreover, by private sale disposed of one hundred and sixteen Testaments to individuals entirely of the lower classes, namely muleteers, carmen, *contrabandistas*, etc. My accounts will follow in a few days. . . .

Brandram wrote immediately on receiving this to say how pleased he was – 'peculiarly welcome' was his phrase – and then, in his second paragraph: 'Mr Graydon meets with much encouragement in the towns. Valencia and Alicante have purchased between them more than a thousand copies, and Mr G. has found a great cry for the whole Bible. . . . We were all deeply interested in your ten gentlemen of Oviedo. . . .' Graydon's thousand, Borrow's ten – was this Brandram needling him? Borrow beyond doubt felt that he was. He was enraged. He was thirty-five by now. He was seasoned. He had been through much. He began to act forcefully – even impoliticly.

Madrid was not the place it had been when he had set out on his foray. Calatrava had gone in August. The Count of Luchana had briefly succeeded him. But when Borrow arrived in the capital on 31 October Don José Maria Pérez was in the middle of his brief authority, himself to be succeeded on 30 November by Count Ofalia. This last was a man sympathetic on the whole to the clique of Maria Cristina and unlikely therefore to have much to say in favour of this pestilential and interfering giant from Norwich. But Borrow was in no mood to practise humility. He had spent five difficult, dangerous months fighting for the cause in areas where the cause had little backing. His ten gentlemen of Oviedo were worth any ten thousand Graydon might or might not drum up in fickle Andalusia. And why should Brandram bother him, a sick, suffering but still determinedly active man, with niggling talk about accounts? Was he, Borrow, a counting-house man, a crooked man given to embezzlement if opportunity offered? By God he was not. He would show them that he was a clean fighting man, and no crawler. He would set up a shop in Madrid, and sell openly the Holy Word. And the change of government? And Count Ofalia? Both deserved nothing but contempt. Ofalia was a timid nonentity, a man good for nothing but looking over his shoulder, a man whom a month or two later Borrow was to describe, making use of a picturesque form of words used by the staunch Sir George Villiers: 'if there be any truth in metempsychosis, the *anima* of Count Ofalia must have originally belonged to a mouse. . . .'

He rented a shop in the Calle del Principe. Admittedly the rent was high – eight *reals* a day – but he was not in a frame of mind for cheeseparing or shopping around. On 5 November a letter appeared in *El Español* fiercely attacking the activities of the Bible Society – 'an infernal society' the writer said, and possessed of an 'accursed fecundity'. In answering this Borrow went in with fists flailing, and on 20 November gave Brandram an account of what had clearly been to him an enjoyable encounter. 'I deemed it my duty . . . not to permit so brutal an attack . . . to pass unanswered. You will doubtless deem it too warm and fiery, but tameness and gentleness are of little avail when surrounded by the vassal slaves of bloody Rome. . . .' Borrow's shop was an open affront to the authorities, and even the faithful Villiers thought Borrow was being – was he not? – a little imprudent. He appointed a man from Galicia, José Calzado, to look after the shop; he furnished the place forthwith with no close regard to expense; he paid attention to window-dressing; he ordered chandeliers. If Brandram was worried about Borrow's accounts, let Brandram have something to worry about. He wrote briskly to him on 28 November:

I write these lines in a great hurry, as no time must be lost. The shop opened yesterday, and several Testaments have been sold, but three parts of the customers departed on finding that only the New Testament was to be obtained. . . . I *must* therefore be furnished with Bibles instanter. Send me therefore the London edition, bad as it is, say 500 copies . . . the most advisable way would be to pack them in two chests placing at the top Bibles in English and other languages. . . . *Pray do not fail.* . . . I start tomorrow for Toledo with 100 Testaments, for I must spare no exertion in such a cause. I go as usual on horseback. . . . You must likewise renew my credit on Messrs O'Shea and Company. . . .

Never had Brandram been treated so high-handedly, yet, a tough man himself, he was almost hypnotized by these instructions barked out from far away by someone even tougher than he was. Was the Reverend Andrew Brandram, an evangelical of the strictest principles, being asked to descend to dirty tricks, to become in effect a smuggler? Indeed it seemed so. Well, he would do it, because it was *ad majorem Dei gloriam* – what harm could there be in adapting a slogan of the detestable Ignatius Loyola to English Protestant evangelical causes? And in committee it was also resolved 'that a Credit of £200 be opened in his [Borrow's] favour with Messrs O'Shea and Co., Bankers at Madrid'. On the second day of opening Borrow crossed the street and leant against the opposite wall with his arms folded, looking at his handiwork: 'Pope of Rome! Pope of Rome! look at thyself. That shop must be closed; but oh! what a sign of the times, that it has been permitted to exist for one day. . . . See I not in yonder letters a *Mene, Mene, Tekel, Upharsin*? Look to thyself, Batuschica.' Then, with the delay of hardly more than a day, he sent ahead a muleteer with a cargo of a hundred Testaments, and, accompanied by Antonio, set off himself on horseback for the toilsome ride to Toledo.

Why, having thus vigorously stirred the pot in Madrid, did he suddenly fling off and let his stratagems boil over into hiss and steam and cloudy confusion – if that was to be the way of it? Was it simply in order to try the effect of a hundred Testaments on the Toledaños, to see if he could find a bookseller of the calibre of Rey Romero? That, certainly, is the way Borrow tells it in *The Bible in Spain*, but a reader familiar with the strange quirks of the Borrovian temperament will find this difficult to accept. He knew that by opening his shop in Madrid he had shouted defiance at the clergy – as well as at what authority there was. Surely his first task was to stay close and play out as skilfully as he could the hand he had chosen to pick up? He must have known that Spain, torn and divided though she was, could not for ever allow her nose to be tweaked not by one zealot but by three – because Graydon the inflammatory bungler, was busy in Valencia not selling Bibles but giving them away, and the Revd W. H. Rule had set up a meeting-house in Cádiz in order to preach to people he thought of as heathen.

The explanation must lie in the strange nature of the man. Although no man was less of a coward, he nevertheless was in a sense running away. What Borrow was doing, if in a briefer, less indefinitely committed way, was re-enacting the summer of 1825 when on an impulse he had put London behind him. He was suddenly sick of bickering and Bibles and Brandram, so he flung off to Toledo. There, in the little church of San Tomé hung El Greco's greatest masterpiece, *The Burial of Count Orgaz*. He could stand and admire in that papist place for as long as he liked (although he lacked his brother's painter's gifts he knew a great picture when he saw one, and 'I should say it would be cheap at five thousand pounds'). The Toledo bookseller too turned out to be a comfort, a big man, an officer in the national cavalry and, better still, a horsebreeder who told him he would help with Bible-selling. '"Will not your doing so bring you into odium with the clergy?" "Ca!", said he; "who cares? I am rich . . . they cannot hate me more than they do already. . . . Who cares for the cowardly priests? I am a liberal, Don Jorge, and a friend of your countryman Flinter. . . ."' The joy of his stolen week was completed with his being able to mingle once more with the gipsies.

Beyond the bare announcement before he went, he said nothing about his wonderful week in Toledo to Brandram, but returned to Madrid more eager than ever to act disobligingly, and caused Villiers serious anxieties. Madrid was the 'centre of old, gloomy, bigoted Spain', and Borrow was ready to do battle 'in the midst of furious priests and Carlists'. He 'printed three thousand advertisements on paper, yellow, blue, and crimson, with which I almost covered the sides of the streets, and besides this inserted notices in all the journals and periodicals, employing also a man after the London fashion to parade the streets with a placard, to the astonishment of the populace.' By Christmas Day 1837 he had sold between seventy and eighty New Testaments and ten Bibles and the turnover was quickening. He was riding the wave, fighting off the inner certainty that the sliding-down was bound soon to begin. '. . . were it right and seemly for *me*, the most insignificant of worms, to make such a comparison, I would say that, like Paul at Ephesus, I am fighting with wild beasts. . . .' On 16 January Brandram wrote back to say that the letter about the sales drive had afforded the Committee no little merriment. He was even pleased to give approval to the idea of the sandwichman. Publicity was not something to be dismissed as undignified or as inappropriate, but – never unqualaified praise from Brandram – 'I hope it may not be prejudicial. . . .'

Before Brandram's letter had had time to reach him, however, the wave had begun to break. On 31 December Antonio Buchini, most faithful of all his Sancho Panzas, gave notice that he was about to quit. Antonio admitted that he was a man fond of change 'though it be for the worse', and since the return from Galicia he could not settle; he was tired of the same lodgings, tired even of Maria Diaz, and so, at four dollars less a month, he had hired himself out as a cook. But there was no ill-feeling towards Borrow himself. 'Should you chance, however, to have any pressing need *de mes soins* send for me without hesitation, and I will at once . . . come to you.' Borrow hired a Basque from Hernani in Guipuzcoa, Francisco, in his place without any difficulty. By now he was becoming familiar in Madrid – not a very large place in those days; Valencia and Barcelona were much bigger. Once seen and listened to, he was not of course a figure easily forgotten: he was Don Jorgito, el Ingles. A hero?

Borrow was not a man self-satisfied enough, foolish enough, ever to think so. He knew that in the eyes of the more bigoted Catholics of Madrid – quite a large body – he was no heroic figure but rather the spawn of the devil himself. His gaudy shop and his sandwichman were an offence to the true faith. Was there truth in the rumour that he was busy translating Holy Writ into the heathenish gabble of Romany? Of course there was. Might he be in the thick of a plot to bring down Catholic Spain in ruin? That was probable rather than just possible. Spain, it must be remembered, had reached those limits of chaos when whisperings and fantasies flew overhead hand in hand. He knew also of course that there were those whose curiosity he had aroused who leaned more to admiration than mistrust, and so he kept as close as he could to those who, if it came to a collision, would stand by him. He listened to Maria Diaz; of Francisco the Basque he made a strong ally. Early in January 1838 'one of the ruffians of Madrid, called *Manolos*, came up to me one night in a dark street, and told me that unless I discontinued selling "my Jewish books" I should have a knife *"nailed in my heart"*; but I told him to go home, say his prayers, and tell his employers that I pitied them, whereupon he turned away with an oath. . . .' But it was Borrow's size, not Borrow's Christian advice, that turned away the bully-boy.

But if tough, undercover tactics would not work against the tougher evangelist, there were other agencies, perhaps more effective, that could be turned to. On 15 January writing from his lodging at Maria Diaz's, Borrow gave Brandram some disturbing news, and merriment in Earl Street would doubtless have been cut off short. 'Revd. and Dear Sir, The priests have at length "swooped upon me," and I have received a peremptory order from the Political Governor of Madrid to sell no more New Testaments. . . .' And did London offer counsel and support? Not a bit of it. Brandram wrote testily to say that with his tri-coloured placards he had asked for what he had got.

This was unfair. Borrow's placards doubtless counted for some-

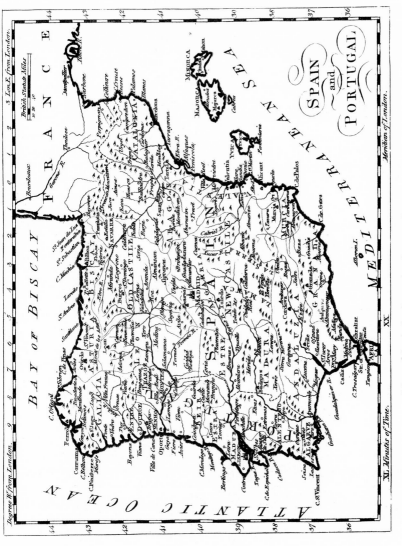

Map of Spain in the early nineteenth century.

Right. Richard Ford as a *majo* ('gallant') at Seville in 1832 by J. Becquer.

Below. The Calle de Alcalá, Madrid.

thing in the exacerbation of official disapproval; but ultimately Graydon's tactless and excessive zeal counted for far more. Villiers, powerless to do anything against the ban, felt this strongly. It was true that Graydon had disposed of more than 5,000 copies in 1837; but this was the result of his giveaway tactics in Valencia and Barcelona – and it had never been the Society's policy to spread the Word for nothing: the Orangeman's generosity with other people's money, combined with his ranting and roaring against the Roman Catholic Church, had been by far the greater influence in pushing Ofalia's feeble government into some show of action.

Meanwhile, Borrow's translation of the Gospel according to St. Luke into Romany went well and he went to the palace in order to present Ofalia personally with a handsome, specially bound copy. '. . . a dusky, diminutive person, between fifty and sixty years of age,' Borrow thought, 'with false hair and teeth', affable – but certainly mouselike, as Villiers had said. It is possible to feel sympathy for Ofalia, caught between six Spanish bishops, including the Primate on the one hand, and Villiers, representative of a very powerful nation and allied to a gigantic wild man on the other.

Confident apparently that no decisive action would be taken against him by this inconsiderable little man, Borrow planned further sorties. 'Shall I,' he asked Brandram on 17 March, 'wait a little time longer in Madrid; or shall I proceed at once on a journey to Andalusia and other places? I am in health, strength and spirits thanks be to the Lord! and am at all times ready to devote myself body and mind, to His cause. . . .' He made no mention in this letter of the two pestilential trouble-makers, Rule, based primarily in Cádiz, Graydon all over the place but more particularly in Seville, Cádiz, and Málaga, yet there can be no doubt that it was on account of these two that Borrow was eager to head south. Brandram had earlier reassured him that Graydon was about to leave Spain on account of his health. On 30 March however Borrow informed Brandram that Graydon had changed his mind and was out and about sowing the wind. Rule, to add to the trouble, had converted a Roman Catholic priest called Marin who, by reason of his apostasy, was now penniless and with a mother to support, and would Borrow help since most unfortunately Graydon did not happen to be at hand to offer assistance? 'I therefore this day [30 March] have sent him a small sum on my own account to relieve the pinch of utter need,' he told Brandram, adding not without cause, that he (Borrow) had 'a heart full of trouble and doubt'. But still Brandram refused to recognize that Borrow was being badly done by. 'I doubt exceedingly whether Mr Rule has that perfect knowledge of Mr G. which he supposes that he has, and I scarcely think that either of you are at all alive to his real worth which is undoubtedly hidden beneath his peculiarities. . . .' Then in April Rule asked Borrow to take Marin on in Madrid as a salesman. Not taking the trouble wholly to conceal from Brandram that he was seething with fury, Borrow wrote again to London on 23 April. '. . . it will be as well to remind you that all the difficulty and danger connected with what has been accomplished in Spain have fallen to my share, I have been labouring on the flinty rock and sierra, and not in smiling meadows refreshed by sea breezes. . . .' So-called friends and avowed enemies alike seemed to be uniting to snap at him and bring him down. 'I repeat that I was grieved to have Marin saddled upon me, in a place where I am surrounded by spies and persecuted by many and vindictive enemies.'

On 30 April 1838 things came to something of a head. A fortnight before, two police officers, sent by the Civil Governor, had raided Borrow's shop in the Calle del Principe and seized twenty-five copies of his Romany St. Luke. Without delay Villiers wrote to Ofalia to say that this was an unjustified act and that Borrow should be indemnified. No attention was paid to Villiers' strong words, and while Borrow was eating Maria Diaz's breakfast on that morning of the 30th, officers arrived with an order to search. Borrow took the visit robustly, telling this Pedro Martin de Eugenio to be off and take his warrant with him. 'I shall go when I please. . . do you know to whom you are speaking? Are you aware that if I think fit I can search your apartment, yes, even below your bed? What have we here?. . .' poking a heap of papers which lay upon a chair, '. . . are these also papers of the gipsies?' By then Borrow had had enough, and 'led him out of the apartment; and then still holding him, conducted him downstairs from the third floor in which I lived, into the street, looking him steadfastly in the face the whole while. . . .' He had left his hat behind, and Maria was sent down to hand it to him. Borrow makes it all sound dignified and even stately, but doubtless what happened was a rough, tough scuffle which Borrow thoroughly enjoyed. Maria Diaz was sure though that this would not be the end of the affair, and was anxious for him. This Martin de Eugenio, make no doubt about it, was an *agent provocateur*. He would go back with a story.

Feeling that Maria was right – she so often was – Borrow left his lodging then and there and spent the night 'in a celebrated French tavern in the Calle del Caballero' – a fashionable and well-attended place, and the last one, he argued, where the *corregidor* would think of looking for him. At ten that night Maria came round to warn him that the constables had just been round with a warrant for his arrest. The next morning, 1 May, Borrow went to Villiers and told him in detail how things stood. Villiers offered him the protection of the embassy. Borrow declined. 'I assured him that I was under no apprehension whatever.' And knowing the man, one has no difficulty in accepting this as absolute truth. He paused on the way out to chat to Southern, secretary of embassy, and before he had finished, his servant Francisco the Basque rushed breathlessly in to inform him, in his own mysterious language – which by now of course Borrow had thoroughly got the hang of – that the *alguacils* (constables) were on the rampage again. Southern was all anxiety. 'But perhaps these fellows will arrest you.' Borrow was imperturbable. 'I must take my chance as to that . . .' and presently afterwards departed.

He was arrested in the Alcalá quite close to Villiers' headquarters, and told Francisco in rapid Basque so that the constables should understand nothing, to cut straight back to the embassy so that Villiers should know that the great axe had indeed fallen. Then he was taken to the *jefatura*. The tone of his narrative characteristically gives one to think that he was enjoying the whole business immensely. Characteristically, too, he seems to have on the whole enjoyed his twelve days in gaol. There were bugs in plenty of course, and an ever-present risk of catching typhus, but it was interesting. He was treated as an honoured guest. He was offered a large empty room and Maria Diaz was allowed to hire someone to bring in furnishings. There were diverse characters to talk to and he enjoyed drawing their colourful histories out of them. He was the centre of attention – something again which he always enjoyed. Villiers threatened the might of England and poor Ofalia began to be afraid. It was made clear to the *corregidor* that he had blundered. Would Borrow please go? 'Vamos, Don Jorge, a la casa, a la posada' they said – Vamos anywhere, indeed, provided it could not be said that Borrow, countryman of Sir George Villiers, countryman indeed of the great Lord Melbourne, was lying wrongfully a prisoner in a Spanish gaol. But Borrow, although physically far from well, would not budge. He was in the news back home. *The Times* had noted that, having done no wrong, he refused to quit prison even when the doors had been flung open for him, and congratulated him. Here was a man whom Palmerston, Melbourne's Foreign Secretary, liked the sound of.

My arch-enemy [Borrow told Brandram] the Archbishop of Toledo, the Primate of Spain, wishes to give me the kiss of brotherly peace. He has caused a message to be conveyed to me in my dungeon [typical of Borrow to be misleading about the size of his accommodation] assuring me that he has had

no share in causing my imprisonment, which he says was the work of the civil
governor, who was incited to that step by the Jesuits.

He adds that he is determined to seek out my persecutors amongst the
clergy and to have them punished, and that when I leave prison he shall be
happy to co-operate with me in the dissemination of the gospel!!!

As for Marin and Rule and the other bothersome fanatics, he felt
himself in a position now to dismiss them as loud-mouthed seekers of
publicity. 'To do a great and good thing requires a heart cooled by
experience and knowledge of the world; both of which desiderata I
consider incompatible with a will to shine.' So that was Graydon
slapped down. Bitten by bugs, fleas, lice, and all the old familiars of
prison life, Borrow remained in very high spirits and reluctant to
leave the *carcel* which however he finally did on 12 May. The very
next day Sir George Villiers asked to see him at the embassy and
having heard the details, 'Sir George has commanded me' – thus
Borrow wrote to Brandram,

to write to the following effect:- Mr Graydon must leave Spain, or the Bible
Society must publicly disavow that his proceedings receive their encouragement. . . . A formal complaint of his conduct has been sent up from Málaga,
and a copy of one of his writings. Sir George blushed when he saw it, and
informed Count Ofalia that any steps which might be taken towards punish-
ing the author would receive no impediment from him. . . . I have never had
any other opinion of Mr Graydon than that he was insane – insane as the
person who for the sake of warming his own hands would set a street on
fire. . . .

Borrow considered that he had conquered all his foes, that his actions
and opinions had been justified. He was free to act.

This was delusion. It was true that Ofalia wanted to cool things
down, that he had no wish at all for a high-level row with the might of
Britain; it was true also that highly-placed ecclesiastics of the Spanish
Church could see no point in wrangling openly with an unbelieving
buccaneer like Palmerston – to such an extent that the Primate
himself, the Archbishop of Toledo, gave Borrow an interview and
was affable, and dazzled even that staunchest no-popery man with
the lustre of his amethyst ring. But Borrow was never by nature a
negotiator; he never learnt to distinguish between temporary tactical
manoeuvrings and the unconditional volte-face. He advertised again.
On 17 May 1838 he hired space in the *Correo Nacional* and made a
long statement signed by 'George Borrow, Sole authorised Agent of
the British and Foreign Bible Society in Spain', in which he 'publicly
declared' that the Society had no connection with over-zealous

trouble-makers. A week later he wrote in high fettle to Brandram saying 'In the name of the *Most Highest* take steps for preventing that miserable creature Graydon from ruining us all.' Now he could march onward unfettered, the solely authorized Christian soldier.

But it did not turn out like that at all. Ofalia still regarded Borrow's caches of Testaments here and there over the land as a commanding officer might regard the scattered sowing of minefields over a wide battle-area. He wanted to ensure that subversion was impounded and locked away or destroyed. He wished Borrow would go home. Graydon did not by any means go suddenly quiet, and the authorities could see no conclusive difference between the Irish demagogue and Borrow. The Bible Society, at a full meeting on 28 May, with Lord Bexley in the chair, did decide to ask Graydon to leave Spain, but solely 'on account of his personal safety'; furthermore in informing Borrow of this decision, Brandram chose to be cool and sharp and critical, not of Graydon but of Borrow who had borne imprisonment for the sake of the faith. '. . . you have written,' Brandram told him, 'with what appears to us unmitigated severity of his conduct.' Graydon, Borrow was reminded, was working not for a salary but for nothing. And if he was working for nothing what rights or control did Borrow suppose the Society had over him – even supposing that Graydon had, because of his selfless devotion to the Cause, perhaps overstepped the limits of prudence? And at the end of this letter Brandram jabbed his hardest. '. . . you thought yourself fully justi-fied by the distinction of salaried and unsalaried Agents, in speaking of yourself as the alone accredited Agent of the Society. Possibly when you reflect a little upon the matter you may view it in another light.' Neither man would budge from his position. Further letters were exchanged, Brandram's cool and full of thrust, Borrow's over-wrought and boisterous. He felt inclined to leave Madrid and all the bother in order to begin a selling campaign in Castile. Maria Diaz came from there and could ensure that he would not be a traveller without friends. This was an important point and one that weighed much with him. He felt suddenly deserted. He had been through long, exhausting months in the Society's service, had returned to Madrid and to a prison cell. And then, with release and, as he thought, freedom of action and its attendant rewards in prospect, rejection and rebuff had come instead. Villiers was sympathetic, but Borrow's ups and downs were not by a long way the only serial story he had to give his attention to. To add to his troubles, Borrow at this time lost Francisco, the faithful Basque who caught typhus in gaol and died horribly. (It should be noted how, all through the years of his Spanish

wanderings, Borrow was able consistently to inspire afffection and
loyalty in his servants.) It seemed to him that Earl Street was making
no effort to understand the difficulties of his situation.

On 16 June he wrote to express his grievances and his intentions
with a clarity which would allow him no means of extrication if the
Society chose to take him at his word.

Take now in good part what I am about to say, and O! do not misunderstand
me! I owe a great deal to the Bible Society, and the Bible Society owes
nothing to me. I am well aware and am always disposed to admit that it can
find thousands more zealous, more active, and in every respect more adapted
to transact its affairs and watch over its interests. Yet with this consciousness
of my own inutility I must be permitted to state that linked to a man like
Graydon I can no longer consent to be, and that if the Society expect such a
thing, I must take the liberty of retiring, perhaps to the wilds of Tartary or the
Zigani camps of Siberia.

He did not finish there but went on with detailed complaints about
the manner of his imprisonment and comparisons between Madrid
and Petersburg. 'I had as many or more difficulties to surmount in
Russia than I originally had here, yet all that the Society expected or
desired was effected without stir or noise, and that in the teeth of an
imperial *Ukase* which forbade the work which I was employed to
superintend. . . .'

Brandram buzzed like a wasp on receiving this. The best thing
would be that Borrow should return to London forthwith 'for a
personal conference', and he tartly added: 'I trust that we shall not
easily forget your services in St Petersburg; but suffer me to remind
you that when you came to the point of *distribution*, your success
ended.' Borrow must have choked at the injustice of this, but all the
same, by mid-July when he received this fighting stuff from Brandram, his temper must have cooled a little. By then he did not at all
like the Society's brisk announcement of immediate recall to London.
'You hint,' he wrote, choosing to ignore the bluntness of Brandram's
prose,

that a desire is entertained at home to have a personal conference with me. In
the name of the Highest I entreat you all to banish such a preposterous idea.
A journey home (provided you intend that I should return to Spain) [This
was the alarm-bell sounding in his ear] could lead to no result but expense
and the loss of precious time. I have nothing to explain to you which you are
not perfectly well acquainted with by my previous letters . . . the plain
unvarnished truth is seldom agreeable. . . . It was unkind and unjust to taunt
me with having been unsuccessful in distributing the Scriptures . . . no other
person . . . would have distributed the tenth part. . . .'

He then made ready to resume a sales campaign outside Madrid. Buchini returned to him, and Juan Lopez, Maria Diaz's husband, went as well. He would go first to Maria Diaz's home, Villa Seca out on the Meseta, where the Carlists were strong. But Borrow was prepared to risk any sharp encounters in order to establish or re-establish – it was shameful that his bat-eyed employers back in London should see any need for this – his valour and his good faith. He took comfort in his two companions and in his two horses to whom he would chant the Muslim creed in Arabic. They plunged down into the Tagus valley and spent three days selling frenziedly from door to door in the green leafiness of Aranjuez, then back to the uplands where the July heat was paralysing. Muleteers fell dead from their saddles, clubbed down by the sun, but Borrow and his two partners went indomitably about from village to village making sales and spreading the word. '. . . nothing is beyond my capacity' Buchini assured him, and Lopez, just as tough, supported him with 'Don Jorge, yo quiero engancharme con usted' – 'I want to be your enlisted man.'

But the wounding letters continued to fly out from London, and they found their mark even though Borrow had ridden out of Madrid to avoid them. So he was off, the tone of these implied, riding around very dangerous country like a demented bagman. And would he please stop going on and on about Mr Graydon? He rode back to Madrid to write a reply – a determined one, but calmer in tone than the earlier ones. 'Have you not, to a certain extent, been partial in this matter? . . . It was God's will that I, who have risked all and lost *almost* all in the cause, be taunted, suspected, and the seat of agony and tears which I have poured out be estimated at the value of the water of the ditch or the moisture which exudes from rotten dung. But I murmur not. . . . I *will not* leave Spain until the whole affair has been thoroughly sifted. . . .'

Then he was off to Ocaña, not far from Aranjuez, sending Lopez on ahead with between two and three hundred Testaments. But in the outskirts, 'a man appeared from under the porch . . . [he] placed himself before my horse so as to bar the way, and said *Schophon*, which in the Hebrew tongue signifies a rabbit [how handily his multilingualism pops up to help him at awkward moments.] I knew this word to be one of the Jewish countersigns, and asked the man if he had anything to communicate.' Indeed he had. Lopez had already been taken up, and the net was spread in readiness for Buchini and himself. He should turn his horse's tail to his enemies 'and neigh in derision of them'. This was the kind of advice, delivered mysteriously and with a touch of the occult, which he always tended to heed. With his carriers he turned for Madrid. Daylight had gone but danger was everywhere, not simply in Ocaña. On a low bank close to their left near the village of Antigola they saw three men. All three were stark naked but each carried a long gun. Common assassins and fighting for no cause, Borrow decided, and therefore cowards whom you tackled head on. He told them to cross to the right-hand side of the road or the horses' hooves would immediately trample them. One of them was for firing, but a second shouted 'No! Hay peligro!' and the coward's cry of danger was the more persuasive and the next morning Borrow reached Madrid where a released Lopez shortly arrived. Let no chairbound London bureaucrat dare to insinuate that George Borrow was not worth his salary, that he ever flagged in devotion to his mission.

The party made a fresh sortie. They sold five hundred Testaments in a week. Then, hearing that again authority was close behind him, they bivouacked in the open for a night and the next day reached Labajoz, between Valladolid and Madrid. But Balmaseda, chief of the Carlist marauders thereabouts, was on the rampage. '. . . he [Borrow wrote] made his desperate inroad into the southern part of Old Castile, dashing down like an avalanche from the pine woods of Soria. I was present at all the horrors which ensued – the sack of Arrevalo – and the forcible entry into Martin Munoz and San Cyrian. . . .' Lopez went missing, and Borrow set out alone on horse-back to find him. Buchini, scared at last, had made off for Madrid. Lopez was found in custody at Vilallos. On 23 August Borrow wrote to Lord Hervey, chargé d'affaires in Madrid (Villiers by now was in England and about to become Earl of Clarendon) to inform him of how he, a British citizen, had reacted to this situation. The *alcalde* of Vilallos held on to Lopez; he was keeping him for Carlist vengeance. 'Taking these circumstances into consideration, I deemed it my duty, as a Christian and a gentleman, to rescue my unfortunate servant from such lawless hands, and in consequence defying opposition I bore him off, though perfectly unarmed, through a crowd of at least one hundred peasants. On leaving the place I shouted "Viva Isabella Segunda".'

He was severely ill with fever by then, but by force of will he crossed the high Guadarrama in the blistering August heat and reached Madrid on 29 August, and what lay waiting for him there was not praise, not congratulation, but simply Brandram's final word. At a subcommittee on 6 August it had been 'resolved that it be recommended to the General Committee to recall Mr Borrow from Madrid without further delay'. Only Browne, one of Brandram's assistants, having perhaps some intuitive understanding of what Borrow had been through, added a personal, kindly note: 'believe us sincerely desirous of doing full justice to your motives, and of cherishing towards you nothing but the most frank and friendly spirit.' Was Borrow grateful for this? The likeliest guess is that he was past caring. At all events nothing now would serve except obedience. On 19 September he wrote to Brandram: 'for the last ten days I have been confined to my bed by a fever. I am now better, and hope in a few days to proceed to Saragossa, which is the only road open. . . . I hope my next letter will be from Bordeaux. . . .' He took his time, spent a fortnight in Paris, and reached London, by steamer from Boulogne, about 18 October.

Once back, he sat down to compose the long and splendid defence of his actions in Spain during the second tour. It is spirited, forceful, and dignified. Borrow never wrote better. Did he, after all those years of labour and close concern with the texts of the Scriptures, see himself as a nineteenth-century St. Paul, not of Tarsus but of Dumpling Green? Perhaps not, but the Pauline harangues might well have been running in his head: 'In perils in the city, in perils in the wilderness, in perils in the sea, in perils among false brethren. . .' 'There was given to me a thorn in the flesh, the messenger of Satan to buffet me. . . .' He did not mention Graydon, saying only: 'I had scarcely opened my establishment in Madrid when I began to hear rumours of certain transactions at Valencia, said to be encouraged by the Bible Society . . . transactions, as they were reported . . . in the highest degree absurd and improper. . . .' But he did mention 'the ex-priest Pascual Marin, who arrived in Madrid the very day in which I was committed to prison. His narrative served to confirm all the rumours which I had previously heard. . . .' And he did stress his tenacity. He was not a man to be deterred from what he saw as his appointed duty, even after the hostility of the authorities had been thoroughly aroused by the thoughtless and unnecessary antics in the south. And he did refer to his final campaign in Old Castile: 'here my success was almost miraculous, nine hundred copies of the Holy Book being sold in less than three weeks, but not in peace and tranquillity, as the province became suddenly a scene of horrors, which I shall not attempt to describe. It was not the war of men, or even of cannibals, which I witnessed; it seemed a contest of fiends from the infernal pit. . . .' In his peroration he insisted that what he had said could be vouched for. 'And lastly, for my zeal in the Bible Cause, whilst employed in the Peninsula, I can have the evidence not only of some of the most illustrious characters resident in Madrid, but likewise that of the greatest part of Spain, throughout which I believe my name is better known than in my native village in East Anglia.' This was true. The name of Don Jorge went from lip to lip in Spain as readily as the name of Wellington three decades earlier.

In November he sent them another, somewhat shorter, letter, in which he presumed to look forward. The thing to do, he told them, was to concentrate upon the peasantry. He reminded them of his own sales talk at village pumps and in market-places. 'Peasants, peasants, I bring you the Word of God at a cheap price. I know you have but little money, but I bring it you at whatever you can command, at four or three *reals*, according to your means. . . .' It was true that here was a country plagued by civil strife, a country where a missioner would be at risk. But he made it clear that still, in spite of all he had been through, he remained a man never for one moment tempted to shrink from danger.

. . . it does not become a real Christian to be daunted . . . moreover if it be not written that a man is to perish by wild beast or reptiles, he is as safe in the den even of the cockatrice as in the most retired chamber of the king's palace; and that if on the contrary he be doomed to perish by them, his destiny will overtake him notwithstanding all the precautions which, like a blind worm, may essay for his security. . . .

In short, George Borrow, badly used though he had been, was prepared to go back.

CHAPTER 8

A MAN OF PROPERTY

BORROW took a holiday with his mother in Norwich, spent some time also with Mary Clarke at Oulton (she was glad to see him), and read *Oliver Twist* and *Nicholas Nickleby*. Quite a lot had been happening to Mary Clarke during his long wanderings. Between 1835 and 1837 both her parents, as well as Breame, her brother, the inheritor, had died. Breame by his will had appointed trustees who were now pressing for the sale of the estate and the division of the proceeds among Breame's six children. But Mary Clarke, executrix and mortgagee, objected to this plan. After wrangling, both sides agreed to the sale of the estate to Joseph Cator Webb for £11,000. Then there were second thoughts. Was £11,000 enough? Was it not likely that the estate would rise in value? Webb went to law in order to force them to carry out the sale. Mary Clarke was in the middle of all this when on 14 December the Society invited Borrow to make a third journey. Brandram, not a man to submit to bullying, who was as tough in his own pietistic way as Borrow in his never-blunted self-sufficiency, was cool. But Borrow had made out a case so Borrow should go. There is no doubt at all that Mary would have preferred to keep him at her side; after all Borrow was by now a very forceful and dominating man. But in spite of her efforts at persuasion, Borrow went.

As usual he had a stormy passage. He also had the horrors on the way, but none the less reached Cádiz on the last day of 1838, and settled in at the Hotel de la Reina in Seville on 2 January. Seville, he felt, was the right place to choose as headquarters for this third campaign. Seville, for one thing, was where the gipsies were in greatest abundance, and Borrow was by now deep into his 'Gypsies in Spain' (*The Zincali*). The Bible Society, however, would expect their representative to be in Madrid, and to Madrid, if reluctantly, he went on 12 January – but not before finding time to further his researches for the book. He met Antonio Bailly, a courier who knew the gipsies and something of the Romany language too. Bailly must make notes and observations and send them on to him in Madrid.

Bailly also introduced him to a lottery-ticket salesman called Mañuel who interested himself much in Romany songs, fake or otherwise, so that in all Borrow quickly found congenial company. For the furthering of the Society's business, however, it did not seem to be a propitious time. Borrow had stocked a Seville bookshop with Testaments before going home, but these had been impounded by the ecclesiastical Governor who refused to release them. He went northwards by post-coach and reached Madrid on 16 January 1839. He persuaded Antonio Buchini to take on again the hazardous job of distribution, and settled down once more in the Calle de Santiago with Maria Diaz. He paid a call on Lord Clarendon. Maria's husband, though not willing this time to co-operate actively, sent him an old peasant, Victoriano, to act as henchman, and he brought with him into the city Borrow's magnificent Arab horse, Sidi Habismilk. A second horse, which he had kept in reserve at Salamanca, came too, and depression lifted from him if temporarily. He was a man who loved horses more than women. But the general situation had not improved. Ofalia had gone the way of all the others, but the official attitude towards evangelists remained as cold as ever. Still, praying earnestly to God, Borrow determined to try again. He went out into the country, faithful to the advice he had given to Brandram in London. 'I was dressed,' so he wrote to London on 15 February,

in the fashion of the peasants of the neighbourhood of Segovia in Old Castile, namely, I had on my head a species of leather helmet, or *montera*, with a jacket and trousers of the same material. I had the appearance of a person between sixty and seventy years of age, and drove me a *burrico*, with a sack of Testaments lying across its back. On nearing the village I met a genteel-looking young woman leading a little boy by the hand. As I was about to pass her with the customary salutation of 'Vaya usted con Dios,' she stopped, and after looking at me for a moment she said; 'Uncle (*Tio*), what is that you have on your *burrico*? Is it soap?' I replied, 'Yes; it is soap to wash souls clean.'

Then she was offered one to read, which she did for ten minutes on end in a loud voice, remarking 'Que lectura tan bonita, que lectura tan linda!' But the price of three *reals* was more than she could manage, and so Borrow moved away. 'I had not, however, proceeded thirty yards, when the boy came running behind me, shouting out of breath: "Stop, uncle! the book, the book." Upon overtaking me he delivered me three *reals* in copper, and seizing the Testament, ran back to her, who I suppose was his sister, flourishing the book over his head with great glee.'

This was a good day. But as one looks at Borrow tramping roads and taking risks on this third and final mission, the impression of a discouraged man persists. His thoughts were turning more and more to the gipsies, and less and less to his job. He tackled the poor of Madrid, hoping for a response like that of the young country girl and her brother; but then he heard that Victoriano, sent off to Guadalajara, had been arrested and Buchini had to be detached from town business in order to make the journey to Guadalajara to arrange, if possible, his release. All the same he did make headway in Madrid, and increased his sales staff to eight, three men and five women. He had a longing to go to the valley of Batuecas because the gipsy colonies of Extremadura beckoned him; and indeed he did set out on the Talavera road, making first for his cache of Testaments at the village of Naval Carnero. But here he heard that word had gone out ahead of him. *Alcaldes* of all the places along his route had been warned that this dangerous white-haired subversive, who could cover incredible distances in a single day, was on the march again: no violence was to be used, but nevertheless the constituted authorities were ordered to make things as difficult as they could for him. Borrow galloped back to Madrid, taking comfort from the fact that the clericals seemed still to be frightened of him.

From Brandram he received further discouragement in a letter sent on 4 March: 'They [the Committee] smiled . . . but having smiled began to grow grave. . . . Perhaps some little failing in dignity began to manifest itself, so that where they would cheerfully employ a . . . peasant, they were doubtful whether it became them to have the likeness of one going about in their name. A word to the wise, they say, is enough, and you will understand what I mean. . . .' Borrow understood perfectly well, but he was beginning to have had enough of the Bible Society and the niggling. Anyway, he was beginning to see a clearer, more positive career for himself as a writing man. Time and again Brandram had told him how entertained the Committee had been by his long and detailed letters to them. Very well, when he got home he would ask for those letters back and make a book out of them on his own account.

And there was Mary Clarke. Did he become engaged to her in December 1838, before returning to Spain for the third time? Nothing was made public, either by Borrow or Mary Clarke. That would be Borrow's way, and Mary at this time might well have been willing to accede to his strange secretiveness. But she must sooner or later have told Ann Perfrement of some sort of understanding because later on there is a letter to her from the old lady in Willow Lane: 'I am not surprised, my dear Mrs Clarke, at what you tell me. . . . So far all is well. I shall now resign him to your care, and may you love and cherish him as much as I have done. I hope and trust that each will try and make the other happy. You will always have my prayers and best wishes. Give my kind love to George and tell him he is never out of my thoughts. . . .' Was Mary anticipating things in 'what she told' Ann? Impossible to say, but it is quite characteristic of Borrow that he should be satisfied for his mother, whom he treasured and honoured, to hear this vital piece of news concerning himself from Mary and not by his own hand or from his own mouth. Certainly he wrote to Mary telling her she should be firm and unyielding faced with assaults on her rights. And once back in Seville in January 1839 he wrote to her to say that it would be, he thought, a wise move that she should get away from the harpies for a while, and come out to him in Seville, bringing with her of course Henrietta who played so nicely on the guitar and so would be a great help to him in his efforts to win over the confidence of the gipsies of Triana . . . At the end of March 1839 Mary wrote to him the conclusive letter. She was taking him at his word. She was embarking for Seville. She was bringing Hen with her. Borrow beyond doubt was glad to have his mind made up for him, and welcomed the chance to get away from Madrid.

He sat down in the Calle de Santiago on 10 April, and wrote to Earl Street a typically circuitous letter. 'Revd. and Dear Sir, In a few days I shall leave Madrid for Seville. . . .' He went on to outline yet again the inhospitable, unpropitious state of affairs in Spain. He would send Buchini with the Testaments with a convoy starting for Andalusia on the 13th; and he would follow with the courier. He had meant to go by way of Extremadura, but now Carlist bandits were out there in strength and so he thought it best to avoid that route and the risk of being shot or being held to ransom for a thousand pounds. He had taken risks enough and was his skin worth a thousand pounds to Brandram? (This last question did not actually appear, but it was implied.) But he did say a moment later something very characteristic. 'I am willing to confess that I am what the world calls exceedingly superstitious; perhaps the real cause of my change of resolution was a dream, in which I imagined myself on a desolate road in the hands of several robbers, who were hacking me with their long ugly knives. . . .' He had now given up trying to sell Testaments in Madrid, but there was no overt suggestion that he had had enough of working for the Bible Society. He pointed again to his achievements – 'a large edition of the New Testament almost entirely disposed of in the very centre of old, gloomy, fanatic Spain, in spite of the opposition and the furious cry of the sanguinary priesthood and the edicts of a tyrannical, deceitful Government. . .' He offered some criticisms of Morrison's Chinese version of the Gospel according to St. Matthew, with the intention, probably, of reminding his masters that he still hungered for a journey into Tartary and for employment there. There was no word about Mary Clarke, no suggestion that he was going to Seville primarily to meet her, that soon he would be a married man – and with a comfortable middle-aged heiress for a wife together with an accompanying twenty-one year-old-daughter. Perhaps at Mary's age it would be unlikely – and certainly this would be from his point of view strongly desirable – that she would be sexually demanding.

This is not at all to say that Borrow was a calculating man where money was concerned, a man liable to prey upon women for what they had in the way of material possessions. Borrow in the role of stalker of heiresses is quite unimaginable. It was rather she who wanted him. He was strong and she needed protection. She was a woman suddenly pushed into what was in the 1830s pretty exclusively a man's world – the world of legal jousting and financial manoeuvring. She had strong intelligence and plentiful force of character, but she knew she would fare better if she operated with a man walking in front of her. Furthermore it is reasonable to make the guess that Ann Perfrement had told her that her George was a strange one, a man vigorous,· decisive, and utterly fearless in the face of danger and threat, and at the same time a man who would all his life be in need of a mother rather than a wife.

He found a big, solid two-storied house in the Pila Seca Square in Seville which would do splendidly for himself, he thought, for the present, and for himself and the two women when they finally arrived. Brandram continued to nag. On 2 May, after his arrival in Seville, Borrow wrote him an abundantly adventurous letter.

He had had to bring off successfully an extremely hazardous smuggling operation in order to get his Testaments into Seville; an accompanying missionary friar, bound for the Philippine Islands, had been terrified by all the violence and all the butchery he had witnessed on the journey, and had been sustained by the man from Norwich, who brought this Roman priest to Seville in safety and then took leave of him 'telling him that I hoped to meet him again at Philippi...' Once again Borrow is thinking of himself as a nineteenth-century St. Paul. Brandram replied on the 22nd, vinegary as ever: ' you are in a very peculiar country – you are doubtless a man of very peculiar temperament. . . . What shall we say to your confession of a certain superstitiousness. . . . Strangers that know you not would carry away strange ideas. . . .' And what of the unseemly

Borrovian boastfulness? '. . .you say at the beginning of the description, "my usual wonderful good fortune accompanying us. . ." This
. . . savours, some of our friends would say, a little of the profane. . . .' And indeed Brandram is perfectly right. Borrow's letters
and reports to him around this time do have the flavour of the
piratical rather than the evangelical Borrow.

He hired a collection of oddities to sell his unwanted wares. 'One
of these,' he told Browne in a letter of 12 June, 'is a very remarkable
person: an aged professor of music, by birth an old Castilian. . . .This
venerable individual has just brought me the price of six Testaments
and a Gypsy Gospel which he has this day sold under the heat of an
Andalusian sun. . . .' And then there was 'a labouring bricklayer, a
native of Morea. . . . Though entirely destitute of education he has,
by his strength of character and by a kind of rude eloquence . . .
obtained such a mastery over the minds of the labouring classes of
Seville that to everything he asserts they assent . . . so that should I
employ him, which I have not yet resolved upon, I may entertain
perfect confidence. . . .' It was all a bit airy, somehow, so Earl Street
felt, so lacking the purposeful seriousness they looked for and
admired. And Borrow was startling them with views they did not like
to hear.

It is unwise to print Testaments, and Testaments *alone* for Catholic countries. . . .The Catholic, unused to Scripture reading, finds a thousand things
which he cannot possibly understand in the New Testament . . . though an
English labourer may read a Testament and derive from it the most blessed
fruit, it does not follow that a Spanish peasant will enjoy similar success, as he
will find many dark things. . . .

Had Borrow lost his fire? Certainly there was less tramping about.
He shut himself up in the house in the Pila Seca through the heat of
the day, wrote about the gipsies, and at the hour of the *paseo* in the
cool of the evening, rode around on Sidi Habismilk to take the air.

On 16 June 1839 Mary Clarke and Hen arrived in Cádiz, and on
the following day Borrow installed them in the Pila Seca. The house
had twenty rooms, so that there was no shortage of space for all three
of them. Did he sleep with Mary? The answer must be a confident
No. Borrow kept his bed to himself. Because the Sevillanos winked
and quite failed to believe in the realities of this strange *ménage à
trois*, he had to talk to people of his wife and daughter. This was
accepted though it was noticed that in Hen there was little – indeed
there was absolutely nothing at all – to suggest that here was the
daughter of her father. Yet still it was accepted; it was a very brave

person indeed who, in Borrow's own presence or anywhere in the city, would make a remark that contained the slightest hint that Borrow was a liar. He gave the ladies Bibles to sell if they could, but they both could see that not much evangelism was being carried out just then on Borrow's part. He had a room for his writing table and he shut himself up there and went to work at his book about the Spanish gipsies.

He wrote to Brandram on the 28th a propitiatory letter. Yes, he agreed that he had perhaps been 'profane' in talking of his 'wonderful good fortune'. The expression – he saw this quite clearly now, was 'objectionable, and, as you very properly observe, savours of pagan times. . .' He had been thoughtlessly repeating what a courier had said to him: 'La mucha suerte de Usted tambien nos ha acompañado en este viaje.' (Your Honour's great destiny has been shared by us also throughout this journey.) He also in this letter – and this, in all the vast mass of his correspondence with the Bible Society, is extremely rare – brought himself to introduce an expression of humility. 'I am sorry, and I will endeavour to mend,' he said. And he thought also that, in case the news filtered through to Brandram by some other channel, he ought to make mention, however dis-ingenuously, of the business of Mary Clarke and Hen. He began his paragraph by saying, 'We go on selling Testaments at Seville in a quiet satisfactory manner,' and a little later, 'Two or three ladies of my acquaintance occasionally dispose of some amongst their friends, but they say that they experience some difficulty, the cry for Bibles being so great. . . .' A characteristic of Borrow is often to stalk the truth as if it was some quivering antelope to be approached deviously, and never to achieve a close and complete coming together. But in spite of his reassurances Borrow knew, and Brandram knew, that the eventful association between the two of them was coming to its term. Official Spain was beginning now to set its face quite decisively against Don Jorge. On 1 July he parted from Antonio Buchini because he could see no busy future for him. On 8 July the *alcalde*, with his en-forcement officers, visited him and seized his Testaments. These were the remains, between a hundred and a hundred and fifty volumes, of the smuggled cargo. He sent Brandram some cumulative sales figures – about three thousand, he thought, had been sold 'during the last twelve months'. On 29 July it was resolved at Earl Street 'that as it appears . . . that the object of Mr Borrow's present Mission is nearly attained . . . it be recommended to the General Committee to request him immediately to take measures for selling such copies as he may still have on hand, or for placing them in safe custody, and to return

without loss of time to this Country.' Borrow meanwhile sent notice
of his intention (Seville having turned a blankly uncooperative face
towards him) to cross the straits and try to dispose of what stocks he
had remaining amongst the Spanish living along the Barbary coast.
And when that had been accomplished he still wanted to return to La
Mancha, risk peril, famine, and what he called 'unnatural assassination' in order to clear his copies – something under a thousand –
still unsold in Madrid. On 8 August he sailed from Gibraltar to
Tangier – before the dismissive letter from London had set out on its
way.

He left the women in Seville and found lodging in Tangier 'in the
house of a Christian woman'. There were not many Christians,
however, some two hundred and fifty in all. The Muhammadans
were in command, and Borrow was shocked, or professed to be
shocked, by what he saw of their rule:

The Sultan collects armies and marches against this or that province . . . if
successful, a thousand heads are borne before him on his return in ghastly
triumph . . . if vanquished his own not unfrequently blackens in the sun
above the gate of some town . . . here pleasure is sought in the practice of
abominations or in the chewing of noxious and intoxicating drugs; here men
make a pomp and parade of their infamy; and the cavalcade which escorts
with jealous eye the wives and concubines of the potentate on the march . . .
is also charged with the care of his *zammins*, the unfortunate youths who
administer to his fouler passions. . . .

He did not rush immediately into evangelism, but studied carefully
the conditions and paused before making any positive move. He
enjoyed himself. Here was another language barrier which he found
he could leap without losing momentum. 'I was glad to find that I
could make myself very well understood . . . the wild people, who
arrive from the far interior . . . invariably understand me best. . . .'
He spent five weeks in all in Tangier and helped by a young Jew from
Fez and a Negro slave, he could say by then that 'The blessed Book is
now in the hands of most of the Christians of Tangiers.' On 21
September he arrived back in Cádiz, and brought his young Jewish
assistant, Hayim Ben Attar, along with him. Brackenbury, the British
Consul-General, handed him the letter of recall. Before replying to it
he returned to the Plaza de la Pila Seca where Mary and Hen were
anxiously waiting for him along with another peremptory letter from
Brandram forbidding him to go to North Africa. In his reply of 29
September, Borrow showed no disposition to be rushed. He had
unfinished business. (There had been a letter also from Browne,
always much more conciliatory than Brandram, waiting for him in

Cádiz, and to this Borrow had replied immediately, saying that the news from London had left him 'sorrowful, disappointed and unstrung'.) He went on to show that he was no longer unstrung in any way. 'I am very glad that I went to Tangiers for many reasons.' He noted that Brackenbury had received a circular letter from Lord Palmerston forbidding British consuls in Spain 'to afford the slightest countenance to religious agents'. Brackenbury, however, wrote a long letter from Cádiz on 19 September defending his singular evangelist. Borrow had won his total support just as he had won Clarendon's. Graydon and Rule and the hotheads were the ones who had finally soured the Spanish authorities and made a wreck of Borrow's endeavours.

... our severe disappointments are derivable from the indiscretions of those who ... have acted in opposition to the advice and judgment of others who knew the habits and propensities of the Spaniards better than themselves. ... These opinions, so often heretofore expressed by me, are concurred in, I am happy to say, by Mr Borrow, who has an intimate knowledge of the Spanish character, and whose zeal and judgment have gone hand in hand throughout this Province.

But testimonials and Borrow's tenacious sticking to his task alike failed to bring about a change of heart in Earl Street. On November, with his defence and Brackenbury's confident praise in front of them, the answer remained the same: 'this Sub-Committee cannot recommend to the General Committee to engage the further services of Mr Borrow until he shall have returned to this Country from his Mission to Spain.'

He replied to this one from the Seville gaol, dragged there, he said, for having tried to get a passport for Córdoba for himself and Hayim Ben Attar. He had had a tremendous row with the Alcalde del Barrio, 'the greatest ruffian in Seville' – he was still peddling Bibles, the *alcalde* claimed, and would 'cause me to be knocked down if I made the slightest resistance'. He dared the *alcalde* repeatedly simply to have a try. 'Viva Inglaterra, y viva La Constitución' Borrow shouted, and the *alcalde* 'quailed before me as I looked him in the eyes defying him'. Borrow's utter fearlessness and might are nowhere better displayed than at this moment, surrounded in a far foreign land by a crowd officially hostile though with pockets of people who felt, however serious the risks attached, admiration for him.

He was only twenty-four hours a prisoner, and again he enjoyed the chance to hobnob with outlaws, 'the celebrated thief Palacio, the most expert housebreaker and dexterous swindler in Spain', a 'hand-

some, black-haired man, the modern Guzman D'Alfarache', and
Salvador 'the brawny man who sits by the *brasero* [it was the end of
November by now] . . . the highwayman of Ronda, who has committed a hundred murders. . . .' Did he shrink, as a well-schooled
evangelist might be expected to, from such scum? Not a bit of it. 'I
have never found myself amongst more quiet and well-behaved
men. . . .' Quite briefly, at the end of his zestful tale of woe, he
acknowledges his receipt of Brandram's dismissive letter. 'I received
your letter, which I read with great pleasure. You are quite right in
most of your observations. . . .' Submissive? Mocking? What was the
Bible Society to do with such a man?

Set free once more, he set out for Madrid with a retinue of gipsies.
There, before the British Representative (now the Hon. G. S. S.
Jerningham) he proposed to lay an account of the outrageous wrongs
he had suffered in Seville. This document goes over much the same
ground as that covered in his letter to Brandram written from prison;
but there are none the less interesting further details. Whilst he had
been locked away, for example, the authorities had raided his house
in the Plaza de la Pila Seca. 'In this house' – so Jerningham, respectably, prudently, and in a Borrovian sense was truly informed – 'I
possess apartments, the remainder being occupied by an English
Lady and her daughter, the former of whom is the widow of an
officer of the highest respectability who died in the naval service of
Great Britain. . . .' And the infamous *alcalde*, not content with
ransacking his rooms in his enforced absence and throwing his papers
about, had 'attempted to force his way into some apartments occupied by the Ladies, my friends. . . .' In conclusion Borrow made it
clear to Jerningham that he wanted the *alcalde*'s blood . . .

From Maria Diaz's house in Madrid he wrote again to Brandram
on 28 December. The mood of this one was that of a man about to
depart. He felt forgiving towards Graydon and Rule, those zealots
who had rushed in, roused a wasps' nest of popish fanatics, and put
Borrow's own prudent policies into disarray. 'I am not ashamed of
the *Methodists of Cadiz*; their conduct in many respects does them
honour, nor do I accuse any one of *fanaticism* amongst our dear and
worthy friends. . . .' On these italicizations Brandram was clearly
being invited to put any interpretation he pleased – provided he stood
in no doubt about how Borrow himself viewed the matter. On the
second day of the new year, 1840, he wrote the last letter he was ever
to write from the Spanish capital to Earl Street. He was first returning
to Seville because he had an account to settle with the *alcalde*; he was
also going, of course, because Mary Clarke was still in the Pila Seca,

and so was Hen, strumming on her guitar. Borrow made no mention of his domestic complications in the letter. He loved mystification almost more than extremely foreign languages; and yet it is in the highest degree unlikely that Brandram was entirely ignorant of the departure of these two ladies in the direction of the Pillars of Hercules. After all Cunningham was still in Norfolk, and Cunningham's connection with Bible Society officials was sufficiently close. On all sides it was probably felt that, in the face of a most unusual situation, silence all round was the safest reaction. In the same letter Borrow did acknowledge that he had received orders to quit. 'I hope that in a very short time I shall be able to bid adieu to the shores of Spain, which I shall quit with as little regret as the tired labourer at nightfall quits the filthy ditch in which he has been toiling during the whole of a dreary day. . . .'

Yet still Borrow strangely dawdled. In mid-March he heard, through Brackenbury, that the Society without news, was wondering what had happened to him. 'This intelligence astonished me,' he told them in a letter from Seville on 18 March. Two letters of his must have gone astray. As for his return, he had adequate reasons for putting this off. English winters were bad for his rheumatism; by staying on thus far he had managed to get the high- and rough-handed *alcalde* the sack; and finally there had been the matter of getting his papers in order after the raid. (This was Borrovian effrontery. Mary Clarke would have soon put the Pila Seca house to rights. What Borrow was concerned about was not the re-ordering of his house but the final, on-the-spot touches to his manuscript.) And indeed later in the same letter he did announce that he had 'a work nearly in readiness for publication'. But he did also – which was what Earl Street was chiefly concerned about – find room to mention that 'I embark on the 3rd of next month.' And to this he added that he wished very much 'to spend the remaining years of my life in the northern parts of China'. Did he suppose that the Bible Society would be eager to find fresh work for him after all the many shindies and after the intervention of Lord Palmerston himself? Had he brought Mary Clarke and Hen all the way out to Spain – surely a most compromising *déplacement* – just in order for them to enjoy a tranquil change of scene? It is likely that he asked himself no such questions. Putting himself in another person's place and viewing the same situation from the new angle – this was never an exercise he was good at.

The embarkation at Cádiz on 3 April as promised must have caused some stir. It was not without some ceremony that Borrow finally left the Peninsula after four and a half tempestuous years. There were

Mary Clarke and Hen and her guitar of course, there was the young Jew Hayim Ben Attar, his latest henchman, and lastly there was the Arab steed which he so loved, and which eventually had to be slung aboard. On 16 April they docked in London. On Monday 20 April he was carpeted. The next day Brandram wrote: 'Your later communications have been referred to our Sub-Committee for General Purposes. After what you said yesterday in the Committee [and he had cleansed his bosom of perilous stuff] I am hardly aware that anything can arise out of them. The door seems shut. . . . I do not myself at present see any sphere open to which your services in connexion with our Society can be transferred.'

It was all over. On 23 April – a rush job – George Henry Borrow and Mary Clarke were married at St. Peter's, Cornhill. He had married a comfortably endowed middle-aged person with a property in the East Anglia he loved. He even had a grown-up stepdaughter. Tartary looked further off than ever before. The vagrant days would never come again. Well, they might, perhaps, but not in any determined, neck-or-nothing way.

The couple went, almost immediately, to live at Oulton Cottage. Oulton Hall had been let and was bringing in an income. Borrow did not, at any rate in the early stages, have to ask for any dole. He had savings from his Bible Society stipend, and the regular sums he had sent back to Ann Perfrement in Norwich had not been spent by her but put by for his return. The cottage was a solitary place. Oulton Broad lapped it on one side. You had to use a footpath in order to reach a road; 'girt with dark firs, through which the wind sighs sadly,' wrote Richard Ford after a visit. And in the grounds there was a gazebo which Mary Borrow fitted up as a study for George; Captain Borrow's sword and uniform hung on the door. Hayim Ben Attar was housed in a lean-to. But would Borrow settle? About this there never ceased to be doubts. Borrow liked company – rough company for preference – whilst Oulton was more suitable for a hermit. If company did turn up there, he could not be depended upon to act the part of a comfortably-off country gentleman. He would, perhaps, start singing in his high, unlovely voice, or he would offer a guest a book written in an unlikely language and ask for it to be read aloud – and be unreasonably petulant when the request was declined. He could be quite convivial, but if he took a party out for a walk he tended to forget about them and stride away, a powerful motor-boat leaving a covey of canoes.

But Mary was fond of him – 'loved' is scarcely perhaps the word – and mothered him. She even fussed over him. Powerful though he was, he had been through many fevers and sicknesses and strains during his long time in Spain, so she fed him well and accepted his singularities. He would go off, on foot or on Sidi Habismilk, to visit his mother and Lucy Brightwell in Norwich or other friends round about; sometimes he would simply go off – revert, in fact, to the early wandering – and return only after many days. When this happened he liked Mary to treat the affair as if it had been a matter of an hour's brisk march round the property, and she learnt to do this. Because she knew little or no Spanish she was even quite pleased to be called 'Carreta', although this is Castilian for a long, narrow cart. Probably this is an example of Borrow's linguistic carelessness and he meant 'carita' – a little dear; possibly he meant 'querida' which would be the likelier Spanish word. Whichever way it was, Mary Borrow was satisfied; she knew he meant well. The long winter evenings passed in cushioned cosiness behind drawn curtains. Mary read or knitted; Hen busied herself with indoor plants, wrote stories, accompanied the Spanish songs she had learnt on her guitar. Borrow listened, held them with ghost stories, or told them of his adventures – experimenting how to be most effective in future books.

Yet the future books were slow in coming. He fiddled about in the gazebo, but when would *The Zincali* be finished? Old literary loves – Kaempe Viser, ap Gwilym – awoke to charm him. He could not be persuaded that lumpish verse translation of ancient balladists was not his *métier*. Mary kept her husband more or less on course by making a fair copy of *The Zincali*. It would be full of 'ridiculous errata', he considered, but she was clever enough to ignore this ingratitude and push on. By November he was ready to put on his best black, go up to London, and call on Mr Murray in Albemarle Street. He had tried to see 'Glorious John' many times seventeen years earlier during his first assault on literary London, but had never then reached the presence. This time however it was different. He was decently clad, clearly a man of some substance. He was granted an audience.

John Murray II, 'Anak of publishers' as Byron had called him, was by now a man of sixty-two, with only three more years to go. He agreed to consider *The Zincali*. It seemed a ragbag sort of book, but it was about foreign parts and he was already having great success with his guide-books. Moreover Borrow's fortitude and endurance on behalf of the Bible Society in Spain had earned him some small fame in London: Glorious John would have heard his name mentioned. So he sent the manuscript off to Devonshire, inviting Richard Ford, busy with his *Handbook for Travellers in Spain*, to give an opinion on it.

Ford advised publication. Ford was the man who first saw that in Borrow, the eccentric literary misfit, there lay strong and undeniable genius. *The Zincali* on its own was nothing – how characteristic of the man that he failed even to get its Romany title right: he should have written *Zincala* – but there was evident to the discerning man this author's gift for the evocation of wild outsider people, for the writing of strange, enchanting, stylized dialogues. Ford in fact saw someone who might be bullied, or coaxed, into writing a masterpiece. Murray printed 750 copies of Borrow's book. It had a modest success. The *Edinburgh Review* said it was 'a hotch-potch of the jockey, tramper, philologist and missionary' which was accurate enough and not perhaps as damning as the notice intended it to be. The book went on selling, modestly and slowly. A fourth edition of 7,500 copies came out in 1846 and as late as 1870 a fifth edition of 1,000 copies was issued.

But Ford was not greatly interested in the fortunes of *The Zincali*. He was concerned much more about what might follow. He met Borrow in London in December 1840. He gave advice – always a risky thing to do where Borrow was concerned, but Borrow felt an immediate affinity to this rich, wandering, generous dilettante. Ford, in effect, told him to get on with the tale. He suggested – this was brave – that he should avoid poetry; he made it clear that his writing would benefit if he avoided abstractions, fake-philosophizing, and his unappeasable itch to quote at great length from unknown and almost always boring authors. He urged finally the basic thing: that Borrow should be himself, that he should do his best to recreate on paper not the man he sometimes thought he was, nor the man he often thought he would like to be, but the man who, in differing situations acted not in accordance with policies and convictions previously worked out and decided upon, but *like that*.

Borrow was braced. He returned to Oulton and his ladies determined to work on his big Spanish book. Naturally there came waverings in his resolution. The winter of 1841 was harsh, and the shores of Oulton Broad emphasized its harshness. Local sorties failed to satisfy his large restlessness. He thought of trips to Berlin, to Constantinople, vaguely of some fanning-out in Africa beyond the Tangier he knew. Hasfeld wrote and told him to come out to Denmark. Ford suggested he should return to Seville. But Carreta's little income would not run to anything on this scale, and indeed he would never dream of suggesting any such disbursement. He tried Clarendon, Lord Privy Seal by now, to see if he would be willing to sound Palmerston about the possibility of a consulship – Stendhal, another literary man, was in that very year to suffer his first stroke in dismal Civitavecchia, but Borrow was not to know about that. They never met of course, and unquestionably it was fortunate for Stendhal that they did not: five minutes in each other's company would have been quite enough time for Borrow to have felled him almost as finally as the stroke.

Much of *The Bible in Spain* was already in some form down on paper. He wrote to Brandram to ask for his letters back, and Brandram, less obdurate than usual, agreed to this, provided no whiff of disagreement between the Society and their employee should appear in anything he chose to write. Mary assembled scattered papers, recopied his angular handwriting, and in January 1842 he sent Glorious John a sizeable manuscript. It contained extracts from the Society letters together with a first draft of *The Bible in Spain* as we now know it. This again was passed to Ford whose reaction was as before: more sharpness, more action, more people, more drama. Borrow's gifts as a writer of dialogue were recognized, but Ford thought that some of the conversations were too stilted and should be reshaped. Borrow took fairly kindly to all this, though understandably he showed no wish to enlarge on the final Sevillan phase of his mission. Within six weeks a revised version was in Murray's hands. But Borrow had grown unused to writing concentratedly and continuously and at home he began to get wild and ungovernable. A quarrel about a dog arose with the Oulton dissenting minister. Notes in the third person were exchanged between the two and Borrow's attitude became so extreme as to border on the irrational. He relieved his pent-up feelings by spending a week breaking in a horse. '. . . he can be bought for eight pounds but no person will have him; it is said that he kills everybody who mounts him. I have been *charming* him, and have so far succeeded that he does not fling me more than once in five minutes. . . .' Ford though was pleased with the laboriously revised version. '*Gil Blas* with a touch of Bunyan' he said – and that can still stand as the best seven-word summary of *The Bible in Spain*.

During the summer, waiting for his book to come out, he turned again to what he had already written about the distant days of 1824 and 1825. *Lavengro* and *The Romany Rye* had not as yet any presentable shape, but already they had got much further than simply existing as dozings in his head. He found composing slow. Truth and fantasy both plucked at his sleeve, urging him on but not always in quite the same direction.

In December he received his review copies of *The Bible in Spain: or the Journeys, Adventures and Imprisonments of an Englishman in an attempt to circulate the Scriptures in the Peninsula.* He sent one to his mother, dated 13 December: 'Ann Borrow with her son's best love'; and in January the book came out properly. It was a great and immediate success. A second edition was called for that same month, a third in March, a fourth in June, a fifth in July. The French wanted a translation; so did the Germans. The United States became excited about it. Borrow found himself with so much sudden fame that he hardly knew what to do with it. Was it the wealthy and evangelical party that caused the book to take wing in the way it did? It is hardly likely. Peel mentioned the book in the House of Commons, and he, it is true, stressed the missionary element. 'It might have been said, to Mr Borrow with respect to Spain, that it would be impossible to distribute the Bible in that country in consequence of the danger of offending the prejudices which prevail there; yet he, a private individual, by showing some zeal in what he believed to be right, succeeded in triumphing over many obstacles.'

His sudden fame was a consolation during the long winter. But his mood would change swiftly and drastically. Melancholy thoughts of his end crowded on to him. He took singing lessons. Carreta caught cold and this increased his gloom because it emphasized his dependence on her. When spring came he got on Sidi Habismilk at dawn and rode from village to village till night. The horse came back exhausted ; the rider's spirits remained far from tranquil. The admiring letters that flooded in were all very well, but why did no one offer him a job, a cause he might fight for? Might he not lead a campaign against the papists who were becoming uppity, encouraged by the rise of the arch-fiend Daniel O'Connell plotting away in Ireland? Was not Nicholas Patrick Wiseman the mischief-maker, hand-in-glove with him? Carreta lived calmly with his tantrums, his despairs, and his glory. She urged him to be positive and to take action. How well already she understood him. In May he went to London.

The reception he got was enough to turn a head steadier than Borrow's. Everybody who mattered wanted to meet him. He attended receptions given by important people and what hostess could possibly feel that a man of Borrow's stature and colouring did not, by his mere presence, give good value for his entertainment? Yet still huge depressions could sweep over him. 'I did wrong,' he wrote to Carreta in May 1843, 'not to bring you when I came, for without you I cannot get on at all. Left to myself a gloom comes over me which I cannot describe. . . .' He dined with the Murrays and Glorious John talked of another edition running to 10,000 copies – to sell to the Colonies and to dish the piratical Americans who were

living handsomely and for nothing on the backs of both Murray and
Borrow. He walked in Richmond Park with his publisher, and
Murray, naturally enough with a big success on his hands, urged him
to give presentable shape as quickly as possible to the autobiography
which already existed cloudily and in jottings. On the last day of May
– in five weeks he would be forty – he felt adrift in London; he felt he
had come to the end of a life filled with feverish industry, dreamlike
adventure, and strange wanderings; what now lay ahead was the
problem of how to handle a long and featureless aftermath. London
was not for him – not the grand salons, not the literary sociabilities of
the Murray circle, not even the enthusiastic championing of him by
Ford who had come at least part of the way towards understanding
him. He sat down, heavy with all this, and wrote a melancholy,
strangely grudging, letter to Carreta.

I passed last Sunday at Clapham with Mrs Browne [wife of Brandram's
assistant], I was glad to go there for it was a gloomy day. They are now glad
enough to ask me: I suppose I must stay in London through next week. I have
an invitation to two grand parties, and it is as well to have something for one's
money. . . . I have nothing more to say save to commend you not to go on the
water without me; perhaps you would be overset; and do not go on the
bridge again until I come. Take care of Habismilk . . . kiss the little mare and
old Hen. . . .

They are not the words of a lionized man.
    In June he was back in Oulton. Daniel O'Connell continued to be a
worry. Should he rake up some volunteers, put himself at their head
mounted on Habismilk, cross the water and face him? By autumn the
impulse had faded, but Hayim Ben Attar in his little annexe began to
have depressions like his employer. The climate of the Norfolk
Broads was one he could not get used to. He had to be returned to
Tangier. Borrow paced about his property and became exceedingly
quarrelsome towards trespassers, inviting them to put their fists up.
The reaction is odd, because half of him – or more than half of him –
always felt kinship with vagabonds, poachers, and trespassers. If
Ambrose Petulengro and his gipsies were in the neighbourhood the
welcome they got from Borrow was of the warmest; even George
Wombwell with his travelling circus and his seedy little menagerie
was received with delight. However, it took him a long time to get
George Borrow the landed proprietor, and George Borrow who was
Don Jorge and Lavengro and Romany Rye to march harmoniously
side by side. In the end he decided to accept that he was a man with
two faces. He would be the sober, comfortably-off, Church of

England man who turned a stern face against violence and lawlessness and the wearing of the green and the spreading strength of popery; and he would also lounge in pubs with cronies, swilling beer in great quantities and talking of wagering and fist-fights. And he would write the book that John Murray III, successor now to Glorious John, so wanted.

Ford visited him in January 1844 and stayed four days. They went about by coach through the endless rain, and drank and smoked in the evenings conspiring to keep each other's courage up. But after the departure of his guest the deepest melancholy dropped down on him. At any cost he felt he must soon be on the move again. The book would have to wait. He would begin to make preparations. Mary encouraged and helped to get him ready. She herself had bronchitis badly – Oulton was so damp – but she summoned enough strength to persuade him to work for a while on *Lavengro* before he went, so that Murray's impatience could be allayed. Ann Perfrement came from Norwich to be with her while he was journeying; and then, in March, he was off, staying briefly in London. He met Lady Eastlake there, a sharp, imperious lady of the same breed as Harriet Martineau. She brought out all the boorish aggressiveness in him – as she noted in her Journal: 'March 20. Borrow came in the evening; now a fine man, but a most disagreeable one; a kind of character that would be most dangerous in rebellious times – one that would suffer and persecute to the utmost. His face is expressive of strong-headed determination.' Lady Eastlake was not wholly wrong, but not wholly right either. She did not know about his horrors; she did not know about that streak of utter dependence on women which is there for anyone to see in his relations with his mother, with Maria Diaz, and with Carreta.

He was abroad until 16 November 1844, and it is a time of his life we know little about. He wrote home to Carreta giving selective accounts of what he was doing; he also wrote to John Murray III, but there is nothing upon which to base a continuous narrative. It is reasonable to guess though that the chief purpose of his journey (one perhaps not plainly admitted even to himself) was to seek out the Hungarian gipsies and to fraternize with them. He wrote to Carreta from Budapest on 14 June. 'Hungary is a widely different country to Austria, not at all civilised, no coaches etc. . . . however it is all the same thing to me as I am quite used to rough it. . . . I have also been about another chapter and get on tolerably well [this to reassure her]; were I not so particular I should get on faster. . . . Kind remembrances. . . .' Nothing about gipsies of course because he knew that that was unlikely to go down well, but writing from Debreczen on 8 July he does bring them in, although guardedly. 'I have already met with

several Gypsies; those who lived abroad in the wildernesses are quite
black; the more civilised wander about as musicians, playing on the
fiddle . . . they speak the same languages as those in England, with
slight variations, and upon the whole they understand me very
well. . . .' He ended with an account of a visit he had paid to a man
about to be hanged – blood-curdling circumstances, but Borrow tells
it all in a quiet Sunday-schoolish way, probably to keep the ladies
from worrying. However Charles Brace, who published a book
called *Hungary in 1851* had something to say of him which is closer to
the mark than anything to be deduced from his letters.

My companions, as we rode along, related some marvellous stories of a
certain English traveller, who had been there, and of his influence over the
Gypsies. . . . He did more good among them, all said, than all the laws over
them, or the benevolent efforts for them, of the last half century. . . . They
described his appearance – his tall, *lank*, muscular form . . . and I saw that
must be . . . Mr Borrow.

He crossed into Transylvania where again the gipsies were numerous,
and thence to Bucharest. By September he was in Constantinople,
brushing up his Turkish which had been neglected, and from here on
the 16th he wrote to Carreta. He wanted money and he hated asking
for it since she was still, for all his fame, the keeper of the purse. He
talked urgently of home. He had given up the idea of revisiting
Russia.

The people here are very kind in their way, but home is home, especially such
a one as mine, with true hearts to welcome me . . . your letters . . . quite
revived me. . . . I count so on getting into my summer-house again, and
sitting down to write; I have arranged my book in my mind. . . . My journey,
with God's help, has done me a great deal of good. I am stronger than I was,
and I can now sleep. I intend to draw on England for forty or fifty
pounds. . . .

He fills up with picturesque details, yet somehow it is a jaded
Borrow, a man still not quite himself. Two more letters followed, one
from Venice and one from Rome, but still snippety and lacking the
old zest – except when he climbed to the top of Mount Olympus and
'saw a whole herd of wild deer bounding down the cliffs, the noise
they made was like thunder' and then, by 16 November he was home
at Oulton, with another English winter ahead, and his moodiness still
strong. He returned determined none the less to abide by his promises and to finish the autobiography which he was to call *Lavengro*;
but in spite of what he had said to Carreta about that beckoning
summer-house, he was still reluctant to settle – and too eager to pick a
quarrel.

CHAPTER 9

CELTS AND THE BEGINNING
OF TWILIGHT

FORD wrote in December, welcoming him back; there was nowhere quite like one's own paddock, he thought. However the Borrows' paddock was about to be sliced in two by a rail-link that would plough its way right between Oulton Hall and Oulton Cottage, a prospect too monstrous to contemplate. Borrow lamented that coaches would be driven off the road and that soon the population would be possessed by the *envie de se déplacer*, to be somewhere other than their proper place which was the place they had been born in (he was a fine one to talk). Yet when Ford sympathized with him about the railway – 'Sell and be off' was his advice – Borrow took offence.

In the spring of 1845 he had bad feverish attacks which were probably recurrences of the malaria he had come back with from Spain. Ford sent him his *Handbook for Travellers in Spain*, hoping that he would review it for the *Quarterly*: 'You will do it magnificently. "Thou art the man".' The book reminded Borrow of all his own Spanish troubles and frustrations, but he laboured at the review and by June had thirty-seven folio sheets ready for Murray. Carreta however was not happy with what he had produced and she wrote to Murray: '[the article] must not be received as a specimen of what Mr Borrow would have produced had he been well. . . .' Murray handed the bulky manuscript over to his editor, Lockhart, who found that it contained far too much about Borrow and his Spanish griefs and not enough about Ford's *Handbook*: 'I am very sorry . . . that I must return his paper. . . .' Carreta perhaps wondered whether tact ought in rightness to be so strenuously exercised. Ford assured Borrow that he was not to worry at all about this rejection; however, Borrow had got to the unappealing stage of life when the tendency to find small matters that can be counted irritating, has a way of becoming strong.

In 1846 he flung off again without much warning and walked the length of the Thames. In 1847 he made fresh efforts to get himself appointed Justice of the Peace: was he not now a considerable landed proprietor since in 1846 Carreta had become the owner of Oulton Hall; was not the whole district overrun with poachers and evil-doers? He put his case to Clarendon. All that Clarendon was able to do however was refer the matter to the Lord Lieutenant, and after some while Stradbroke wrote back to say that they had good magistrates and what was more, quite enough of them. The fact was that Borrow's oddities and wildnesses were quite well known by now in his part of the world, and the sound of George Borrow, JP seemed to them ridiculous.

Borrow was famous – and at the same time rejected. He belonged to two mutually exclusive worlds and could not bring himself to give up one in favour of the other. It was this struggle battling inside him which was the cause of the nine restless, quarrelsome, unhappy years he spent after coming back from Spain. It made him uncivil to people who had no wish to wound him and who even admired him. Bowring was picked on. Bowring was doing well for himself – a busy MP and, as he told Borrow, his son had just been elected fellow of Trinity College, Cambridge. Borrow informed him sourly, with no supporting evidence, that Trinity dons married their bedders. Bowring was scheming to get himself nominated commercial representative in Egypt, Syria, and Turkey, and he wondered about trade possibilities with Siberia. He asked Borrow's advice because had not Borrow given it out long ago that he had been as far as Kiachta? Borrow hastened to be helpful, seeing in Bowring a man who might land him that longed-for consulship in China. Bowring thought that there might be a possibility, but no summons to London for interview came. Was Bowring passing off all the information Borrow had accumulated as his own? At the end of 1847 Bowring got his job but still there was no breath of a word about a consulship for Borrow. Bowring, it appeared, had done his genuine best for him, but Borrow chose to be enraged. Men were deceivers. All the Spaniards (Maria Diaz and perhaps Usoz excepted), Lockhart (perhaps Borrow was not far off the mark there), Bowring – untrustworthy, swindling rogues all of them. Everywhere you looked there was villainy. Old England – Thurtell's England – which had been rough and open and manly, where you could ride your horse without its bolting from the noise of a whistling, steam-driven monstrosity (the cutting was finished, with a bridge for Borrow to cross to church) – was becoming effete and corrupt.

Bowring, the purposeful, perfectly well-meaning Bowring, was written into the Appendix to *The Romany Rye*, Borrow's lament at his remembrance of things past, as

a thin and weaselly figure, [with] a sallow complexion, a certain obliquity of vision and a large pair of spectacles... [he] uttered the most desperate Radicalism.... Being informed that the writer was something of a philologist, to which character the individual in question laid great pretensions, he came and sat down by him, and talked about languages and literature. The writer, who was only a boy, was a little frightened at first....

He doubtless had Bowring in mind too, on writing:

What constitutes a gentleman? ... there are no distinctions in what is gentlemanly, as there are in what is genteel. The characteristics of a gentleman are high feeling – a determination never to take a cowardly advantage of another – a liberal education – absence of narrow views – generosity and courage, propriety of behaviour.... Is the emperor a gentleman, with spatters of blood on his clothes, scourged from the backs of Hungarian women? Are the aristocracy gentlefolks, who admire them? Is Mr Flamson a gentleman, although he has a million pounds? No! cowardly miscreants, and people who make a million pounds by means compared with those employed to make fortunes by the getters up of the South Sea Bubble might be called honest dealing, are decidedly not gentlefolks....

Flamson was his name for Peto, the initiator of the railway line and there are certainly signs of a genuine persecution mania developing in Borrow at this time. The Appendix to *The Romany Rye* reeks of it. He snubbed people for no cause whatever.

In 1847 he was present at a party along with Thackeray. And chatting fluently as was his way, Thackeray said something about what a bore it was to have to make money so as to provide for one's daughters by delivering lectures – they were to appear later as *The English Humourists of the Eighteenth Century* – but from Borrow there came no response but sourness. So Thackeray tried another tack – quite innocently because by then Thackeray had reached the stage when there was no need at all for him to pace about casting flies in order to catch compliments – 'Have you read my Snob Papers in *Punch*?' 'In *Punch*? It is a periodical I never look at.' It seemed indeed as though he was beginning to lose the capacity to establish reasonable, friendly relations with anybody except for the women at Oulton Cottage and his mother, by now in her middle seventies and still hanging on at Willow Lane. Like that other, later, troubled creature T. H. White he began to find solace only in the company of animals.

He worked at the autobiography only in sudden spurts, turning

Portrait of George Borrow by Henry Phillips, 1843.

Oulton Cottage from the Broad. Sketch by Henrietta MacOubrey.

The only known photograph of George Borrow,
taken in the garden of Mrs Simms Reeve in 1848.

THE BEGINNING OF TWILIGHT

over and over what had been running in his mind for so long. John Murray III kept pressing him – the likeliest way to make him even more stubborn. In the Advertisement, or preface, to *The Romany Rye* in 1857 he wrote: 'It having been frequently stated in print that the book called *Lavengro* was got up expressly against the popish agitation, in the years 1850–51, the author takes this opportunity of saying that the principal part of that book was written in the year '43, that the whole of it was completed before the termination of the year '46, and that it was in the hands of the publisher in the year '48. . . .' It is true that in October 1848 he sent his work – unfinished – to be set up by the printer Woodfall and that by December 1848 Murray had arranged for it to be subscribed for. But Borrow still wanted more time. Instead of sticking to his book he went tramping. This was not from idleness – no man was ever less idle – but from a desperate attempt to shake off melancholia.

The whole of 1849 went by, and still no book. By now his mother had grown too old to manage for herself and that summer he moved her to Oulton Hall to lodge with his tenant farmer there. In December Murray did his best to soothe the subscribers but he must have wondered if his author was ever likely to deliver. Woodfall fretted too; he wanted the setting finished. Borrow invited him to Oulton Cottage, and for once he was able when he got back to London to report that he had found a Borrow hard at work and outwardly at least cheerful. Very soon, he thought, copy to complete would be arriving. But then followed another bout of depression. Mary and Hen did their best to revive his spirits. They took him off to Yarmouth, and without her husband's knowledge Mary wrote both to Murray and Woodfall imploring them to be patient even still, and not to nag their author. Bravely they consented to bottle their feelings up. Ford wrote to tell him, 'I am sure it will be *the* book of the year when it is brought forth.'

At last Borrow got to the end of his third and – according to the agreement made – final volume. But *Lavengro* of course does not end at all. Borrow simply stops in mid-career. He has not yet taught Belle how to say 'I love you' in Armenian. It ends in fact with a long inserted story about Mumbo Jumbo, told to Belle and Lavengro as they sit together in the tent beside a fire of scattered red coals over which Lavengro has scattered a small portion of sugar. 'No bad smell,' says the postillion, and plunges into a tale about 9,000 words long. At the end of it he says: 'Young gentleman, I will now take a spell on your blanket – young lady, good-night.' And at that point, just for the hell of it, Borrow throws down his pen, packs up the sheets, and tells Mary to be off with the parcel to London. That was in November 1850. As Saintsbury put it, 'Lavengro itself ends with a more startling abruptness than perhaps any nominally complete book before or since.'

Borrow's grip upon the book had suddenly slackened. He had got himself into a muddle between that distant dream-summer of 1825 and his anti-popery obsessions of 1850. Newman had announced his conversion that September, Pius IX had re-established the Roman Catholic Church in England, had named Wiseman as Archbishop, and was soon to raise him to the cardinalate. Borrow wrote a hurried preface to his manuscript warning his considerably excited countrymen – Pius and Wiseman had frequently been burnt in effigy around the country – of Spanish turmoil as he had himself experienced it springing up in England. Murray urged him to tone this down; Borrow did so (and, as we have seen, he tried to dissociate the book from those issues still further in 1857), and Murray, thankful to have at last got three volumes out of him – Lavengro runs to about 200,000 words – gave Woodfall his go-ahead. Long-promised, Lavengro appeared on 7 February 1851.

Borrow was in his forty-ninth year. His book ran counter to the Zeitgeist and was a flop. It is a sound maxim amongst publishers that a highly successful book needs to be swiftly followed up. Pickwick Papers began serialization in 1836; in 1837 Oliver Twist was set on his way. Borrow had not this kind of business flair; he fantasized too much. Eight years had gone by since The Bible in Spain had so greatly taken the public fancy. Times had changed much more rapidly than in any eight years since 1641. In 1851 the last ditch was no longer a popular place to make for. In spite of those scattered effigy-burnings, the general feeling was that it was right to be willing to accept change, to be 'progressive'. 1851 was the year of the Great Exhibition. It was also the year, perhaps more positively than any other year of British history, when social problems became recognized as challenges to be taken up with vigour and delight. Dickens was thinking very much of how to support a Guild for Literature and Art – forerunner of a welfare Ministry of the Fine Arts – and was at the same time enjoying himself with his amateur play-productions designed to raise money for such a project. It was a time when people in far larger numbers than ever before were beginning to find time to take life seriously. People – all people – mattered; and tolerance was an expression of one's faith in the notion that people mattered. Borrow's Lavengro took no account of any of this. The Dickens-Kingsley attitudes were not and never could be his.

The critics damned it or disregarded it. There were a few voices prepared to give it praise, but these were for the most part friends and local Norfolk people. Dr Gordon Hake, who, it will be recalled, gave an account of Borrow's rescue in the *Bury Post*, wrote a letter to the *New Monthly Review* to announce that '*Lavengro's* roots will strike deep into the soil of English letters,' but Harrison Ainsworth, who edited the paper, had already on his own account given it a lukewarm reception. Ford, the great encourager, had to confess that he was 'somewhat disappointed' and John Murray III who had been so remarkably patient and who backed his belief in Borrow by printing 3,000 copies, wrote to Carreta to say that Borrow's preface was 'quaint', adding reassuringly, 'but so is everything Mr Borrow writes'. It was a backward-looking book – that was the general view. Should any book, in the mid-nineteenth century, have quite so improvised an air? Were not all the rogues and vagabonds Borrow wandered about with people dragged out of a time long past, a ranting, roaring, pugilistic, beer-swilling age quite out of keeping with the sober earnestness of the young Queen and her Consort? *The Bible in Spain* was full of adventures, certainly, and most enjoyable to read about, but the man at the centre of it all was moved by praise-worthy evangelical principles: who was this new man come to replace him, who told tall stories and was shifty?

Borrow's persecution mania grew stronger. He was, he felt, the victim of a conspiracy of hate. He wanted to retreat, to become anonymous. He was reluctant even to sign his name: an enemy might steal the signature and – in some way which he never explained – use it against him. Back from London and cornered in Oulton Cottage he glared out at a hostile world. Even the level-headed Carreta became concerned and decided on the nineteenth-century cure-all, a change of air. In March she took him off to Yarmouth again, and there every morning Borrow walked out of the town to a beach where he could be alone. There he took his clothes off and plunged into the sea and swam out using his dog-paddle stroke. The winds were keen and penetrating but he took no notice of that. Out he went, distancing himself from his detractors.

Back in Oulton that April he was gradually coaxed out of his resentments by Carreta. No writer ever owed more to a woman than Borrow to Mary Clarke. She was fifty-five by now, wore a bonnet trimmed with lace which was quite out of fashion, but she was good-humoured, easy to get on with, difficult to ruffle, and a first-rate manager not only of household affairs but also of her husband's tormented literary scramblings. As East Anglia slowly pulled itself clear of winter she was able to give him back some confidence. During that summer she sent him up, with Hen, to see the Great Exhibition, and although he hated Peto and his railway he was swept by sudden enthusiasm. Here, laid out magnificently for all to see, was proof of British originality, inventiveness, and might. Perhaps he had been wrong to cry ruin so loudly. Foreigners of course were there in great abundance and this delighted him. He felt like one of the Apostles at Pentecost; once again he had the chance to speak with other tongues, and he charged about quite unselfconsciously doing just that, causing amazement because indeed his linguistic range was remarkable. He was a Tower of Babel come to life. Hen had to calm him down and persuade him to come away.

The following December Palmerston took it upon himself to congratulate the French ambassador on Louis Napoleon's *coup d'état* without first seeking the views either of the Queen or of the Prime Minister, Lord John Russell. He had in consequence to relinquish the Foreign Office; and Borrow, always a staunch Palmerston man, for once with the majority of his countrymen, was greatly dismayed. Early in 1852 he had to watch Harriet Beecher Stowe enjoy a wildfire success with *Uncle Tom's Cabin*. Why, he asked himself, was it proving so extraordinarily difficult to dispose of the 3,000 copies of *Lavengro* which Murray had printed? If this was the public attitude towards him, what point was there in going on with *The Romany Rye*?

In 1853 he came to know Whitwell Elwin, who as well as being rector of Booton in Norfolk, was from that year the editor of the *Quarterly Review*. The disgruntled Borrow of the 1850s, still feeling deeply aggrieved at the cold reception given to *Lavengro* by the important papers, was eager to pick a quarrel with the absentee parson on meeting him for the first time. He advised him frankly to choose as his second job something less cut-throat than editing the *Quarterly*. Then, in the hectoring manner he had come to cultivate, he asked about Elwin's churchmanship. 'What party are *you* in the Church – Tractarian, Moderate, or Evangelical? I am happy to say that I am the old *High*.' Elwin, a kindly, unassuming man whom Thackeray, recalling *The Vicar of Wakefield*, called 'a grandson of the late Dr Primrose', was nevertheless not a man prepared to allow himself to be browbeaten. 'I am happy to say that I am not,' he replied. Borrow, used by now to seeing people get flustered by his conversational tactics, was a bit taken aback and changed course. He started to boast about how good he was at handling the Norfolk dialect and gave Elwin a demonstration. 'I told him,' Elwin later reported, 'that he had not cultivated it with his usual success.' This bluff, no-nonsense stance of Elwin's was of course entirely the right one to adopt when dealing for the first time with Borrow, and thereafter the two got on well and promised to visit each other. Indeed that October Elwin wanted him to write for the *Quarterly*, but Borrow was not yet willing to play cards with the devil. 'Never,' he told Elwin. 'I have made a resolution never to have anything to do with such a blackguard trade.' For this second meeting Borrow had walked over to Booton from Oulton. It was a long way – all of thirty miles – and Elwin was astonished to see him tramping up to his fine new rectory, green umbrella in hand. 'But Mr Borrow, where is your horse?' 'I've walked it,' Borrow told him in high good spirits, and apart from the little outburst about the blackguard trade, harmony and peace prevailed throughout the visit. He sang Romany songs to the Elwin children, talked about *The Romany Rye* in the tones of a man determined to go on and confident of finishing his book, and was encouraged by Elwin who promised to review it when the time came. Back at Oulton he wrote to Elwin to say how much he had enjoyed himself, and sent him a packet of tea.

Gordon Hake, always his supporter, was now admitted to close friendship, and it was Hake as a medical man who advised him about Carreta. Oulton, he was sure, was much too damp a place for her in the winter; and this was enough to stir Borrow to swift action. He sought out rooms for the three of them in Yarmouth, a place with a bracing climate which suited both well enough to hold them there for an extended stay of seven years. Here – and almost immediately – took place the famous rescue from drowning which introduces readers of this book to its wayward hero and which gave him a lift. He would go on with his autobiography, even if only in a private way; he would do all he could to conquer his depressions and surmount his sense of grievance. He was still, he told himself, a doer of great deeds. The six winter weeks spent in Cornwall by invitation amongst his Cornish cousins as a result of his new Don Jorge-type adventure further revived him. There was a new Celtic language to be investigated – a challenge to his antiquarianism because Cornish had been officially pronounced dead only in 1777, when tough young Thomas Borrow was already nineteen. There were dolmens and pixies and folk-tales to delight him, and he got, as he put it, 'a hospitable reception, with a log on the fire' because, at any rate for the small literary-minded few amongst his welcomers, he was a famous writing man coming home.

At the beginning of February 1854 he started back, with travel-notes from which to make a book, once *The Romany Rye* – for so long a work in progress, written only in scraps by fits and starts – was out. And he stayed for a fortnight in London to work in the British Museum, digging out material for the Appendix to that work. The Cornish exhilarations dropped away from him, and he became gloomy again. Murray and Woodfall were all kindness and encouragement – monumentally patient men they both must have been – but Borrow's tetchiness refused to be soothed away. He brooded over his wrongs, struggled with the Appendix – and the two processes ran side by side. Even the letters he wrote home to Carreta were full of spleen.

I am in rooms . . . for which I pay thirty shillings a week. I live as economically as I can. . . . Please to send me a five pound note by return of post . . . the letter which I received from you this morning . . . was hardly worth while making me more melancholy than I am. . . . With respect to literature, I am tired of it and believe that there is little to be got by it, unless by writing humbug, which I can't and will not do. My spirits are very low and your letters make them worse. I shall probably return by the end of next week; but I shall want some more money. . . .

Carreta had much to put up with, but she never faltered in fidelity or support.

His revived passion for the Celtic arts and the Celtic past made Wales a source of interest. That summer the journey was made, and this time Carreta had a hand in it. Lone tramps, she had clearly decided, were not always good for her husband's state of mind. She went on ahead and rented a splendid, spacious house in Llangollen which would comfortably accommodate all three of them. Borrow, of course, would have to be allowed off the leash for his vast pilgrimages in search of dead bards and living legends, but she would be there, reasonably close at hand, to regulate the routines of life and to keep an eye on him.

It is undoubtedly the presence of the two women which makes the book *Wild Wales* – not finally published, and even then reluctantly, by John Murray till eight years had gone by – the happy, flawed masterpiece it undoubtedly is. In it Borrow is himself again, the scatty, dreamy adventurer who speeds about untamed places and makes improbable people live. He tracked down the grave of Goronwy Owen, he climbed to the top of Caer Gybi Head in Anglesey, meditated on the wars and tumults of the Welsh past, remembered how Suetonius had savaged the Island of Mon, the mother of Wales. 'I figured to myself long-bearded men with white vestments toiling up the rocks, followed by fierce warriors with glittering helms. . . .' As guide he employed a Llangollen weaver who spoke no English. The boots in the hotel at Holyhead turned out to be a poet. How delightful, and peculiarly Welsh, that was. He heard sailors in a pub in Port Dinorwic talking about sea-serpents. Were there such creatures? Borrow could not resist bursting in with an 'Of course there were' – all this, in Welsh naturally – and no longer ago than 1805 something 'like an immense worm' had been seen undulating skittishly along the surface of the Menai Straits. The subject was gone into thoroughly and then, having finished his jug of ale, Borrow headed briskly on for Caernarvon. . . . At the Castle Inn there he talks to an ailing young Englishman up for a long stay amongst the mountains and hoping to better his health, and this encounter caused him to 'think how insensible I had hitherto been to the possession of the greatest of all terrestrial blessings. I had always had the health of an elephant. . . .' Here, at the top of his form, is Borrow the joyous and the buoyant who presents himself to us always with exhilarating force in his best writing. The prostrating glooms, the near-insanity, the fevers, the obsessions – all these are swept away. He is on his own, being inquisitive, pacing swiftly about strange places, looking, listening, discovering wonders and oddities which the dulled eyes of the vast majority of travellers would never seize on, being defiantly and deliberately inexact – Moel Hebog, for example, rises to the west of Beddgellert and not, as he says, to the south – but always attuned to the spirit of the place and responsive to the attitudes of people who live out their lives in remote places, tethered to a small patch of ground and free to let their individual peculiarities flourish – or even bolt – in a manner which has become by now almost impossible in so-called developed Europe.

Developed Europe was, of course, by 1854, already something strong and real and not easily avoided. Even wild Wales was experiencing vast and sudden changes. Slate quarries were being blasted in Snowdonia. In Anglesey copper and lead mines were being worked again after long disuse. Country people from the north were coming down to the South Wales valleys to find work in the new booming industries of iron and steel and coal. Welshmen exiled in London but doing well there supplied funds and organizing abilities in order to re-establish the ancient bardic festivals like the Carmarthen Eisteddfod of 1451, but to make of them a grand, annual national affair – a coming-together of the nation as a whole. Borrow is not really interested in any of this. It is true that at the end of his sixteen weeks he penetrated south as far as Merthyr Tydfil and saw the iron works at Cyfartha Fawr. 'I saw enormous furnaces. I saw streams of molten metal. I saw a long ductile piece of red-hot iron being operated upon. . . . I saw an immense wheel impelled round with frightful velocity by a steam engine of two hundred and forty horse-power. I heard all kinds of dreadful sounds. The general effect was stunning. . . .' But 'I had best say but very little. . . .' It was all beyond him. It was all hateful. He stood gazing open-mouthed but unresponsive, and 'after strolling about for some two hours . . . I returned to my inn, called for a glass of ale . . . flung my satchel over my shoulder, and departed.'

He is happier sitting in an inn near Pont Bettws and discovering that the landlord has a dog he calls 'Perro'. '"Perro," said I, "is a Spanish word and signifies a dog in general. I am rather surprised that a dog in the mountains of Wales should be called by the Spanish word for dog." I fell into a fit of musing.' This kind of linguistic daydreaming is always his passion and can lift him above transient cares and less transient grudges. He remembers that in 'the oldest of Icelandic sagas, Hallgerdr, widow of Gunnar, is called a Puta by Skarphedrin and is so stung by the insult that she works for his destruction. So how did the Spanish word for whore find its way north into the high latitudes?'

Wild Wales remains one of his most delightful books. It is self-indulgent – and this always suits him. His strange personality is recaptured once again and we can see him as we see him in *The Bible in Spain*, *Lavengro*, and the better parts of *The Romany Rye*. The book is far too long, and this is because he tries to combine a narrative of personal travel with a history of Welsh literature. Borrow always lacked the organizational ability to write a cogent, convincing history of anything, and his knowledge of Welsh, although it was remarkably good, was neither wide-ranging nor exact enough to enable him to speak with authority. It would have been better if he had disciplined himself and not spoken of the literature at all. Borrow the landowner is also apparent in *Wild Wales*, but he never becomes obtrusive. There is just enough of him, in fact, to give piquant contrast to the general run of the narrative.

After wide wanderings in north and mid-Wales, he returned to Llangollen on 7 September for a more settled stay. He felt relaxed, in better shape mentally and emotionally than he had been for a long time. Carreta, 'the best woman of business in East Anglia', was faithfully there to see that everything was comfortable and in order. It was high time that he put the final words to the continuation of *Lavengro*, and now, she urged, was the time to do just that. He

worked at it, not much put out of his stride by the news from the
Crimea – even when, on 3 October, the bells rang out too soon to
celebrate the taking of Sebastopol. At the end of September the two
women returned home to Yarmouth. On 21 October he set off
southwards alone, through Bala, past the sources of the Rheidol,
Severn, and Wye and down to the coast at Swansea: then westward to
Chepstow where he took train to London. The MS of *The Romany
Rye* was in his baggage, and he left it with Murray at 50 Albemarle
Street. By mid-November he was home again. The hated winter was
not far away. Uneasiness of mind and restlessness of body took
command of him almost immediately. What was Carreta to do with
him? Could she contrive to keep him occupied with the writing-up of
his Welsh excursion? She was in part successful, but, before Christmas, Murray plucked up his courage and wrote to him about *The
Romany Rye*. He spoke his mind, with the result that, although far
from being a timid man, he could not bring himself actually to send
the letter until 27 January 1855.

It is my firm conviction then, that you will incur the certainty of failure and
run the risque of injuring your literary fame by publishing the MS as it
stands. . . . It seems to me that you have dwelt too long on English ground in
this new work, and have resuscitated some characters of the former book
(such as F. Ardry) whom your readers would have been better pleased to
have left behind. Why should you not introduce us rather to those novel
scenes of Moscovite and Hungarian life respecting which I have heard you
drop so many stimulating allusions. . . .

Murray went on with suggestions for omission. The 'Jockey story'
was 'terribly spun out'; there was altogether too much about the
Postillion, the chapter about learning Chinese was repetitious, and, in
general, 'condensation is indispensable. Many of the narratives are
carried to a tedious length by details and repetition. . . .' Murray's
criticisms were perfectly fair. *The Romany Rye* is a very fine book in
so far as the greater part of it is simply a continuation of the unfinished business of *Lavengro*; but the interpolations are longer,
more frequent, and less interesting than those of *Lavengro*; the
doings and discourses of the Man in Black, the papistical proselytizer,
are contrived and tedious; Borrow turns his back on his own natural
gifts in order to launch into outbursts of forcible-feeble fiction. Yet
how mistaken Murray was to complain, in that letter, about the long
dialogue with Ursula under the hedge, and the songs, which 'border
on the indelicate', but which in fact represent Borrow at his purest,
inimitable best. There is much unhappiness in the book: a wilful,

violent, opinionated man refuses to recognize that he has been crushed somewhat out of shape under the world's coarse thumb. The Appendix, intended as a trouncing of all his foes, becomes rather an exposure of his own weaknesses.

He chose to disregard Murray's criticisms. Carreta replied to the letter, but in terms that sound very much like Borrow's.

Mr Borrow has not the slightest wish to publish the book. The MS was left with you because you wished to see it. . . . Mr Borrow can bide his time. He is independent of the public and of everybody. Say no more on that Russian subject. Mr Borrow has had quite enough of the press. . . . He has written a book in connection with England such as no other body could have written [Murray, a fair man, would have found this undeniable] and he now rests from his labours. He has found England an ungrateful country. It owes much to him, and he owes nothing to it. . . .

On 5 April 1856 she wrote to Murray again, asking that the MS should be returned. Murray complied with understandable alacrity. No publisher ever had the handling of a tetchier author. 'He is independent of the public and of everybody'; that sentence, whether it was from Carreta or from Borrow himself, lies at the heart of Borrow's trouble all through the long, quarrelsome decades that follow the publication of *The Bible in Spain* in 1843. If he had had only a meagre salary in his pocket – and even perhaps another Sir Richard Phillips to hound him on – his life, both personal and literary, might have been happier.

He worked at *Wild Wales*. In the summer he walked about Norfolk and covered 180 miles in a week. He called on Anna Gurney the philologist, eight years older than he, who lived at Northrepps just south of Cromer. The Reverend Arthur Upcher wrote a letter to the press about this visit in 1893.

He told us there were three personages in the world whom he had always had a desire to see; two of these had slipped through his fingers, so he was determined to see the third. 'Pray, Mr Borrow, who were they?' He held up three fingers of his left hand and pointed them off with the forefinger of the right: the first Daniel O'Connell, the second Lamplighter (the sire of Phosphorus, Lord Berner's winner of the Derby), the third, Anna Gurney. The first two were dead and he had not seen them; now he had come to see Anna Gurney. It was an invitation: the lady wanted him to clear up for her some difficulty she was having in Arabic grammar.

But here again – according to Upcher who had the story, he says, from Borrow himself – what he encountered was not the wished-for meeting of minds, but something of a small disaster.

When . . . he had been but a very short time in her presence, she wheeled her chair round and reached her hand to one of her bookshelves and took down an Arabic grammar, and put it into his hand, asking for explanation of some difficult point, which he tried to decipher; but meanwhile she talked to him continuously; when, said he, 'I could not study the Arabic grammar and listen to her at the same time, so I threw down the book and ran out of the room. . . .'

He did not stop, apparently, till he reached the Old Tucker's Inn which was in Cromer, where he ate five excellent sausages and gradually regained his poise. Anna Gurney, Harriet Martineau, even Belle Berners – how terrifying women were, and how prudent of him to run from them all except his sheet-anchor, Carreta. In King's Lynn he found a horse fallen between the shafts, with his driver beating it. The beating was summarily put a stop to. Borrow sent a pot of ale for the horse, and, that consumed, sent for another, which brought the horse to its feet and to duty. Borrow believed in ale – for himself, for horses, and for publishers. He wrote to John Murray III: 'take long walks and drink plenty of Scotch ale with your dinner'.

The take-it-or-leave-it letter from Carreta in January 1856 had elicited no response from Albemarle Street. Borrow got his MS back, and Murray seemed disposed to accept the lull unexcitedly. In February 1857 Borrow wrote to say that 'the work must go to press', and if Murray would not undertake this, then Borrow would see to it himself. Murray then obediently got to the stage of proofs and showed these to Elwin. Elwin thought that Borrow had been unnecessarily unkind and hostile to his old champion Ford. Murray felt it was time to take a strong line with his author and wrote on 8 April:

You are the last man I should ever expect to 'frighten or bully'; and if a mild but firm remonstrance against an offensive passage . . . is interpreted by you into such an application, I submit that the grounds for the notion must exist nowhere but in your own imagination. The alternative offered to you is to omit or publish elsewhere. Nothing shall compel me to *publish* what you have written. . . .

Borrow wrote him a grumbling letter back, but was persuaded by Carreta at last to see reason in what Murray had said. On 30 April 1857 *The Romany Rye*, the oddly cantankerous yet still for the most part utterly delightful pendant to *Lavengro*, made its appearance in an edition of 1,000 copies. There is no doubt that Borrow hoped for great things from the Appendix: the hostility shown to *Lavengro* would be humbled; he would achieve success again as in 1843; he would sweep on with books about Cornwall, about the Isle of Man which he had recently visited, about Russia, about the gipsies of Hungary; in that snippety, note-jotting way he had, he could point already to a book on Wales. But Borrow had miscalculated – with that *sancta simplicitas* of his which can be as endearing as it can be irritating. Nobody could stomach the Appendix. He sent copies of the two volumes to FitzGerald: from him surely, a friend and supporter, he might expect approval and encouragement. But he too found much to object to, mainly in the Appendix. What FitzGerald could not see was that, although Borrow was, like himself, a maverick, he was a maverick of an entirely different kind. FitzGerald was cultivated, literary, bred to a life of gentlemanly ease and plenty. Borrow's defiant unbookishness, which comes out so strongly in *The Romany Rye*, was hardly likely to please him. The chat which Borrow has with the corpulent, middle-aged man whom he has found deeply asleep in a meadow would not go down well.

'I was fearful . . . that you might catch a fever from sleeping under a tree. . . . what may induce you to come and sleep in this meadow?' 'Owing to the anxiety to which my mind had been subjected . . . sleep forsook my pillow. . . . I took opiates . . . . About three weeks ago a friend of mine put this book into my hand, and advised me to take it every day to some pleasant part of my estate, and try and read a page or two, assuring me, if I did, that I should infallibly fall asleep. . . . I came, and lying down, commenced reading the book, and before finishing a page was in a dead slumber. . . . It consists of poetry.' . . . 'Not Byron's?' 'No, this is not Byron's poetry, but the inimitable —'s. . .'

This is a typical bit of Borrow; a slow but agreeable joke, an absurd blank when it comes to the proper name, because he goes on to make it perfectly clear that he is talking about Wordsworth. FitzGerald would not have warmed to slapstick of this sort about Wordsworth, but Borrow is being perfectly himself – longing always in one sense to be the accepted literary man, yet in another robustly mocking what he chooses to think of as the sedentary sloppiness of the writer's trade. FitzGerald's letter, however – gentle in reproof as his writing almost always is – could scarcely have provoked even Borrow to touchiness.

Well, lying in a Paddock of his ['his' was Kenworthy Browne, the love of FitzGerald's life, who died young and terribly from an accident whilst out on horseback], I have been travelling along with you to Horncastle etc., – in a very delightful way for the most part; something as I have travelled, and love to travel, with Fielding, Cervantes, and Robinson Crusoe – and a smack of all three there seems to me, with something beside, in your book. But, as will happen in Travel, there were some spots I didn't like so well – didn't like *at all*: and sometimes wished to myself that I, a poor 'Man of Taste', had been at your elbow (who are a man of much more than taste) to divert you, or get you by some means to pass lightlier over some places. . . .

With what feather-light precision FitzGerald here allocates praise and blame to *Lavengro* and to *The Romany Rye*. In his inimitable way he wraps up, in a few deceptively casual sentences, all that needs to be said about Borrow's two great books.

CHAPTER 10

ICHABOD – OR VERY NEARLY

Borrow did not take readily to the idea of growing old. And in 1857 Borrow at fifty-four still had plentiful years of robust activity ahead of him. All the same, the long perspective of over a century and a quarter enables us to say that the year 1857 marks for him the beginning of a long diminuendo. He sulked over the reception accorded to *The Romany Rye*. To Murray he wrote defiantly in September. The Appendix 'denounces boldly the evils which are hurrying the country to destruction, and which have kindled God's anger against it, namely the pride, insolence, cruelty, covetousnes, and hypocrisy of its people, and above all the rage for gentility. . . .' Gentility – Borrow was contemptuous of it all his days. Earlier, in July, Hasfeld had visited him, and both blew hard if unavailingly on the fires of youth. Hasfeld left, and that was the last time they saw each other. Borrow went off on another trip to Wales, this time leaving Carreta and Hen in Shrewsbury whilst he explored to the south, tracking down places where Goronwy Owen had ministered. When he got back he tried Murray again with his translation called 'Visions of the Sleeping Bard' which he had made almost thirty years earlier. Murray hedged, thought it might be improved if Cruikshank illustrated it, kept it a while but then after ten months returned it.

In August 1858 urgent word came to Yarmouth. Ann Perfrement, now aged 86, was dangerously ill of pneumonia at Oulton. He got there just before she died. Thus he lost the first of the three great female props of his life. Maria Diaz was still alive but far away and unattainable and in any positive sense lost to him also. Carreta he still had, but she was sixty-two and in the mid-nineteenth century women of that age were thought of as old. Borrow was distressed beyond measure by his mother's death. She had supported him long ago in the face of his father's disapproval; she had condoned his refusal to settle down and be conventional; she had rejoiced when after long wanderings *The Bible in Spain* had scored a mighty success. She adored him but she could also guide and criticize. After the Captain's death in 1824 Thomas Borrow's voice could be said to have gone on speaking through her and for the first time to have been listened to by the moody, hard-to-handle son. She left Borrow land together with a thatched house and outbuildings at Mattishall Burgh, and later on he used to enjoy walking over the Mattishall land with his tenant, Henry Hill – the kind of man Borrow always liked – someone determined to give his talents – cello-playing, watch-repairing, bee-keeping – the fullest rein.

There could be no cure, Carreta thought, for Borrow's despondency, save perhaps yet one more bout of wandering. She proposed Scotland. So he took ship from Yarmouth on 16 September and spent the following day prowling gloomily round Newcastle until he was suddenly hailed matily by a couple of fisherman-friends from Yarmouth, and that made his day. By the 18th he was in Edinburgh where he was able to recognize changelessness from his boyhood days, note with disapproval how much admired still was that contemptible courtier Sir Walter Scott, and recall with sad affection the grisly end of his boyhood friend David Haggart. He pushed on northwards to Inverness, and from there tramped the Highlands where strong cold winds were already beginning to bring snow. He hunted for the Scotland of legend, for Viking traces and Runic inscriptions. What he found, or what he considered he had found, was Scotland on the make in true Victorian style, a land eager to turn its back on the old stories and the old ways. He thought much about Carreta and wrote to her. He went to Mull and picked specimens of moss and heather for Hen. On the way back to Inverness by rail he got out to stretch his legs at a stop, and the train went on without him. '. . . the train drove off *purposely*,' he wrote to Carreta. '. . . I instantly said that I would bring an action against the company, and walked off to the town, where I stated the facts to a magistrate. . . . He advised me to bring my action. I went back and found the people frightened. They telegraphed again and the reply was that the things were safe. There is nothing like setting oneself up sometimes. . . . I got them, and my old umbrella too. . . .' That was the famous green one that never left him. Drenched and storm-beaten, he still marched about. In November he was on Orkney. He was fascinated by what he considered to be 'Druidical and Pictish remains'. By Christmas, he was home. He left memories behind him. A Shetland-islander, one snowy day towards the end of November, passed an old castle almost surrounded by the waters of a marsh flooded by autumn rains. He saw a tall man up to his thighs in water, wearing a summery shirt and with unbuttoned jacket flapping: it was Borrow on the trail of the Picts.

Through the winter of 1859 he worked hard at *Wild Wales*. In the summer he took Carreta and Hen to Ireland with him, dumping them – in his usual way – in lodgings at 75 St. Stephen Green South, and then, on his own, stepping westward, Ennis, Galway, Connemara, and on to the Giant's Causeway. But nothing could conquer his depression, his sense of having come to an inexpungeable fullstop. He wrote a letter to Carreta from Ballina in County Mayo, but it is spiritless stuff with nothing Borrovian about it except for the request – so often repeated throughout his correspondence with her – that she send him on some money.

Back at Yarmouth in the spring of 1860 he decided to publish – at his own cost since Murray still so resolutely declined – 250 copies of *Visions of the Sleeping Bard*. Murray was persuaded to agree that his name should appear on the title-page. Nobody took any notice of it. But Murray the ever-patient did accept a piece by Borrow called 'The Welsh and their Literature' for the January 1861 issue of the *Quarterly*. In this Borrow took the opportunity to write on his own account a review of *The Sleeping Bard*, and by this means managed to dispose of all the copies. This stands out as the most humiliating literary transaction of Borrow's life. Slaving away at *Celebrated Trials* for Sir Richard Phillips seems by comparison heroic, Herculean labour.

Through this time Carreta was busy making practical rearrangements. The Yarmouth climate was beginning to be too rigorous for her. Perhaps a sudden jolt would be the cure for her husband's lapsing into sulky anonymity. (There were people who thought that the famous author of *The Bible in Spain* was dead.) She decided to try living in London. By the autumn of 1860 she had found 22 Hereford Square, Brompton, and Borrow, Carreta, and Hen became tenants there from the beginning of the Michaelmas quarter. Borrow mooned about and accepted. To him now, once so responsive to his surroundings, one place seemed as good, or as bad, as another.

It was of course a thoroughly respectable address, and the neighbours thought a freak had arrived. White-haired, unwrinkled, as tall as Mr Thackeray, slightly bulbous eyes, a chimney-pot hat, a black overcoat buttoned all the way down, white cotton socks, low shoes, the enormous green umbrella, always on the march hither and thither at an enormous speed – this was not the sort of man Hereford Square was used to.

And where now did he go to? He went mostly in search of the roving, raffish unconventional life that had always attracted him. He went to gipsy encampments in Wandsworth, to the Bald Faced Stag in Kingston Vale to drink with the regulars and to tell them tales of the highwayman Jerry Abershaw (long ago Borrow had learnt, and learnt the hard way, a great deal about highwaymen) whose sword still hung on a wall at the inn. He dropped in on his neighbour on one side, a painter called Robert Collinson, to drink ale with him, careful always to bring his own pot with him because the stuff did not taste right drunk out of one of Collinson's glasses. Gordon Hake had recently set up in Richmond after a long stay in the New World, and he and Borrow used to walk in Richmond Park together.

It was through Hake and his family that Watts-Dunton, who long ago had watched from afar Borrow's plunging about in the North Sea at Yarmouth, at last came to know the man he so much admired and was thus enabled to write much about him, in friendly, reminiscent style after Borrow had finally slipped out of life with little in the way of public fuss or tribute.

One day when I was sitting with him [Hake] in his delightful home near Roehampton, whose windows at the back looked over Richmond Park, and in front over the wildest part of Wimbledon Common, one of his sons came in and said that he had seen Dereham [his name for Borrow in this context] striding across the common, evidently bound for the house. 'Dereham,' I said, 'is there a man in the world I should so like to see as Dereham?' And then I told Gordon how I had seen him years before swimming in the sea off Yarmouth, but had never spoken to him. 'Why do you want so much to see him?' asked Gordon. 'Well, among other things, I want to see if he is a true Child of the Open Air.'

Amongst Watts-Dunton's many glimpses of him comes one from near the end of his Hereford Square time.

At seventy years of age, after breakfasting at eight o'clock at Hereford Square, he would walk to Putney, meet one or more of us at Roehampton, roam about Wimbledon and Richmond Park with us, bathe in the Pen Ponds with a north-east wind cutting across the icy water like a razor, run about the grass afterwards, like a boy to shake off the water-drops, stride about the park for hours, and then, after fasting for twelve hours, eat a dinner at Roehampton that would have done Sir Walter Scott's eyes good to see . . . his conversation, unless he happened to be suffering from one of his occasional fits of depression, was [bracing]. . . . Its freshness, raciness, and eccentric whim no pen could describe. . . .

Steadily though, over the London years, Borrow's way of life narrowed. *Wild Wales*, of which a reluctant Murray was persuaded to print 1,600 copies in 1862, did not do as badly as Murray had feared. There was a profit of over £500 on the first edition. Encouraged,

Murray brought out a second edition of 3,000 copies in 1863. But by then the small spurt of support had faltered, and thirteen years went by before the edition was exhausted.

In 1865, suddenly, Hen married. The bridegroom was sixty-five and Hen was forty-seven. His name was William MacOubrey, and he was an Ulsterman. When signing in after the marriage he declared himself to be a doctor of medicine; on his gravestone however he is described as a barrister. There is no reason of course why he should not have been both. But MacOubrey, Hen, the marriage itself – all are mysterious. How they met and why they married – these are questions which have to be left unanswered. Whether from the law or from medicine, MacOubrey appears, naturally enough, to have been a retired man by 1865; Hen has vanished leaving few traces by which to judge her. She played the guitar in Seville, she collected sea-shells when opportunity served, and as shown by the tribute Borrow gave her in *Wild Wales*, she had his strong affection, which by itself says much for her. 'I generally call her daughter, and with good reason, seeing that she has always shown herself a daughter to me – that she has all kinds of good qualities, and several accomplishments, knowing something of conchology, more of botany, drawing capitally in the Dutch style. . . .' She went off to live in Belfast and Borrow missed her, and probably felt no warmth of regard for MacOubrey. After all, the man had suddenly carried off a woman whom Borrow, quite reasonably, had come to regard as a safely permanent member of the ménage. Indeed the gap she left was so great that in 1866 Carreta and he went on a visit to them in Belfast. Once arrived however, Borrow, at sixty-three, showed himself faithful to the familiar pattern. He fled from the lot of them on his travels.

He crossed from Larne to Stranraer and then tramped the Scottish Lowlands: Dumfries, Gretna Green, a dip down to Carlisle, and thence to Kirk Yetholm, a village in the Cheviots where the Scottish gipsies held an annual gathering. Here he met Esther Blythe, 'the Queen of the Nokkums'. Borrow wondered in his wayward unscientific way about the meaning of 'nokkum'. '"Nokkum?" said I, "the root of nokkum must be nok, which signifieth a nose . . . and I have no doubt that your people call themselves *nokkum* because they are in the habit of *nosing* the gorgios. . . ."' This wild but interesting guesswork he includes in *Romano Lavo-Lil*, a book which he worked at fitfully over a long number of years but which did not finally appear until 1874. It was, he said, a 'word-book of the Romany or English Gypsy language . . . illustrative of the way of speaking and thinking of the English Gypsies; with specimens of their poetry, and an account of certain Gypsyries or places inhabited by them [this the result largely of those long walks of his out of Hereford Square to any of London's surrounding villages – by now long absorbed – where the gipsies had encampments], and of various things relative to Gypsy life in England. . . .' That 'various things relative' is characteristic. It is still the essential Borrow that speaks in *Romano Lavo-Lil*, but with the vigour and vivacity somewhat enfeebled. The characters and conversations deriving from his visit to the border gipsies at Kirk Yetholm come in the best and final chapter.

By mid-August he was back in Belfast. Carreta, seventy now, was ailing. Years of coping with her difficult husband seemed at last to be having their effect on her nervous, even mental, health. Borrow took her back to London, and the MacOubreys decided to give up their Belfast home and to set up in London too, so as to be on hand. But Borrow still found it impossible to stay quiet. In the autumn of 1867 he took her to Bognor: perhaps it might do her good. She was left much alone, however, whilst her husband went off alone to explore the New Forest – and already in the spring of that year he had been away, on a third, briefer, Welsh journey. Still, Bognor seemed to set her up, and in 1868 she declared herself well enough to make the journey to Oulton; there were awkward matters concerning the estate to deal with.

Dealing with business matters did nothing for Carreta's health, and on 24 January 1869 she became suddenly worse. Borrow reacted instantly by having a bad attack of manic depressiveness. What was he to do? Their regular doctor was out of town. He sent to Curzon Street for Dr Playfair who wrote the next day to his colleague. Clearly Carreta's case had baffled him – a state of mind common with the medical profession in Victorian times. 'I found great difficulty in making out the case exactly. . . . Mr Borrow himself was so agitated that I could get no very clear account of it. . . . It seemed to me to be either a very aggravated form of hysteria, or, what appears more likely, some more serious mental affection. . . . I doubt very much whether she gets [careful nursing and management] . . . with her present surroundings. . . .' He clearly thought that Borrow would be better out of the way.

Carreta died on the 30th, and the death certificate said, 'valvular disease of the heart and dropsy'. She was buried in Brompton Cemetery on 4 February and on the gravestone was inscribed 'To the Beloved Memory of My Mother, Mary Borrow, who fell asleep in Jesus, 30th January 1869.' It is astonishing that the tribute should be Hen's alone and that Borrow should not be associated with it. The suspicion lingers, even though not backed by any solid evidence, that he was more thoroughly soured than is supposed by her marriage to MacOubrey – a man older by much than Borrow himself. All the same, inscription or no inscription, Carreta's death left Borrow distracted and bereft. He went to Norwich after the funeral to talk to lawyers and three friends went with him. He said no word during the journey, and later, when they reached the gate of his Oulton property he took off his hat, beat his breast, and groaned. Then they went in, and Borrow seemed less distressed. They sat down, with an empty chair facing Borrow. He pointed at it and told them that it was there he had seen his wife for the first time. Then they talked business where Borrow, without Carreta, was entirely lost. He went back to Hereford Square. He had twelve and a half years still to go, but for the most part they were dismal, empty years. The link attaching him however loosely to the real world had gone, and his habits of dreaming and wandering, and fighting, and generally standing up for himself did not suit his sixty-six years. He had outlived himself. He was a man born to live the life of a Lavengro or a Don Jorge, a hard, aggressive, rackety life – a life quite oblivious of all routine, all convention. Temperamentally he was not a man born to be old, yet the limitless toughness of his constitution forced old age on him.

He tried to shake off his glooms by poking about the London bookshops, by keeping on with his notes and scribbles which before, Carreta would have taken from him and put into order. He went to the Savile Club, but he could never be properly clubbable anywhere except in a four-ale bar. He slaked his philological thirst in the Reading Room of the British Museum. He studied to be quarrelsome. Miss Lloyd from next door asked him in to tea, but affability, even with this gentle soul, was more than he could manage.

Gordon Hake was a reliable and trusted companion in the first years of the 1870s. When Hake left the country to live in Germany in 1872 Borrow missed him. Borrow was beginning to be very lonely indeed. But still, there was Theodore Watts-Dunton. This, indeed, was a strange alliance, but then Watts-Dunton, guardian and protector of an ailing aberrant Swinburne, seems to have been designed by nature to be a specialist in strange alliances. Borrow, although always hungry for success, was too fond of going his own way ever to feel the need of cronies and satellites. But Watts-Dunton was fascinated by gipsies and gipsydom and this provided a strong link. Matthew Arnold's *The Scholar-Gipsy* had been published twenty years earlier, but characteristically Borrow knew nothing of it. Watts-Dunton read it to him. Borrow was full of admiration. It would be a good idea, he thought, if Watts-Dunton and he should hunt down the gipsies again so as to be able to read this remarkable poem to them and note any reaction. Certainly Watts-Dunton was eager to follow, so far as he was able, the lengthy strides of the master. He hunted out old remembered tents, with Watts-Dunton in tow, and found an acquaintance, Perpinia Boswell. She was smoking a pipe and was carrying a baby in her arms. The child was fretful, suffering, Borrow thought, from the smoke. He briskly took the pipe out of her mouth and told her she was to give up smoking until he made a second visit to the encampment to inspect the baby. He was always able to be high-handed after this fashion, expecting and getting submissiveness. Alongside Perpinia was a lusty young woman whom he gazed at admiringly. She surely would be responsive to Matthew Arnold's poem, and so, with Perpinia's pipe in his pocket, he began reading it to her. The young woman obediently listened, but told him at the end she could make no sense out of it at all. Perhaps Borrow was disappointed. But no gipsy could ever, in any final sense, disappoint him. Whenever a band was somewhere in his whereabouts, there was he in the midst of them. At Ascot Races in 1872 he appeared on the scene when soldiers in some quantity set about sacking a gipsy encampment in revenge for having been the victims of gipsy fraudulence. For Borrow, a set-to remained something enjoyable, and when he was fighting for those belonging to the race of Ambrose Petulengro, his blood-brother, then a battle immediately became more enjoyable still.

After the failure of *Romano Lavo-Lil* in 1874 – 'the [book] is, to speak mildly, an anachronism' said the *Athenaeum*, Borrow gave up trying. He gave up also the house in Hereford Square and retreated to Oulton Cottage. Here he employed a housekeeper, but otherwise lived alone. Henrietta and her ancient husband remained on in London. When the loneliness got too much for him, he took lodgings for a spell in Norwich and sat drinking in the Norfolk Hotel, mostly alone but sometimes with old friends who remembered him. He marched about the flat lands around Oulton, with a squint-eyed sheep-dog. He was much given to sudden tantrums over very little when on these walks, and people avoided him because he was still big enough and strong enough to be terrifying. As tenant at Oulton Hall there was now a mild-mannered man called William Smith. Borrow used to drop in there occasionally with complaints. Knowing his ring or perhaps having seen him march up, the maids would say 'It's Mr Borrow and we dassent go.' Children were scared of him because of his strange ways and because of his habit of singing to himself in strange languages as he tramped about. This was a pity because he always greatly enjoyed the company of children and when with them wanted only to be playful and entertaining. Even the gipsies began to be scarce – during the Seventies there was massive emigration to the United States. Ambrose Petulengro died in 1878. Isaac Heron was one who continued to roam East Anglia, and, although Borrow was fierce against trespassers, Isaac was always free to camp on his property and fish his water. Isaac Heron was of a later generation, but one of the family all the same, and Borrow impressed him, sitting before a fire that never went out, whatever the season. 'Almost a giant,' Isaac said, '– a very noble-looking gentleman, as it might be the Mayor of England. . . .'

Hen and MacOubrey came to live in Oulton, probably in 1878, the year when all that vast physical vigour began suddenly to leak out of him at a great rate. The idea doubtless was that Hen should be on hand to look after him, but long dependence on her mother seems to have left her with no power to organize or direct. Oulton Cottage became squalid and slummy. In 1879 she said that her stepfather was 'unable to walk as far as the white gate'. A new tenant, replacing the affable Smith, was by then occupying the Hall. He was aggressive. He would come round to Borrow demanding repairs and prepared to threaten. It was ironical that a man wholly suitable for knocking down should appear on the scene only at a moment when Borrow at last was no longer capable of doing any such thing. Yet he sturdily rejected the idea of being old. Cowell, a friend of FitzGerald's, called in 1879 and found him gloomy, unresponsive, and resentful of physical incapacity. The vicar of Lowestoft called also, in the way of duty. He asked him how old he was: a question which outraged the secretiveness which was always a strong element in Borrow's character. 'Sir, I tell my age to no man.' The vicar left soon after, and Borrow shuffled off to his summer-house to do just one more bit of writing. 'People's Age' he called it:

Never talk to people about their age. Call a boy a boy, and he will fly into a passion and say, 'Not quite so much of a boy, either; I'm a young man.' Tell an elderly person that he's not so young as he was, and you will make him hate you for life. Compliment a man of eighty-five on the venerableness of his appearance, and he will shriek out: 'No more venerable than yourself,' and will perhaps hit you with his crutch.

In December 1880 he felt it time to make a will. He was after all a propertied man with an unearned income of £500 a year. He left everything to Hen, in trust for Elizabeth Harvey, daughter of a man who had been a fellow-clerk with him at Simpson and Rackham's, Tuck Court, Norwich, long ago. He was making sure that MacOubrey, even if he lived to extreme old age, should never become a beneficiary. He became suspicious to the point of craziness, once again signed no letters in case he should be committing himself to something – he did not know what.

By the summer of 1881 Borrow was very infirm indeed. On 22 July Hen and MacOubrey took the carriage to Lowestoft. On business, they said, but Borrow apparently was querulous at being left. When they got back they found him dead. It was to be expected. 'I have often thought since that it is not a good thing for children to sleep alone.' This comes from the tale of the evangelist, Peter Williams, in *Lavengro*, and there can be no doubt that, by fits and starts, Peter Williams's tale is Borrow's tale too. He was never a father of course, so that this observation must come from some childhood memory of his own. And it is important to remember that all through his long life there was always much of the child in him. This tough, earthy man is always having to fight off childish fears. He is a dream-haunted Romantic: a Gothic man beset by visions which most often turned to nightmares. He chases shadows in bar-rooms, stifles his horrors by exhausting himself physically. He fights bruisers, rides imperturbably through a Spain convulsed by civil war, filling Brandram with alarm, spreading the gospel of peace amongst Sevillan *gitanos*, and at the same time spreading confusion and dismay amongst rulers and ruled alike in the Peninsula. Fantasy, suicidal depression, wild elation, homespun ordinariness – all these have to be fitted in to the compound of contradictions that was Borrow. 'Action will furnish belief, but will that belief be the true one?' Clough's question is Borrow's too, and Borrow brings a kind of childlike wildness to the answering of it. 'Climbing mountains and wading streams I ran wild about. . . .' This again is from Peter Williams's account of himself, and again the parallel with Borrow himself is close. In December 1880 he had ordered a new suit to be buried in. He must, he said, be 'ready for the resurrection'. He was dressed in it, and on 4 August was laid in Brompton Cemetery beside Carreta who had kept him relatively steady for so long.

SELECT READING LIST

Editions

Definitive Edition, ed. H. G. Wright (6 vols., John Murray, 1928)

Norwich Edition, ed. Clement Shorter (16 vols., Constable, 1923–4)

Borrow's Letters to Ann Borrow (printed privately for T. J. Wise, 1913)

Borrow's Letters to his Wife (printed privately for T. J. Wise, 1913)

Letters of GB to the Bible Society, ed. T. H. Darlow (Hodder and Stoughton, 1911)

Biographical

Armstrong, M., *GB* (London, 1950). Hostile.

Bigland, E., *In the Steps of GB* (London, 1951)

Capelin, E., *La Vie errante de GB* (Paris, 1936)

Dearden, S., *The Gipsy Gentleman* (London, 1939). GB the neurasthenic.

Elam, S. M., *GB* (New York, 1929). Hostile and hasty.

Fréchet, R., *GB. Vagabond polyglotte – Agent biblique – Ecrivain* (Paris, 1956). The soundest, most comprehensive book about GB so far. It has not been translated but deserves to be.

Jenkins, H., *Life of GB* (London, 1912)

Knapp, W. I., *Life, Writings, and Correspondence of GB* (2 vols., London, 1899). Knapp, enthusiastic American scholar, never knew GB, but talked with many who had. He is a diligent and resourceful enquirer. Every writer on GB after him owes a lot to Knapp.

Thomas, Edward, *GB, the Man and his Books* (London, 1912). This is rushed hack-work, showing Thomas at far below his best.

Vesey-FitzGerald, B., *Gipsy Borrow* (London, 1953). Argues spiritedly that GB was the son of Ann Borrow and a gipsy.

Walling, R. A. J., *GB, the Man and his Work* (London, 1909). Owes much to Knapp. Good on all the Cornish aspects.

Peripheral articles and books

Birrell, A., *Obiter Dicta*, 2nd series (London, 1890)

Chave, P., 'A Lost Leader' in *New Adelphi* (1929)

Cobbe, F. P., *Life of GB* (London, 1894)

Evans, I., 'GB in life and after' in *Journal of the Gipsy Lore Society* (1938)

Groome, F. H., 'GB' in *The Bookman* (1893)

Hake, A., 'Recollections of GB' in *Athenaeum* (1881)

——, 'GB' in *Macmillan's Magazine* (1881–2)

Hake, G., *Memoirs of Eighty Years* (London, 1892)

Jerrold, W., 'GB's Joseph Sell' in *Cornhill* (1921)

Jessopp, A., *'Lavengro'* in *Athenaeum* (1893)

——, 'Lights on GB' in *Daily Chronicle* (1900)

Johnson, Lionel, *Post Liminium* (London, 1911)

Leland, C. G., *Memoirs* (London, 1893)

Macaulay, R., *They Went to Portugal* (London, 1946)

Monkhouse, A., *Books and Plays* (London, 1894)

Moore, George, *Avowals* (London, 1924)

Murray, John (John Murray IV), 'GB' in *Good Words* (1895)

Napier, E., *Excursions along the shores of the Mediterranean* (London, 1842)

Pritchett, V. S., 'GB in Spain' in *Geographical Magazine* (1942)

Quennell, P., *The Singular Preference* (London, 1952)

Ralli, A., 'GB' in *Fortnightly Review* (1915)

Saintsbury, G., *Essays in English Literature* (London, 1890)

Shorthouse, J. M., *Life and Literary Remains* (London, 1905)

Tilford, J., *Studies for S. E. Leavitt* (Washington, 1953)

Watts-Dunton, T., 'GB' in *Encyclopaedia Britannica*

——, *Old Familar Faces* (London, 1916)

ACKNOWLEDGEMENTS

For help of various kinds, all valuable, I offer my most grateful thanks (in alphabetical order) to Sallie Dunn, Sue Godfree, John Hillaby, Roy Kerridge, John Kerry, Jeremy Lewis, London Library, Judith Luna, Phoenix Trust, Gwilym and Wenna Richards, Gwen Slyfield.

INDEX

GB = George Borrow